ADVANCE PRAISE FOR *Binkley: A Congregational History*

"This is more than just a congregational history—although it is a masterful exemplar of that. It is a story situated in both a particular place and in a larger culture and time. Gardner pays needed attention to a sometimes invisible corner of Baptist life—the world of southern white progressive Christians. And he does so with a critical and caring eye on a real place where real people live out their faith."—Nancy T. Ammerman, author of *Baptist Battles: Social Change and Conflict in the Southern Baptist Convention*

"If Olin T. Binkley Memorial Baptist Church sought to reform and reimagine the 'southern part of heaven' that was Chapel Hill, North Carolina, Gardner himself rectifies as well as reconceives congregational history, rescuing it from the parochialism and hagiography that have so often informed the genre's reputation. . . . While indeed the tale of a particular church, with its own peculiar personalities and in-house happenings, *Binkley* also discloses the courage and resilience as well as the failures and misgivings of Southern liberal Christianity." —Elizabeth Flowers, associate professor of religion, Baylor University

"Surprise! We've been duped to think all Baptists are conservative and reactionary, but not all Baptists are the same. Historian Andrew Gardner reveals how progressive white churches like Binkley Memorial Baptist Church embody a Southern, congregationally based liberalism consistently opposing exclusion and hate. Their ecclesial stance on controversies over race and gender from the past century remains a cornerstone of ministry. Read this book to discover a neglected yet sorely needed history of a white liberal Baptist church persistently striving for a more just and inclusive Christianity." —Gerardo Martí, William R. Kenan Jr. Professor of Sociology at Davidson College

"Andrew Gardner's rich and evocative historical narrative of Binkley Memorial Baptist Church demonstrates the vitality and challenges of a church planted in southern evangelical soil but sown with the seeds of a progressive and justice-oriented vision of faith. Truly, a captivating and informative account that both clergy and scholars should savor." —Scott Thuma, professor of sociology of religion at Hartford International University and director of Hartford Institute for Religion Research

Binkley

Binkley

A Congregational History

ANDREW B. GARDNER

AMERICA'S BAPTISTS   *Keith Harper, Series Editor*

The University of Tennessee Press / Knoxville

The America's Baptists series will bring broader understanding of the places Baptists have occupied in American life. Many of these works will be historical monographs, but the series will embrace different types of primary and secondary works, including but not limited to annotated collections of diaries, letters, and personal reflections as well as biographies and essay collections.

Copyright © 2023 by The University of Tennessee Press / Knoxville.
All Rights Reserved. Manufactured in the United States of America.
First Edition.

Library of Congress Cataloging-in-Publication Data

Names: Gardner, Andrew B., 1990– author.
Title: Binkley : a congregational history / Andrew B. Gardner.
Description: First edition. | Knoxville : The University of Tennessee Press,
    [2023]. | Series: America's Baptists | Includes bibliographical references and
    index. | Summary: "This book examines how a Southern Baptist congregation
    emerged as a bastion of liberal Christianity in late twentieth-century Chapel Hill,
    North Carolina. Andrew B. Gardner narrates a detail-rich history, from the late
    1950s to the 2010s, of the Olin T. Binkley Memorial Baptist Church through the lens
    of its social witness mission. While it is a concrete congregational history of a single
    church community—with profiles of prominent members like the University of North
    Carolina men's basketball coach Dean Smith and influential clergy like Robert
    Seymour and Linda Jordan—Gardner also uses the story to examine how congregations
    more generally change and evolve. He contends that recurring conflicts on various
    issues in the life of a congregation—in Binkley's case, from building projects to civil
    rights, women's ordination, and LGBTQ inclusion—are the primary drivers of its
    development"—Provided by publisher.
Identifiers: LCCN 2022056874 (print) | LCCN 2022056875 (ebook) | ISBN
    9781621907886 (hardcover) | ISBN 9781621908043 (pdf)
Subjects: LCSH: Olin T. Binkley Memorial Baptist Church (Chapel Hill, N.C.)—History.
    Chapel Hill (N.C.)—Church history.
Classification: LCC BX6480.C293 G37 2023 (print)
LC record available at https://lccn.loc.gov/2022056874

Contents

Illustrations

Foreword

REMEMBER A TIME in the not-so-distant past when many churches appointed committees to record and preserve their histories? Such histories typically follow a chronological storyline that celebrates the church's life through a succession of its pastors, building programs, and so forth. These histories are helpful in identifying key individuals in the church's life, but they tend to lack analytical focus. Andrew B. Gardner's *Binkley: A Congregational History* is not that kind of local church history. Gardner chronicles the life and development of Olin T. Binkley Memorial Baptist Church in Chapel Hill, North Carolina. It is a fascinating treatment of an unusual congregation.

Churches have their own distinct character and identity. Over the past couple of decades, many Baptist churches have drawn attention to themselves by their affiliation with the Republican Party and partisan politics. Not so with Binkley Memorial. Since its organization in 1958, Binkley Memorial has self-identified as a "progressive" church dedicated to equality and inclusiveness. Charter members were especially sensitive to racial injustice, and they fought against it in Chapel Hill. They took their name from Olin Trivette Binkley, a well-known, well-educated, and much beloved Baptist minister who had served both in North Carolina churches and taught in North Carolina colleges. To the founding members, Olin Binkley epitomized all they aspired to be, so they named their church after him.

Naming a church is one matter; creating an identity is another. What does it mean to be progressive? Does a "progressive" stance on race automatically translate into a progressive stance on any other social or cultural issue? Does progressivism in a local congregation demand that its membership march lockstep? Is there room for dissent? These are the kinds of questions that Binkley Memorial's membership has faced throughout its history, and Gardner's work will force anyone tempted to dismiss progressive churches as either atheological or theological minimalists to think twice. In fact, this church deliberately tries to apply biblically informed ethics to daily life. It is sometimes messy. It is sometimes difficult. The church's membership, however, will tell you that it is worth it because they believe there is much more to the Christian life than "walking a church aisle" and being baptized.

Andrew B. Gardner's *Binkley: A Congregational History* is the ongoing story of a community of believers who believe that true gospel salvation implies social betterment for those around them. Some would call this "lived religion," and it is an apt description. Gardner's treatment is engaging, sometimes poignant, and always fair. The University of Tennessee Press is proud to welcome *Binkley: A Congregational History* to the America's Baptists series. In fact, we think that Andrew Gardner may be setting a new standard for how to write local church history.

Keith Harper
Southeastern Baptist Theological Seminary

Acknowledgments

THE IDEA FOR THIS BOOK was inspired by the Alliance of Baptists' director of partnership relations, Paula Dempsey, from whom many great ideas have sprung. In 2016, shortly after the publication of *Reimagining Zion: A History of the Alliance of Baptists,* Paula and I took a short road trip together to host a couple of small Alliance gatherings in North Carolina and Georgia to celebrate the book's publication. We had an evening gathering in Durham, North Carolina, to attend, but before doing so, Paula arranged for the two of us to have brunch with Robert "Bob" Seymour, pastor emeritus at the Olin T. Binkley Memorial Baptist Church. Paula, always the great connector, used this brunch to plant the seed of working on a congregational history of Binkley. I was in the early stages of doctoral work at Florida State University and Binkley was in a period of pastoral transition, so the idea took a little while to germinate. In 2019, as I was completing my doctoral work, I reached back out to Rev. Marcus McFaul, the newly called senior minister of Binkley, to see if we could make the history happen. We arranged another brunch. In March 2019, I drove from Greenville, North Carolina, to Chapel Hill to meet McFaul and Seymour at Breadman's, a local restaurant, for brunch. Seymour, in his nineties and clearly a regular at Breadman's, ordered a waffle and two strips of crispy bacon. I followed his lead. Over the course of the meal, we discussed the project and agreed that we would continue a conversation in the coming months. As we got up to leave our table, I remember witnessing multiple individuals stop Seymour in the crowded restaurant. "Excuse me," one gentleman asked, "you're Dean Smith's pastor, right? My son will love this. Please, let me go get him and introduce you." Smith, who had passed away a few years prior, was a national basketball coaching legend and a lifelong faithful Binkley member. Smith's celebrity was one thing, but his pastor's celebrity was another. I looked over at McFaul, who chuckled. "It's like this everywhere we go." I knew I needed to work on this church's history. We soon reached an agreement.

In the fall of 2019, I began working on the project. Thanks to a travel grant from the Z. Smith Reynolds Library at Wake Forest University, I was able to access much of the congregation's early archives. I wanted to write a congregational history that might find readership and interest beyond Binkley's congregants and the most committed of Baptist congregational scholars. Too often congregational histories take on a parochial or hagiographical tone. I did not want that, and neither did McFaul or Seymour. While reading and writing, I strove to delicately thread the needle between a history that could appeal to congregants and one that could appeal to academics. In the process, I felt the need to try and scholastically justify why congregational histories are important to the broader study of religion in the United States, a justification I seek to weave throughout the project.

In my attempt to craft this type of congregational history, Binkley members have been immensely helpful, from engaging in short conversations and emails to participating in longer discussions. I am incredibly grateful for Marcus McFaul and his encouragement during this project as well as for Bob Seymour, who I am saddened will never get to see the final project. Seymour's comments throughout much of the writing process were extremely valuable and insightful. Additionally, I am thankful for emails, conversations, and/or photos from Napier Baker, Howard Lee, Joe and Eva Clontz, Dick and Ginger Clifford, Tom Fewel, Herman Greene, Linda Jordan, Jim Pike, Peter Carman, Stephanie Sanders, Megan Hollenbeck, Ray Speller, John Blevins, and Ayla Volpe. The pandemic prohibited me from spending more time in Chapel Hill with Binkley members, but thanks to Zoom and the digital age, I was able to make things work. I only wish I had the opportunity to speak with more Binkley congregants. Unfortunately, I was unable to utilize a summer research fellowship through the University of North Carolina's Library and Special Collections, but thanks to Matthew Turi and the staff there, I was able to examine much of Bob Seymour's archives digitally.

I am grateful for the numerous colleagues and friends who took the time to read various portions of the manuscript or offered short, off-hand comments over the course of the project, including Lloyd Allen, Mikael Broadway, Deborah Van Broekhoven, Eileen Campbell-Reed, John Findley, Curtis Freeman, Steven Harmon, Bill Leonard, Laura Levens, Andrew Smith, and Doug Weaver. I am also grateful for thoughtful reviews from Mel Hawkins and Glenn Jonas. My colleagues and the faculty at Florida State University generously workshopped the fourth chapter of the project in the religion department's American Religious History Colloquium. John Corrigan, Sonia Hazard, Michael McVicar, and Amanda Porterfield were very encouraging and helpful throughout the writing process. I must also thank my colleagues and fellow graduate students in Dodd 101, Devin Burns, Tim Burnside, Haley Illiff, Taylor Dean, Michael McLaughlin, and American Wolff. I am thankful to consider you all friends as well.

Working on this project during the pandemic proved to be quite challenging as I graduated and moved to another part of the country and began a postdoctoral fellowship working with the Hartford Institute for Religion Research on a truly epic project. The people and team at Hartford helped me think in new ways and provided encouragement at a time when much of the world seemed to be—and, in fact, was—in chaos. Brian Clark, Hans Harmakaputra, Alison Norton, Patricia Tevington, and Scott Thumma are wonderfully supportive colleagues, and I could not ask for better.

Lastly, I am especially grateful for the love and support of my family. I grew up watching my late grandfather, a lifelong Baptist, cheering on Dean Smith and the Tar Heels. Much of this project gave me an opportunity to reflect and remember him. How I wish I could have shared what I learned with him. My parents, Brad and Susie, gave me so much support and encouragement over the course of this project. I continue to wonder how I got so lucky with such great parents.

Introduction

IN HIS MEMOIR, *The Southern Part of Heaven,* the magazine illustrator William Meade Prince recounted growing up in Chapel Hill, North Carolina, in the early half of the twentieth century. Published in 1950, one review described the work as a "human document" portraying the "sleepy university village" that "threatens to become a city." The book's title came from an exchange between a local businessman who, near death, allegedly asked a local Presbyterian minister what heaven is like. The minister paused and reassuringly answered, "I believe Heaven must be a lot like Chapel Hill in the spring." In the decades following the publication of Prince's memoir, many residents of Chapel Hill grew to welcome and celebrate what became their town's nickname—the "southern part of heaven."[1]

Chapel Hill in the 1950s, however, was not heaven for all its residents. Yes, many members of the local white population in Chapel Hill may have agreed with Prince's characterization of the town as "the southern part of heaven," but for many of the area's Black residents, as historian Yonni Chapman notes, Chapel Hill was the "southern part of hell."[2] A deeper reading of Prince's memoir reveals an unsavory celebration of the Old South. What he found appealing about his childhood certainly did not resonate with Chapel Hill's Black residents. Riddled with racial slurs, his memoir celebrated the Southern Confederacy as "the greatest nation on which the sun ever shone" along with its heroes Robert E. Lee and Stonewall Jackson.[3] As local journalist and historian Mike Ogle notes, "It's clear from the illustrations and text that the Southern Part of Heaven, as a book and slogan, was a Confederate monument in the form of a moniker." Contrary to characterizations of Chapel Hill as a southern, progressive bastion, Prince's depiction of the town as the southern part of heaven still welcomed the likes of Jim Crow as one of its dearest saints.[4]

Binkley: A Congregational History recounts the history of a congregation birthed in the years after Prince published his memoir and coined the now controversial phrase. Rather than embrace this southern part of heaven as a perfect manifestation of God's kingdom on earth, Olin T. Binkley Memorial Baptist Church became a congregation committed to reimagining what this southern "heaven" might look like. Drawing inspiration from the University of North Carolina at Chapel Hill and the progressive voices who operated within this academic institution, Binkley's founders sought to establish a religious community that would be welcoming of all people regardless of their racial identity. Shortly after the church's founding in 1958, many of its congregants worked together to challenge the status quo of segregation in Chapel Hill with what little resources they had at their disposal. Although the church remained predominately white well into the twenty-first century, Binkley grew and evolved in the decades following the civil rights movement and became increasingly aware of the ways in which this southern part of heaven failed to live up to its name. From issues of gender equality to poverty and LGBTQ inclusion to climate justice, Binkley sought to build God's kingdom on earth as it is in heaven.

This remarkably unique Southern Baptist congregation looked back to early twentieth-century liberal Protestantism for inspiration. Binkley welcomed ecumenical relations as well as adopted and practiced elements of what was known as the Social Gospel. This movement of the late nineteenth and early twentieth centuries typified liberal Protestantism and advocated for the working class, fueled by an eschatological vision of continuing progress. It prioritized the material and physical needs of individuals alongside their spiritual needs. By the time of Binkley's founding, however, this optimistic liberal Protestant spirit of unfettered progression had been battered by the Great Depression sandwiched between two world wars.[5] Rather than a return to the Social Gospel, many inheritors of this liberal tradition sought to move on from its unbridled optimism. Some inheritors would turn toward the realism of Christian Neo-Orthodoxy, a theological tradition that sought to reemphasize God's transcendent sovereignty over humanity's sinfulness and finitude. Other inheritors of this liberal tradition found renewed community within new thought and spiritualist practices. Binkley, however, returned to the teachings of the Social Gospel and carried this liberal Protestant tradition forward despite critiques of its optimism and presumed naïveté.[6]

At the same time, Binkley held both deeply southern roots as well as a flair for evangelism as a member of the Southern Baptist Convention (SBC). While it may not have been a particularly large movement, there emerged a distinct southern liberal Christianity within the early twentieth century that welcomed

New Deal policies, advocated against Jim Crow, and adopted theological ideas consistent with the Social Gospel. This spirit of liberal Christianity within the South most prominently emerged within the civil rights movement through the work and ministry of certain segments of the Black Church. At the same time, however, a small but vocal minority of white congregations also engaged in the struggle to bring an end to segregation and Jim Crow. A similarly small but vocal progressive evangelical tradition shared many of the same goals and values as its more mainline, liberal Protestant counterparts. Throughout its founding decade, Binkley communicated in this evangelical idiom. As it gained status within the broader community, however, this evangelical identity slowly faded from its congregational messaging. Even so, some congregants continued to carry vestiges of this evangelical spirit well into the twenty-first century.[7] For these congregants, evangelical "Good News" was not limited to one's personal and individual salvation. Instead, this "Good News" entailed a breaking down of social and racial barriers that divided humanity.[8]

Thinking about and characterizing the diversity of Christian identities within the United States can be challenging. It necessitates engaging in broad generalities and similarities. At the congregational level, Christian identity can be equally complicated. Churches contain a wide array of diversity of thought within their membership. Binkley Memorial Baptist Church was and is no different. As a former pastor described the congregation, Binkley "is a living breathing worshipping household of faith," and its members are all at different points on their respective journeys.[9] This book shows some of the ways in which broad and general categories can generate fruitful analysis at the congregational level as well as the ways in which these categories can limit one's understanding of congregational dynamics.[10] Focusing on a singular religious community like Binkley reveals the ways in which an institution's location shapes its identity. The southern part of heaven may not have been heavenly for everyone, but Binkley strove to reimagine that heaven. In the process, the church both shaped and was shaped by the surrounding local community. The liberal and progressive college town spirit of Chapel Hill provided inspiration and intellectual stimulus for the congregation's theological outlook. At the same time, the rot of the Jim Crow South and its Confederate legacy fueled the predominately white congregation's desire to seek change in the southern part of heaven. This congregational history tells the story of Binkley's successes and failures in seeking to be a new and alternative Baptist witness in Chapel Hill.

What is a Congregational History?

At the most basic level, congregational histories provide an account of the life and development of a singular religious community—most often, a Christian church. These works seek to convey the circumstances that led to the institution's founding up to the present or near-present day, showing what remained consistent and what changed in the life of a particular religious community. They provide details into the lives of church leadership and show how these women and men shaped an institution's identity and ministry. Congregational histories chronicle institutional hardships and struggles as well as triumphs and successes. They seek to preserve the story of a particular community of faith.

Just as communities of faith come in all shapes and sizes, so too do congregational histories. Some are larger volumes designed for coffee tables and contain glossy pages and numerous pictures, whereas others are more narrative driven and filled with citations as one might find in an academic monograph.[11] Some congregational histories, significantly shorter in length, are not professionally published and may take the form of a pamphlet, informal paper, or multiple short volumes.[12] Technology has allowed other churches to include brief congregational histories on their websites. For some religious communities, their congregational history does not take a written form, but is instead passed down orally through stories. Others still may not prioritize their history, which remains fragmented and, in some cases, forgotten.

Part of why congregational histories are so diverse, much like the congregations they detail, is because they are all produced by different people and for different reasons. In most circumstances, congregational histories are produced because of the desire of one or more members of the congregation. This desire may often coincide with a congregational anniversary. For instance, Tabernacle Baptist Church in Richmond, Virginia, published a centennial history in 1991 with much of the work completed by a woman who was both a member of the church and the congregation's resident historian.[13] Histories written by congregational members often vary widely as these resident historians have different levels of historical expertise and bring different interests to their project. One individual may prioritize recording a congregation's architectural changes while another may prioritize recording and preserving biographical data on congregational leaders.

Some religious communities seek the help of professional historians or professional writers in the composition of a congregational history. Myers Park Baptist Church in Charlotte, North Carolina, commissioned a local journalist to publish

a history of the congregation at its fiftieth anniversary.[14] Other religious communities might hire a professional historian to compose a history that would contribute to scholarship and engage in academic discourse.[15] This approach to producing
a congregational history largely depends on the resources available to a religious
community. As a result, many examples of professional congregational histories are
skewed toward white affluent congregations. Sometimes a historian may be interested in a congregation because of its history. Churches like the historically Black
Abyssinian Baptist Church in Harlem, New York, and the nearby, multi-racial
Riverside Church on the Upper West Side provide interesting historical case studies
that historians may have independent interests in analyzing.[16] Congregational histories composed by professional historians all skew toward affluent churches with
either the financial resources to put toward producing a historical study or a history
deemed significant enough for further study.

For religious communities, the production of such histories functions to mark
significant milestones in the life of the community and remember individuals who
helped shape and influence the contours and dynamics of the contemporary religious body. As congregational historian Doug Weaver explains, "Local Church history is important because the faith of ordinary believers is the story that describes
most adherents of the Christian faith."[17] The lives of significant or well-known
Christians like the second century's Justin Martyr, the medieval mystic Julian of
Norwich, the Reformation's John Calvin, or civil rights leader Martin Luther King
Jr. can seem distant and unattainable. The lives of those individuals who fill the
pews on Sunday mornings and help to pay the congregation's bills, however, can, as
Weaver suggests, provide another model of examining what religious life looks like
within the broader study of Christianity.

Additionally, congregational histories provide an avenue to reinforce the relationship of the contemporary religious community to its denominational identity.
As Weaver explains, congregational studies can provide "a window toward seeing
how an influential congregation contributed to larger" denominational causes.[18]
Protestant congregational histories may begin with a brief chapter detailing the origins of the church's particular denominational sect.[19] In this way, these histories can
function as educational tools for religious communities. Through these histories,
congregants can learn about their community's denominational identity and how
their community has participated within a larger denominational story. Such histories seek to situate a congregation within the wider religious landscape and show
how a congregation connects to larger religious networks.

For these reasons, congregational histories often have a limited audience that focuses exclusively upon the congregation itself. As a result, these studies remain susceptible to problematic trends. Resident historians writing from within a religious community can easily steer a congregational history away from recounting conflicts or times of hardship and struggle to celebrate victories within the life of the church. These historians may focus on praising the characteristics of strong leaders while downplaying their character flaws. While these hagiographical histories may inspire and instill pride in a religious community, they are far from useful texts to understand congregational dynamics and the relationship between a church and its local community.

Congregational or even denominational histories are often, as one historian describes them, "too narrow in their emphasis" and suffer from "intellectual isolation."[20] By dwelling on the denominational particularities, a congregational history may get caught in the weeds of a dense question of theological doctrine that only interests the most committed of denominational historians. Rather than connect these denominational particularities to broader questions and trends within recent scholarship, they can remain insignificant not only for the individuals who fill the pews of the congregation in question but also for historians working outside of this denominational perspective.

The narrowness that characterizes many congregational histories does not, however, negate their utility. Historian Carol Kammen, a specialist on writing local histories, contends that many congregational histories are particularly successful at documenting or chronicling the "bones" of a historical narrative. "These bones," she suggests, however, "are just that: bones. They lack substantial satisfying context."[21] Part of the art of producing an engaging congregational history, she argues, is incorporating the local context into an understanding of the religious community in question. What does the founding of a religious institution reveal "about the needs of the surrounding community, and how social issues shaped church society?"[22] By asking these types of questions, a congregational history can consider a broader historical context and integrate the history of the congregation into a larger local, regional, and perhaps even national narrative. Such an approach provides a significantly more dynamic and compelling history that offers a more representative picture of a particular congregation's influence.[23]

Congregational histories therefore provide a different perspective of the landscape of American religious history. Often understandings of religion within American culture can drift into what historian James Wellman calls "stately abstractions." Thinking about religion through traditional categories like "Christian" or "Muslim" struggles to capture the nuance and texture contained within these broad classifications. Even within the Christian tradition, categories of Protestant or Catholic and even more specific denominational categories like Baptist or Presbyterian cannot account for the diversity at the level of the local church. Wellman contends that congregational histories provide insight into the "actual experience and factors that make American religion live and die."[24] In this way, congregational histories examine how these broad religious categorizations play out on the ground.

While there are many ways to study religion, approaches that seek to understand how religious life operates on the ground and in the lives of ordinary people occupy a branch of scholarship known as "lived religion." Rather than focusing on formal beliefs and doctrines of a denominational body, lived religion scholars study religion as performed by ordinary, lay practitioners navigating the messiness of daily life.[25] Historian Robert Orsi's *The Madonna of 115th Street* characterizes this approach well. In his work, Orsi describes how the annual "festa" of the Church of Our Lady of Mount Carmel in New York City developed and changed over the course of the twentieth century. Deeply rooted in the lives of the Italian immigrants who made meaning out of the sights and smells and sounds of this annual event, this work might well be seen as a type of congregational history.

According to Orsi, "lived religion directs attention to institutions *and* persons, texts *and* rituals, practice *and* theology, things *and* ideas."[26] It is not that understanding religious practitioners takes priority over religious institutions; rather, lived religion acknowledges an important relationship between individual religious persons and religious institutions. Often studies of lived religion deemphasize religious institutions and congregations and prioritize how individuals practice their religious identity. As sociologist Nancy Ammerman contends, however, such an approach individualizes religion in problematic ways, obscuring how institutions operate in shaping lived religious experience. She argues that lived religion approaches cannot "afford to ignore the religious practices that take place inside religious institutions." For many religious practitioners these institutions significantly shape belief and practice.[27]

Religious congregations are vital to understanding the lived experiences of religious persons in the United States. As sociologists have noted, congregations serve as one of the primary means through which religious life in the US is constructed, especially, though not exclusively, for Christians.[28] This is not to say that the lived religious experience of religious practitioners must intersect with congregational life or that this experience cannot be significantly shaped outside of congregational life, but that for many religious practitioners, their congregational life significantly shapes their lived religious experience. Unique congregations like Binkley both produce and are products of the collective and unique lived religious experience of its membership.

In this way, congregational histories provide an opportunity to think about lived religion differently. Rather than thinking of congregations as static containers of lived religious practice, they become fluid and evolving participants in constructing local lived religious experience. Following the Pauline conception of the body of Christ, congregations are more than the sum of their congregants. Through the corporatization of American religious life, church bodies have their own personalities and interests—their own quirks.[29] Congregations can mature and change as new members contribute their lived religious experience to that of the collective. Congregations can also maintain a collective sense of identity that transcends the individuals who fostered and created that initial sense of collective identity. By focusing on the congregation, scholars of lived religion can see how everyday religious practice operates in community.

Approaching congregational histories in this way provides a more dynamic framework for thinking about a genre that is not altogether celebrated. Congregational histories often play into the assumption that they are inherently hagiographical and confessional in nature—that they lack a particular type of intellectual rigor. While this may often be the case, congregational histories can provide valuable scholastic insights precisely because they require attending to how the lived religious practices and experiences of individuals operate in community. Such attention requires a lot of in-between-ness and attention to relationships. Congregations foster a complex network of relationships between ministers, laity, and the wider local community. As scholars like Orsi contend, "religion is understood as a web not of meanings but of relationships" and "scholars of religion take their places as participants in these networks too."[30] In this way, successful congregational histories must construct interpretations that are intelligible to both congregational insiders and outsiders. Orsi has noted that his scholastic inquiry of the lived religion of Roman Catholics in Italian Harlem has been received warmly by practitioners who recognize themselves and loved ones in his work. Orsi writes in his third edition of the book that "remembering is a devotional act."[31] His highly respected academic engagement of this religious community also struck a devotional and religious chord with his subjects. His work balanced this in-between-ness.

Binkley: A Congregational History seeks to lean into this genre of congregational history and all its messiness and in-between-ness. The project, however, is distinctively not a hagiography. In many ways, the narrative focuses and dwells upon congregational conflicts as a means of revealing Binkley's history and identity. Rather than chronicle every jot, tittle, and potluck (and there were good potlucks as one member fondly remembered), this book at times will focus on the more disruptive elements of Binkley's history.[32] Disruptions and conflict uncover what is unique and different about a congregation's history. They reveal how a congregation changes and grows. In a similar way, the work looks beyond the walls of the church to connect Binkley to its local context in Chapel Hill, North Carolina. Congregations are not islands, isolated in and of themselves. They are enmeshed within their local communities. The context of this southern college town helped define and shape Binkley throughout the course of its ministry, but at the same time Binkley, in turn, shaped Chapel Hill in unique ways.

Given Orsi's claim that "remembering is a devotional act," it may be difficult for any congregational history to rise to the level of being characterized as a "critical" history. Religious studies scholars have devoted much ink to the question of how to position the scholar in relationship to her subjects. The in-between-ness necessitated by a congregational history is not always a welcomed scholastic location. Scholar of religion Russell McCutcheon claims that those who study religion ought to be "critics" and not "caretakers" of the religious traditions and communities they study. The binary of critic and caretaker, however, can be limiting. To resist this binary, some scholars encourage a type of critical caretaking within the analysis of religious subjects. The scholar seeks to preserve, explain, and perhaps even defend their subjects while at the same time illuminating their shortcomings and the ways in which their rhetorical and discursive constructions belie their actions and intentions.[33]

In this history, I seek this more balanced approach and oscillate between the role of critic and caretaker, yet I question whether "scholars" can always claim to be wholly unique in this question. Congregational members themselves also oscillate between critic and caretaker. In September 2019, I attended Olin T. Binkley Memorial Baptist Church's Founders' Day service. When the congregation arrived at the moment of singing the doxology within the order of worship, the entire congregation began not only singing but signing the words in American Sign Language (ASL). Although quite familiar with the tune, I was unfamiliar with the practice of signing the short hymn. The pastor, Marcus McFaul, noticed that I was caught off guard by the practice. Recognizing the service was nearing its end, he paused the order of worship and asked if an individual among the few hundred persons gathered that Sunday morning would explain why the congregation signed the doxology. A member of the choir rose and explained that years ago Binkley's membership included several deaf members and employed an interpreter at services. In an effort to be inclusive, the whole congregation began the practice of signing the doxology each Sunday. Even though those members and that ministry and interpreter were no longer a part of the congregation, Binkley continued the practice of signing the doxology as a reminder of the church's desire to be inclusive of all persons.

McFaul affirmed the congregant's explanation, but one woman rose to offer her critique of such an explanation of the practice. Through the crowd of Sunday churchgoers, the woman explained that signing the doxology was not "being inclusive." Without the presence of an ASL interpreter throughout the entirety of the service, she reasoned, it had been exclusive to persons with hearing loss. Merely signing the doxology was no substitute for welcoming someone with hearing loss into the totality of the congregation's order of worship. She argued that Binkley should not congratulate itself on some symbol of inclusivity. As she spoke, some members of the congregation began to look uncomfortable, while others seemed to roll their eyes. Still others nodded. McFaul thanked the woman for voicing her concern and echoed the sentiment that the congregation still had work to do.

In the middle of a Sunday service, this woman deconstructed the congregation's understanding of inclusivity and highlighted the limitations of the community's collective discourse. How the congregation described and defined itself in that moment was contested. This woman played the role of critic despite being a seemingly involved member of the community and committed to its care. Rising from within the congregation the woman also challenged the church's systems of authority. As one answer was proclaimed from the choir and affirmed from the pulpit, another alternate response came from within the congregation.

This is to say that while scholars provide their own perspectives, those perspectives are not wholly unique—not wholly other from those of their subjects. Both scholar and subject can engage in similar processes of critique and caretaking. As such, this history is merely "a" history of Olin T. Binkley Memorial Baptist Church. Every congregant has their own history of the congregation. Some are more detailed than others, and some may be more critical than others. As one former member, Richard Whitaker, explained at the congregation's fiftieth anniversary, his history and recollections of Binkley were defined by the "community of friends" he cultivated while a member.[34] Founding pastor, Bob Seymour, described the idea of a congregation's history thusly at the thirty-fifth anniversary of Binkley: "our separate stories enter interlocking relationships, criss-crossing like the warp and woof of a weaver's fabric, pulling the threads of our personal histories into patterns and designs with those of

Binkley members signing the doxology on Founders' Sunday in 2008.

others around us who draw us from our isolation into community and change our perspective from MY story to OUR story."[35]

This particular history of Binkley, however, comes from a congregational outsider's perspective and draws upon scholarship within the broader field of American religious history. It seeks to position Binkley and all its complexities within the broader context of twentieth-century liberal Protestantism and the competing interests that characterized and continue to characterize these circles into the twenty-first century. While this history traces Binkley's story up to the second decade of the twenty-first century, the congregation continues its life and ministry in Chapel Hill.

Themes and Organization

Woven throughout this history of Binkley Memorial Baptist Church are three primary themes. The first of these themes focuses upon the role of space and place in the founding of the church. Binkley's founders drew heavily upon the college town aesthetic of Chapel Hill, North Carolina, during its early history. The University of North Carolina's (UNC) progressive brand, while not always as progressive as it may have touted and not particularly welcomed by conservative residents, helped foster a similar progressive outlook at Binkley. As Don Freeman, a charter member, recalled, "The founding members of the church were associated with UNC in so many ways. Many of the first members were faculty or students. Others were graduates of the University, and still others owed their livelihood to the University."[36] UNC did not foster the same type of progressive activism that one might think about at a school like the University of California at Berkley. This was a southern progressivism that many of the founders, and certainly founding pastor Bob Seymour, could both relate to and resonate with. This southern progressivism was shaped by race relations and the injustices of the Jim Crow South.

This college town aesthetic faded as Binkley became more of a recognized fixture of Chapel Hill's religious landscape, but an emphasis on scholarship and the intellect continued to thrive throughout the church's history. Congregational life regularly welcomed new ideas through seminary interns from nearby schools like Southeastern Baptist Theological Seminary and Duke Divinity School. Congregational staff members often held advanced degrees, and many members of the congregation were well-educated, ordained clergy themselves. This theme of space and place works to position Binkley within the context of this southern college town and highlight the ways in which the congregation was shaped by its local community.

Second, the work considers the relationship between theology and identity as well as the processes through which institutions change their identity and accommodate new theological perspectives. Throughout Binkley's more than sixty-year history, the congregation has adopted an increasingly progressive stance on issues like women in the church, human sexuality, and climate justice. Even contemporary congregational appeals for racial justice and Black Lives Matter look far different from the church's founding support for civil rights and desegregation. As Binkley evolved as a religious community, not all its individual membership evolved with it. Through each evolution, the congregation added to its identity in ways that necessitated an intentional and sensitive balancing act. As a predominately white congregation, for Binkley, this identity was largely discreet and siloed rather than intersectional. As a result, these identities, rooted in deep convictions, came in conflict with one another. This work engages the multi-faceted ways Binkley's religious identity evolved over the course of its history as it welcomed and accommodated new theological ideas.

The congregation shaped much of this evolving religious identity in relationship to the changing religious identity among conservative evangelicals in the late twentieth and early twenty-first century. Such a project of identity was not isolated to theological doctrine, either. Scholars like Alison Greene have shown how Southern Baptist projects committed to conservative theological purity were entangled with histories of racism and white supremacy.[37] Other scholars like Seth Dowland and Marie Griffith explain how conservative theological projects embraced "family values" as a means of opposing changing cultural assumptions regarding gender and sexuality.[38] The decision to found Binkley as a different type of Southern Baptist congregation set the church on a trajectory wholly different from and yet wholly connected to this conservative project. In the same way conservative white evangelicals position themselves over and against their liberal Christian counterparts, so too did Binkley position itself in relationship to these more conservative Christian groups. The histories of both groups are intertwined and inescapable from one another.

The third and final theme this work considers is the relationship between religion and politics broadly construed. Binkley's membership, like that of other religious communities, engaged in congregational politics. The congregation developed bureaucratic systems of committees and councils designed to hold a measure of congregational authority, carry out the work of the church, and make decisions. The congregation also affiliated with numerous denominational structures that house their own bureaucratic systems and committees and councils. This project considers congregational politics as well as the role bureaucracy plays in shaping congregational decision-making processes. This is a bureaucracy that people not only accept but one in which they readily and actively participate. In this sense, congregational politics make up a significant component of the lived religious experience of congregational members. For members of Binkley, making decisions about the direction of the religious community, both large and small, is an important part of what it means to be a member of the religious congregation.

The project also considers how the congregation engaged in politics on a larger regional, state, and national level. Many scholars have addressed the ways in which conservative evangelical life has become closely wedded to the politics of the Republican Party, but fewer works have addressed how liberal Protestant groups understood themselves in relationship to the Democratic Party.[39] The congregation's loose connection to Democratic Party politics through the work of individual members serves as a departure from how more conservative Christian groups more systematically became entrenched as a primary base of the Republican Party in the latter half of the twentieth century and early twenty-first century. While Binkley's commitment to the separation of church and state may have kept the congregation from making collective partisan appeals, many individual members were active participants in the Democratic Party, holding positions at numerous levels of local, state, and national government. As congregational politics played out within the local community, they did so in relationship to the larger US political landscape.

These themes pass through to greater and lesser degrees in each of the five chapters that comprise *Binkley: A Congregational History,* and each chapter addresses a particular era within the congregation's history. The first examines the role of Chapel Hill generally and the University of North Carolina specifically in shaping the progressive and inclusive theological outlook of what would become Binkley Memorial Baptist Church. With the prospect of a growing local population in the 1950s, the congregation's founders looked to establish an additional Baptist church out of a small group from within the local Chapel Hill Baptist Church. Inspired by the spirit of southern progressivism that characterized UNC, these founders sought to create a Baptist congregation that would be welcoming to people of all racial identities. The first chapter seeks to show the ways in which a local community can shape and inspire a congregation to adopt a particular theological outlook. As a Baptist congregation, autonomous from the trappings of a rigid hierarchical denominational body, Binkley allowed its locale to shape its vision. From the naming of the church to the calling of its first pastor Robert Seymour to its open membership policy, Binkley sought to be a progressive, well-educated, college-town church.

Chapter two narrates how this college-town aesthetic inspired the congregation's participation in civil rights throughout the 1960s. As a small, young congregation, Binkley did not have the same financial and cultural weight as more established congregations in Chapel Hill. Instead, Binkley capitalized on its nimble and committed membership. Rev. Seymour regularly identified areas in the local community where church members could enter the struggle for combatting segregationist policies within the local community. Through grassroots, local politics, Binkley sought to leverage the time and energy of its membership in its fight for local change. One congregant, Fred Ellis, was elected to the school board to fight for an integrated school system. Binkley member and, at that time, relatively unknown basketball coach Dean Smith worked to recruit a Black basketball player for the Tar Heels. Congregant Howard Lee ran and was elected the first Black mayor of Chapel Hill. Binkley supported each of these individuals in a variety of ways including relieving them of leadership duties within the congregation so they could better serve in the community. Chapter two shows how a small church plant successfully leveraged its meager resources, engaged in local politics, and fought for change in the Chapel Hill community.

Binkley's commitment to the local community garnered the congregation significant notoriety by the end of the 1960s, and chapter three examines how Binkley sought to invest its cultural capital in the 1970s and 80s as it became an established fixture of religious life in Chapel Hill. Binkley continued to expand its progressive outreach within the local community and began prioritizing other issues such as gender equality. Not all of Binkley's membership, however, agreed on what to do with the church's growing standing within the community. With a growing membership and budget, the congregation devolved into a near-decade-long conflict about whether to build a new sanctuary or continue its investment in local ministries that combatted poverty and racial inequality. The church's older membership along with Seymour's desire to see a new sanctuary won out over a newer membership that had been attracted to the congregation because of its community-oriented focus. This chapter traces Binkley's contested evolution from a small, niche, college-town church to a prominent fixture of Chapel Hill's religious establishment.

Shortly after the controversial construction of Binkley's new sanctuary, Seymour retired after twenty-nine years as pastor. The minister who followed had the challenge of forging a new identity for the congregation separate and distinct from the legacy of the congregation's founding pastor. Chapter four addresses the calling of Linda Jordan, Binkley's second senior minister, and the congregation's tumultuous debate over the inclusion of LGBTQ individuals. Shortly into Jordan's tenure, John

Blevins, an openly gay Duke Divinity School student, approached Binkley about receiving ordination. Working through this process divided a congregation that had been divided over building a new sanctuary less than a decade prior. Binkley's decision to ultimately license Blevins to preach the Gospel resulted in numerous families leaving the congregation as well as Binkley's formal removal from the Southern Baptist Convention. This chapter delineates the challenges progressive congregations faced in cultivating a common discourse around human sexuality and illustrates how the church's decision shaped its identity as an unashamedly progressive congregation moving into the twenty-first century.

The final chapter of this work examines the challenges Binkley faced as a progressive congregation in need of balancing its intellectual and denominational diversity. While the latter half of the twentieth and early twenty-first century witnessed the decline of denominational authority, ecumenical congregations like Binkley worked tirelessly to foster a collective identity that welcomed a diversity of denominational and even religious backgrounds. Under Binkley's following two pastors, Jim Pike and Peter Carman, the congregation strove to balance its commitments to racial justice, gender equality, LGBTQ inclusion, and the growing necessity for climate justice among numerous other initiatives. At times these strongly held convictions came into conflict with one another and vied for the congregation's focus. The final chapter examines the challenges predominately white, liberal Protestant churches like Binkley have in establishing an intersectional ethic that remains rooted in a shared sense of religious identity.

Olin T. Binkley Memorial Baptist Church was and remains a unique Baptist congregation. From nurturing the spiritual life of Tar Heels basketball coach Dean Smith to being expelled from the Southern Baptist Convention for affirming the religious calling of a gay man, Binkley's influence stretched far beyond the walls of its church building. As a result, Binkley remained attuned to larger conversations shaping American religious life throughout the country but not at the expense of disregarding its local context. The congregation's history is deeply intertwined with the history of Chapel Hill as well as the University of North Carolina. This southern part of heaven, if it can or even should be called such, marks the congregation's primary site of ministry. In 1958, amidst the backdrop of Jim Crow, Binkley's founding members knew that this "heaven" needed some reforming, so they founded a church and got to work.

Founding a College-Town Church

WHAT KIND OF BAPTIST CHURCH is Olin T. Binkley Memorial Baptist Church? Such a question is an important one, but it is not easily answered. By early twenty-first-century standards, Binkley Baptist Church considered itself a "congregation of active open-minded, progressive Christians."[1] At Binkley's formation in 1958, however, the membership identified themselves as an evangelical congregation affiliated with the Southern Baptist Convention (SBC). Such characterizations of the church from the 1950s to the 2020s might raise questions as to whether the congregation experienced a significant transition over this period of time. Some church members might answer that question with a "yes," while others might answer that question with a "no." On one level, by the twenty-first century, Binkley was no longer affiliated with the SBC, but one could argue that this is more of a result of changes within the SBC than changes at Binkley. The question of whether the congregation remains evangelical is much more difficult to answer, and perhaps the wrong question to ask.

The term "evangelical" is nearly impossible to define through vernacular usage. Etymologically, the term stems from the Greek *evangelion* meaning "good news," and historically, during the Protestant Reformation, Protestants were characterized as *evangelisch*.[2] As Protestantism grew and diversified, the need for a more particular definition emerged. One definition of "evangelical" identifies four distinguishing components to characterize the movement: biblicism, crucicentrism, conversionism, and activism.[3] Such generic characteristics, however, could be used to identify many segments of American Protestantism that perhaps do not identify as evangelical. Some critiques of this definition have built upon it by adding a fifth characteristic centered upon the Holy Spirit, while others have found adding to a doctrinal checklist unhelpful in differentiating conservative evangelicals from more progressive evangelicals or even mainline denominational groups.[4] Journalistic uses of "evangelical" often seek to identity a conservative, white segment of the

American electorate.[5] Progressive evangelicals, like Jim Wallis of Sojourners, however, challenge journalistic definitions by maintaining a more conservative theological perspective but pushing a more progressive political agenda.[6] While at its founding Binkley likely fit into this category of progressive evangelical, such a label does not quite encapsulate the congregation's place in the American religious landscape.

Binkley's identity as a Southern Baptist congregation is similarly difficult to define. While the SBC provides an institutional apparatus to identify a Southern Baptist congregation, the SBC of the early to mid-twentieth century included a diverse composition of theological perspectives within Baptist life in the South. One historian of Southern Baptist life suggests the SBC was composed of a synthesis between four disparate Baptist traditions.[7] Within each of these traditions were those who supported and celebrated the convention's bureaucratic and institutional life as well as those who looked skeptically upon this centralized denominational structure.[8] Binkley emerged amid this complicated and sprawling denominational group. As a result, the label Southern Baptist, while not incorrect, does not serve as a helpful marker of orientation, either, because of the denomination's size and diversity.

Binkley may have initially defined itself as an evangelical and Southern Baptist congregation, but the historical baggage and fraught definitions of these labels are not adequate to understand Binkley's early history. Instead of any institutional affiliation or theological marker, the congregation's location provides better insight into the type of church it hoped to become. Its location clarified and provided texture to comprehending its institutional and theological markers of identity. Baptists practice a congregational polity that celebrates the autonomy of the local church. This means that larger Baptist denominational bodies or neighboring congregations cannot dictate how a local congregation should look or operate. In the same respect, Baptist congregations can also adopt elements and characteristics that can be found in their local context from the politics to the aesthetics to the culture more broadly. Baptists in the Republic of Georgia, for instance, have adopted the use of incense and the appointment of bishops as a way of incorporating Christian Orthodox aesthetics into their worship style.[9] The local context can serve as an alternative means for understanding congregational identity outside abstracted and universalizing terms like "evangelical" and bulky, denominational terms like "Southern Baptist." When local context and these markers of religious identity are viewed together, a clearer picture of Binkley's identity emerges.

This chapter examines the context surrounding the founding of Binkley and suggests that the importance of its proximity to the University of North Carolina at

Chapel Hill (UNC) cannot be understated. The congregation formed amid the growing southern university town of Chapel Hill, North Carolina. This collegiate context shaped the type of congregation Binkley sought to become. More than any idea of what constituted an "evangelical" or even what constituted a representative "Southern Baptist," the congregation's location shaped its identity.[10] Binkley was a college-town church. It met on the campus of UNC and counted numerous students, alumni, faculty, and staff on its membership rosters. The congregation desired rigorous and intellectual sermons from well-educated ministers. Twenty-first-century characterizations of the congregation as "open minded" harken back to a desire for free inquiry very reminiscent of early twentieth-century calls for academic freedom. Binkley was to be a congregation that thought, and studied, and learned together because they were in a context in which thinking, and studying, and learning were prioritized and encouraged.

The Quintessential Southern College Town

Founded near the ruins of an old Church of England chapel in 1795, UNC Chapel Hill was the first attempt at state-sponsored higher education in the United States. The establishment of this school in an out-of-the-way place was intentional. Historians note that state leaders in North Carolina desired for the school to be "at least five miles from any seat of government."[11] These leaders did not want students to be distracted from their studies with politics and other forms of entertainment, so a more rural environment was thought to provide an excellent context for such an institution of learning. The broader state of North Carolina also served as a conducive location for a slower and more rural experience. Geographically, North Carolina did not possess an easy access harbor that could facilitate a large, urban commercial city like Charleston, Savannah, Norfolk, or Baltimore. The location of UNC was decidedly out of the way.

Establishing the school in Chapel Hill predated the rise of what late twentieth- and early twenty-first-century Americans know as the "college town."[12] Scholars of American higher education consider the American college town to be a largely twentieth-century innovation in which a college or university and the "cultures it creates exert a dominant influence over the character" of the local town or city.[13] College towns may have a very integrated collegiate campus or one that sits on the periphery of town. They are youthful and transient places with a highly educated population. In some respect, college towns are unconventional, yet at the same time, a locale's "eccentricity is difficult to calculate."[14] In fact, one scholar has noted that "much of what makes college towns unusual and interesting cannot be quantified in any meaningful way."[15] Identifying college towns can often be reduced to the affective quality of the place or perhaps the Supreme Court's proverbial "you know it when you see it."

One common characteristic college towns often maintain is a unique and "distinct brand."[16] These brands not only "attract new students and new businesses," but they also serve as a mechanism for orienting "campus-community relationships."[17] By the early twentieth century, the University of North Carolina was developing its own unique brand of southern liberalism that centered upon academic freedom. Beginning in the 1920s under the leadership of Harry Woodburn Chase, UNC resisted the calls of individuals pushing an anti-evolutionist agenda. The 1925 Scopes Monkey Trial put this question on national display, but regional debates raged both before and after the well-known spectacle in Tennessee. For Chase, faculty members should have the right to come to their own conclusions in their research. His leadership drew harsh criticism, but it also garnered UNC a reputation and distinct brand across the south and the nation more broadly. The school would not police its faculty on the issue of evolution.[18]

With the economic downturn of the United States in the 1930s, UNC continued establishing their brand of southern liberalism through the Great Depression. Frank Porter Graham, a well-known alumnus who had once served as the university's first dean of students, succeeded Chase as president of the institution. Faculty members under both men's administrations advocated for greater cooperation among local white and Black communities and supported local and national labor movements.[19] Personally, Graham overtly supported a liberal political agenda, and one historian has described him as being "careless about signing political petitions from radically leftist groups."[20] Graham served on a number of federal commissions while serving as president of UNC from 1930 to 1949, including President Truman's 1946 Civil Rights Commission.

Despite this progressivism, the politics of the Jim Crow South continued to inform and guide both the surrounding community as well as the university's policies on segregation. The school refused to admit Black students until 1951, when a court order required the university to admit three Black students to graduate programs that had no public, segregated alternative. As one Black Chapel Hill resident remembered of the 1940s and early 1950s, the school had a "paternalist approach" to the local African American community, almost all of whom "were either working directly for the university, or indirectly."[21] In the summer of 1937, Black workers at UNC staged an uprising focused on better labor rights for the school's Black employees. It led to only minor changes in the relationship between the local Black community and the university. Activist and historian Yonni Chapman explains that although President Graham "supported [B]lack workers and racial student organizers, the trustees limited his power to promote racial justice and labor rights." Chapman argues that the progressive character of UNC did little to "advocate the end of Jim Crow" and rather merely "softened its impact." Much of the university's approach to racial injustice during this period was the product of a well-cultivated "progressive image."[22]

While it may have only been an image, this progressive image was powerful. It shaped local and regional perceptions of the school. Because of Graham's well-known politics as well as those on his faculty, critics of UNC's growing brand of southern liberalism accused the school of harboring Communists. Such accusations only furthered this progressive brand and image. Although the Red Scare of McCarthyism would not begin until 1951, anti-Communist sentiment had been simmering in the broader culture for decades.[23]

While Graham denied that the school employed Communists, he could say nothing of the students who attended the institution. In keeping with the school's protection and promotion of academic freedom, members of the student body were free to explore new ideas and express their political sympathies. Junius Scales was perhaps one of the most well-known Communists to have attended the University of North Carolina during the 1940s. Remembered as the "only American sent to prison for being a member of the Communist Party," Scales joined the Communist Party in America as an undergraduate. He served in the military during World War II before returning to Chapel Hill, where he quickly rose through the ranks of the Communist Party, publicly coordinating political activity in the southern states.[24]

Following increased surveillance by federal authorities, Scales was forced to take his political activity underground, and in 1954, he was arrested in Memphis. Authorities accused Scales of violating the Smith Act, which prohibited the membership of US citizens in groups that "advocated the violent overthrow" of the government. Scales was sentenced and served six years in federal prison, but in 1962, President Kennedy commuted his sentence to fifteen months. During the trial period, Scales became disillusioned with Communism and renounced his party affiliation.[25] Regardless of how progressive the University of North Carolina at Chapel Hill actually was, Scales's political ideology was not only shaped by his experience attending the institution, but his political activities and ultimate arrest also helped shape perceptions of the school. Scales was a product of the school's commitment to academic freedom and this brand of southern liberalism.

Baptists in the College Town

Scales provides a helpful case study for thinking about the kinds of ideas that were able to flourish in Chapel Hill in the decades before the establishment of Olin T. Binkley Memorial Baptist Church. Scales does not simply illustrate the generic kinds of radical ideas and conversations Baptists in Chapel Hill might overhear around town; rather, Scales had a relationship with the local Baptist community. The ways in which his Marxism informed his advocacy for racial and economic justice were directly and personally considered and wrestled with by some individuals in Chapel Hill's local Baptist community. In author Daphne Athas's memoir of her time growing up in Chapel Hill, she recalled once running into Scales while he was "at the Baptist Student Center."[26] He was not an infrequent visitor to the Baptist Student Center (or Union; BSU) either. Years after his arrest, Scales's defense lawyer called upon Julius C. Herrin, the Baptist campus minister who had known Scales since 1946, to serve as a character reference.[27] Herrin was a graduate of Wake Forest College and received his bachelor of divinity from Union Theological Seminary in New York City. During his eight years as student secretary he oversaw the construction of the BSU and would even serve as pastor *pro tempore* for the local Chapel Hill Baptist Church for one summer.[28] Herrin was sympathetic to many of Scales's ideals but approached them from a different perspective, and he exposed Baptist students at UNC to this perspective throughout his tenure as student secretary.

In Scales's memoir, *Cause at Heart,* he recalled that he had frequently appeared on campus or in the local community to participate in debates and panel discussions. Reverend Herrin and the BSU in particular had invited Scales several times "to address the group." Herrin even debated Scales one time in a dormitory. While not a Communist, Herrin pushed the boundaries of Southern Baptist theology engaging in such debate.[29] Both Herrin and Scales found common ground on many issues. Scales recalled "challenging the Baptist students to surpass the Communists in building a better world and in fighting racism and injustice." He told them that if they succeeded, he "would leave the Communist Party and join the Baptist church." Scales did not consider himself to be a "good speaker," but he found these back-and-forth exchanges with religious communities "relaxed" him and improved his "effectiveness."[30] For Herrin, they provided opportunities for BSU students to think critically about their faith and its role in the public sphere.

Scales's relationship with religious congregations was even documented by the FBI, which had been surveilling Scales since the early 1940s. Agents documented Scales encouraging Communist Party members to organize through churches, noting, "[Scales] suggested that one member attend church as part of this mass [organizing] activity." Scales continued explaining to his fellow comrades that he "had attended church every Sunday wherever he happened to be, unless at the time too many of his associates were under surveillance."[31] The bureau held concerns that Communists were attempting to infiltrate American churches, and Scales seemingly provided them a reason to continue to worry about this possibility. Scales's close ties to Baptists like Herrin may not have resulted in any infiltration, but it did indicate that the community of Baptist students at UNC was willing to entertain conversation and debate with Scales's more radical ideology.[32]

Under the leadership of Herrin, Baptist students at UNC pushed the boundaries of Baptist political engagement. They directly addressed questions of racism and segregation that made the local Chapel Hill Baptist Church uneasy. While this congregation may have welcomed enslaved people at its founding in 1854, since Reconstruction, the church had only welcomed white members.[33] Herrin briefly served as interim pastor of the congregation in the early 1950s, but his liberalism eventually became a source of tension between himself and the congregation. Under Herrin's leadership, the BSU challenged, in their own way, the status quo of segregation in Chapel Hill. In the early 1950s, UNC students began inviting students from the local Shaw University, a historically Black institution, to participate in weekly dinners and socials. Since the BSU often met at Chapel Hill Baptist Church, this caused concern among some of the congregation's more conservative members.

One Sunday morning in 1953, at the prompting of Herrin and the BSU, roughly ten Black students showed up for morning worship. Upon entering the sanctuary, Jim Phipps, chairman of the deacons, called an emergency meeting of the church's leadership to take place in the back of the sanctuary. After discussion, a majority of the deacons present affirmed the students' right to attend, and Phipps "stormed out of the meeting," leaving the sanctuary. Following the events of that morning, the church formed a committee on "interracial gatherings" and sought to strike a "middle course" allowing for student interracial gatherings under the leadership and supervision of Herrin but recommending Sunday morning services remain segregated.[34] Such a decision by Chapel Hill Baptist followed in the tradition of many white congregations in the South who likewise opposed the attendance of Black individuals in Sunday services.[35]

Even though the church came to some measure of compromise, some members of the congregation went to the state convention to ask for Herrin's removal before he "caused a riot" in the church.[36] The Baptist State Convention took the congregation's request seriously but remained secretive about its attempts to remove Herrin.

The *Durham Morning Herald* later published a piece of investigative journalism highlighting the tension, explaining that the convention's investigation had "been conducted largely in secret." The paper reported that Herrin "incurred the wrath of many members and leaders in the Chapel Hill Baptist Church on race matters."[37] Despite his liberalism, Herrin remained popular among the students of the BSU. Perhaps because of his popularity among the students, the convention delayed firing Herrin until the student group invited a liberal theologian from Vanderbilt School of Divinity, Nels F. S. Ferré, to speak at a statewide Baptist meeting. The convention received enough complaints from around the state over inviting Ferré that they asked Herrin and two of his colleagues from other schools to resign. All three refused in protest and were subsequently fired.[38] The state Baptist newspaper gave the ordeal little column space. The paper published the recommendation and firing of the three campus ministers but remained positive toward all three. Of Herrin, the *Biblical Recorder* claimed to have the "highest regard" but noted that the continued "friction" between him and the congregation was not conducive to an effective campus ministry.[39] It appeared that Chapel Hill Baptist was not as amenable to UNC's brand of open inquiry and southern liberalism as Herrin was through his leadership of the BSU.

The college-town context of Chapel Hill is important for understanding the identity of Binkley Memorial Baptist Church. While Presidents Chase and Graham as well as Junius Scales predated the establishment of Binkley, they characterize a brand of southern liberalism that would come to inform the congregation's founding. Julius Herrin ensured that Baptists in Chapel Hill engaged this brand even if it may have caused friction with the local Chapel Hill Baptist Church. Herrin guided Baptist students at UNC for eight years, not only making sure that they regularly heard progressive or even radical ideas, but also engaging them in open inquiry and debate. They did not simply reject Scales's Marxism wholesale but saw the elimination of racism and injustice, as Scales wrote, a point of common cause. When a small group of Baptists began the process of envisioning a new congregation in Chapel Hill four years after Herrin was fired, they sought to establish a congregation with a similar brand to UNC—one of southern liberalism centered upon free inquiry and academic freedom.

It was the University of North Carolina's reputable and largely respected brand within the wider world of American higher education coupled with the economic growth following World War II that helped poise Chapel Hill for a sizable increase in population. Such demographic projections had several ramifications for the local town and economy but also for houses of worship in the local area. The few scholars who have analyzed college towns have largely neglected the relationship between congregation and collegiate environment. Geographer Blake Gumprecht has suggested that "college town residents are less religious than the general population" and "are less likely to belong to organized religions." At the same time, many of those who do not belong to formal religious congregations may "consider themselves spiritual."[40] While such statistics may provide a general sociological understanding of individuals who live in college towns, such an observation does not shed light on the religious congregations who reside in these unique settings. Binkley Memorial Baptist Church is one such church and served as the Southern Baptist response to Chapel Hill's growth as well as a response to Chapel Hill Baptist Church's resistance to UNC's brand of southern liberalism. The founding members of Binkley decided to establish a congregation that would work with rather than against this college-town brand.

It was James Cansler, the successor to Julius Herrin as director of the BSU, who reported to the local Yates Baptist Association in 1956 that in ten years' time the estimated "enrollment at Carolina will be doubled."[41] The small college town of Chapel Hill was growing, and the Yates Association needed to allocate their resources properly to keep pace with the growing population. At that point in time, Chapel Hill Baptist Church was the only Southern Baptist congregation in the area. Taking this information into consideration, the following year the association began prospecting a tract of land in the Glen Lennox area of Chapel Hill off the 15–501 bypass just north of the university.[42] Initially the membership of Chapel Hill Baptist was reluctant to consider the possibility of planting a new congregation. After some coaxing, however, Fred and Elizabeth Ellis agreed to lead a small group through the process of conceptualizing the establishment of a new congregation. They saw this as an opportunity to think beyond the limitations and conservativism present at Chapel Hill Baptist. They could instead shape a new congregation in the image of Chapel Hill, and they did just that.

In November, following the Yates Associational meeting, the Ellises enlisted the help of their neighbors and fellow church members, Michael and Cora Lee Berkut and Bill and Hilda Moffitt. Shortly thereafter Leo and Grace Wagoner joined the group.[43] In addition to all being members of Chapel Hill Baptist Church, each family had a close relationship with the University of North Carolina as either alumni of the institution or employees or faculty of the school. For instance, both Fred Ellis and Michael Berkut taught in the School of Medicine. As students, most of them predated Herrin's tenure in the BSU, but most of them were members of Chapel Hill Baptist Church when Herrin was fired. It is possible that neither Herrin's firing

Some of Binkley's founding members at the fiftieth anniversary celebration. *Left to right:* Grace Wagoner, Leo Wagoner, Sam Wilburn, Bill Moffitt, Hilda Moffitt, Mike Berkut, and Nettie Bradley Wilburn.

nor the congregation's policies on interracial gatherings sat well with this group of young families. This group of four families would take the following year to meet with denominational and local leaders to discuss and study Baptist polity as well as the purpose and role of the local church. Through their conversations, the founding members sought to establish a church that would meet the needs of their local community in Chapel Hill. It would be a progressive congregation that built upon the ideals of academic freedom and the liberal tradition of the southern college town in which it found itself. Herrin's legacy would live on. It would do so, however, through another name—Binkley.

Naming a College-Town Church

As the group from Chapel Hill Baptist Church consulted with various Baptist leaders around the state about the nature of starting a new congregation, they met with the academic dean of Southeastern Baptist Theological Seminary.[44] Throughout much of the twentieth century, few Baptists in North Carolina did not know the name Olin Trivette Binkley. The son of a bivocational Baptist preacher and farmer in North Carolina, Binkley excelled in his early studies and felt a call to be a preacher at a young age. He graduated high school at age fourteen and matriculated at Wake Forest College—at the time a prominent Baptist institution in the state. He would later attend Southern Baptist Theological Seminary in Louisville, Kentucky, for his bachelor of theology and Yale University for both his bachelor of divinity and PhD. Over the course of his studies, Binkley developed an affection for theological higher education and would devote much of his career to teaching. During his lifetime, he taught classes at the University of North Carolina, Wake Forest College, Southern Baptist Theological Seminary, and Southeastern Baptist Theological Seminary in Wake Forest, North Carolina, where he concluded his career as dean and later president of the institution. He served as president for eleven years before retiring in 1974.[45]

Many of the members of the small group likely remembered or knew of Dr. Binkley from his time in Chapel Hill when he served as pastor of Chapel Hill Baptist Church. Dr. Binkley took the position of interim pastor at the church upon receiving his doctorate from Yale. After only a few weeks as interim pastor, the congregation offered him the position permanently. He stayed in Chapel Hill for five years. During this time, he not only pastored the church, but he also served as director of the BSU. In 1937, Binkley was invited to teach in the Sociology Department at UNC. He recalled later in life that students initially objected to studying under a "damned Baptist Preacher," but by the spring semester his enrollment numbers surpassed classroom capacity.[46] Binkley fit into the culture at UNC precisely because he had a progressive edge to his theological perspective. When he later taught at Wake Forest College, he introduced students to the writings of Walter Rauschenbusch—an American Baptist of German descent known for his advocacy of the Social Gospel. Many Southern Baptists were apprehensive about emphasizing the social elements of Christianity, but Binkley made this theological liberalism a staple of his teaching.[47]

Binkley's theological progressivism marked a strange amalgamation of competing theological perspectives. He inherited a Southern Baptist evangelical theology that promoted a personal salvation, but during his time at Yale University he studied Neo-Orthodox theology under H. Richard Niebuhr. Along with his brother Reinhold, Niebuhr participated in the rise of the movement known as Christian Neo-Orthodoxy that emphasized God's transcendence and humanity's sinfulness. Both Niebuhr brothers were known for espousing a type of Christian realism that sought to balance humanity's capacity to achieve the good with humanity's sinful nature.[48] This theological position pushed back against the optimism of the early twentieth century's Social Gospel movement but remained deeply concerned with the role of Christianity in addressing social challenges. For Binkley, both theological perspectives—Neo-Orthodoxy and the Social Gospel—were novel theological systems. They were not well known in Southern Baptist circles. As a result, he did not hold the same criticisms of the Social Gospel as his advisor, and because of this, Binkley would come to adopt elements of both conflicting theological schemes. Despite working under one of the country's foremost Neo-Orthodox thinkers, Binkley still came to appreciate elements of the Social Gospel.[49]

Students at UNC may have initially been skeptical of Binkley, but they soon realized he was not the typical Southern Baptist preacher they may have expected. Mixing elements of the Social Gospel and Neo-Orthodoxy into his Southern Baptist upbringing gave Binkley a novel perspective when he returned to the South after graduating from Yale. In his 1945 book, *From Victory Unto Victory,* elements of this theological concoction are evident. On the one hand, Binkley explained that in a post-WWII era, "the primary objective of Christian missions is to bring the gospel of Jesus Christ to bear in a saving power upon the lives of people."[50] Later on in the work, however, he pushed beyond the question of personal salvation and Christian mission to address the challenges of unsolved social "problems of economic injustices, international animosities, and racial conflicts."[51] In *The Churches and the Social Conscience,* Binkley more explicitly discussed Christianity's role in addressing these types of social problems, directly stating, "Religion is a significant factor in social change. It inspires social reform and affects economic and political trends. It produces prophetic personalities, men and women of ethical insight and good will, who disturb the mores."[52] Binkley preached that the social component of Christianity could not be abandoned for an entirely personal Gospel.

Other scholars have noticed that networks of "progressive religious dissenters among Southern Baptists" emerged as the popularity of the Social Gospel gave way to the rise of Neo-Orthodox thought.[53] Binkley modeled this well. He recognized and acknowledged the Neo-Orthodox critiques that "human sin and human finitude" could not "change the social order in the direction of the Kingdom of God on earth."[54] He countered these critiques with what he saw as "evidences of the vitality of the Christian tradition and of the Christian conscience."[55] Coming to embrace the Social Gospel movement after it had fallen from popularity, Binkley embraced a Social Gospel theology fully aware of its limitations and criticisms. He did not completely abandon his Southern Baptist roots, either. Instead, he cobbled together a theological orientation that combined conflicting theological perspectives. As a result, Southern Baptists found that Binkley possessed both a familiarity as well as a progressive novelty.

Binkley's more progressive outlook on his Baptist faith inspired the small group from Chapel Hill Baptist Church that was planning to establish this new church. After meeting with numerous Baptist leaders around the state in addition to Binkley, the group began pondering a name for the new congregation. They desired to "find a name for the Church in harmony with their religious beliefs and their understandings and qualifications of the Christian ministry."[56] Dr. Binkley fit their vision of the congregation. At the end of June in 1958, members of the group met with Dr. Binkley to inform him that he was to be the congregation's namesake. Following this meeting, Binkley chronicled his feelings on a couple of index cards. He scribbled that he "expressed appreciation of their confidence," but also found himself "surprised and humbled and somewhat bewildered" at their decision. He told the group that he would need some time to process and consider their request.[57]

Over the next ten days, Dr. Binkley considered whether to grant the congregation permission to utilize his name. During that time, he also contemplated the proposed versions of the name. The group was torn between naming the congregation "The Olin T. Binkley Baptist Church; The Binkley Chapel Baptist Church; or The Binkley Memorial Baptist Church."[58] After consideration, Dr. Binkley wrote to Fred Ellis offering his own thoughts on the specifics of the name. He suggested that "the term 'Chapel' has been used occasionally, but it appears that the term memorial has been used more frequently in the names of Baptist churches in this State." Binkley concluded his letter granting the group permission to use his name "in any way that may seem appropriate to you in the new venture." Binkley acknowledged that he was "not worthy of the honor" the group granted him in their request but would make himself available should they find a way that he could be helpful in their endeavor.[59]

Seeking to take advantage of Dr. Binkley's offer, the church asked him to serve as the interim pastor of the congregation until they hired a permanent minister. Such a request was more than Dr. Binkley was willing and able to provide at the time, and he cordially declined.[60] Instead, he secured the help of another faculty member of Southeastern Theological Seminary, John T. Wayland, to fill the pulpit of the church for three months, or roughly by the first of the new year, until it could secure a pastor.[61]

On September 21, 1958, a service of organization was held for Olin T. Binkley Memorial Baptist Church in Hill Music Hall on the campus of the UNC. At this inaugural service, the membership of the new congregation would clearly state their intention and purpose to establish a new Baptist church amidst the "rapid expansion" of Chapel Hill's residential community in addition to the "increasing number of students." They desired to "re-examine" and "re-evaluate" their Christian faith in "relation to the problems of the day."[62] The new congregation resolved:

1. To lead unsaved people to Christ.
2. To guide and inspire professing Christians to more abundant living.
3. To attract children and young people and stimulate their spiritual development by a program of Christian fellowship and recreation.
4. To provide a Church home for college students, and aid them in their search for a satisfying interpretation of the Christian faith.
5. To encourage family unity in home devotion, in Church worship, and in wholesome recreation.
6. To participate in the fulfillment of the world-wide mission obligation of the Church.
7. To relate the principles of Christianity to all matters of human concern in such a way that the Christian's intent will be strengthened to keep his secular life in harmony with his religious life.[63]

While elements and understandings of these principles would change and evolve over the course of the congregation's history, it is important to highlight the role of UNC in shaping the congregation's mission and purpose. The growth of the school and surrounding area was pivotal in establishing Binkley. At the center of the resolutions outlining the congregation's purpose were college students and the desire to help them find a "satisfying interpretation" of Christianity.

Speaking at the inaugural service, Dr. Binkley challenged the new congregation to avail themselves of all the resources available to them. He highlighted the congregation's "disciplined and dedicated minds" and expressed a desire that they would use their "intellectual powers in the interest of the kingdom of God." Binkley also pointed to the "enormous storehouse of learning" housed within the nearby UNC library—a collection that, while significant, he noted could not compare to the brief yet profound teaching of Jesus that has "enlarged and enriched the intellectual life of mankind." Lastly, Dr. Binkley encouraged the congregation to seek the help of the Holy Spirit to "draw believers together . . . and interpret the mind of Christ."[64] In this collegiate setting, Binkley encouraged his namesake congregation to rely upon their intellect but not without also appealing to the Holy Spirit.

The congregation's emphasis on its relationship and proximity to the university shaped its identity. In retelling the congregation's founding, members have often highlighted Binkley Baptist's commitment to inclusivity. In a brief historical essay on the first ten years of the congregation, one member wrote that from the congregation's beginning, "there was no stated nor hidden barriers based on race, color or national origin."[65] While this certainly was a strongly held desire within the congregation, it was one among many. Likely their focus upon the collegiate environment gave rise to a complimentary desire to welcome people of all racial backgrounds. Black students, although few, were now attending UNC. The school reluctantly accepted a few Black students to both the law school and medical school in 1951 because there were no public alternatives. It was not until after *Brown v. Board of Education* (1954) that the undergraduate program began to admit African American students.[66] It took until 1968 before the total number of Black undergraduate students approached 1 percent of the total student body.[67] While the university did not serve as the best model of racial inclusivity, the presence of Black students on campus provided Binkley a means of envisioning their campus congregation as a welcoming community for all people regardless of racial identity.

Additionally, Binkley members were well aware of the policies enacted by Chapel Hill Baptist Church that led to the firing of BSU director Herrin. That church's uneasiness with biracial BSU gatherings in their sanctuary also likely influenced the Binkley's decision to create a community without membership restrictions based upon race.

Binkley founders undoubtedly supported these advances by UNC, however glacial they may have been. At the same time, the congregation's founding documents did not make racial inclusivity as explicit of a priority as those documents sought to prioritize other things. The topic of race, for instance, made no appearance in Binkley's "Resolution of Purpose." In the congregation's affirmation of faith, they expressed a belief that anyone who confessed their sin and professed faith in Jesus, "regardless of creed or race," became a child of God.[68] The church covenant similarly explained that members agreed to "recognize the dignity and sanctity of every person." At the conclusion of the inaugural service of organization, the congregation sang from the well-known hymn "In Christ there is No East or West," which includes the line "Join hands, then, brothers of the faith, what e're your race may be: Who serves my Father as a son is surely kin to me."[69] Such platitudes, while not insignificant, were not as forceful as they could have been. Such language did not even rise to the wording used by the Southern Baptist Annual Convention that year when it explicitly made a call for racial reconciliation. The convention encouraged Southern Baptist congregations to "meet the imperative need for racial reconciliation and seek the restoration of communication and fellowship with people of every race and nationality."[70]

Regardless of how explicit or implicit, vocal or taciturn the newly founded congregation was on the question of accepting Black members, the idea was present within the congregation from its founding. Three months into the life of the church, Binkley turned their idea of a congregation that welcomed members regardless of race into a reality. In January 1959, Binkley welcomed its first Black member into the church. George Grigsby was from Holly Springs, North Carolina, and was one of only twenty-three Black freshmen admitted to UNC's undergraduate program that academic year. He joined Binkley in January, a few months before the congregation called its first pastor, who remembered Grigsby as a "soft-spoken lad" who "seemed very comfortable in a predominately white group." Little fanfare was made of his membership and, as a result, the local paper reported the news of the congregation's acceptance of a Black member five months late.[71]

Grigsby's status as a student was important. Binkley was first and foremost founded as a college-town church. The congregation's commitment to welcoming members regardless of racial identity was rooted in what they saw as the progressive brand of both UNC and the Baptist tradition of the church's namesake. The congregation sought to champion a progressive Baptist identity shaped by individuals like Dr. Binkley and Rev. Herrin. Both men pushed the theological boundaries of Baptist life, and both were able to do so because of their context working in close relationship to institutions of higher education. This is not to make a claim that UNC or colleges and universities in general are inherently progressive and liberal institutions, but rather to claim that the brand and perception of these schools can be formative. At its founding, the fight for racial equality and civil rights remained an implicit or even unspoken part of the congregation's larger mission. Binkley would seek to make the issue of race a more explicit priority through the calling of a college-town preacher eager and ready to lead a congregation committed to the equality of all people.

Calling a College-Town Pastor

While the church may not have strongly stated in their founding documents that they intended to be a congregation inclusive of all races, the decision to welcome George Grigsby reveals that Binkley did intend to welcome and admit non-white members into the congregation from the very beginning. Perhaps the most significant decision that signaled this intention was the search for and selection of a senior minister. It took the congregation only a few months of searching before they settled upon calling Dr. Robert "Bob" Seymour, a pastor from Mars Hill Baptist Church just North of Asheville, North Carolina, on the campus of Mars Hill College. Seymour had been one of the leaders that Binkley's founders had consulted during their planning phase in the months leading up to the congregation's inaugural service.[72] He, his wife Pearl, and their two children would leave a roughly one-hundred-year-old congregation that had recently completed a building expansion providing the church with over sixty rooms of office and meeting space to lead a small church plant that did not even possess a permanent church building.[73] Little did the Seymours know, they would commit the rest of both their professional and personal lives to Binkley Baptist Church.

Bob Seymour grew up in South Carolina. He was born at the Greenwood County Hospital in the summer of 1925. Greenwood was a growing textile center in the state, but it also had the highest rate of lynching in South Carolina during the era of Jim Crow.[74] As Seymour recalled in his memoir, *"Whites Only": A Pastor's Retrospective on Signs of the New South*, his parents did their best to shelter him from this racial violence, and he never recalled hearing about lynching growing up. Even so, he wrote, "indoctrination in racial differences began for me from the day of my birth. . . . White supremacy reigned supreme."[75] Seymour was born breathing the air of white supremacy and would spend the rest of his life and career attempting to make sense of his experience and to correct, as he put it, the "prejudicial conditioning of those first formative years."[76]

South Carolina had been home for Seymour's family for multiple generations. His maternal grandfather had the opportunity to begin a career at the local telephone company, and he was able to provide a comfortable life for his family. Growing up, the Seymour family attended the First Baptist Church of Greenwood, where they sat on the first pew every Sunday morning. Seymour would come to describe the church as a "conservative congregation without a strident tone of voice and where everything was done decently and in order."[77] It was not a biracial congregation, and local Black residents only attended for the occasional funeral.

In his home life, Seymour recalled numerous Black employees who lived and worked on his family's property. Sadie was "the cook at the big house" and Uncle Henry and Aunt Ada lived a short walk down the hill from the main residence. When Seymour's parents moved into a house next door, Rosa came to work for Seymour's mother and consequently took care of Seymour as well. Rosa's two oldest sons, Frank and James, would be Seymour's playmates until they reached school age and societal rules separated them. Reflecting on his childhood experiences, Seymour remembered the "special relationship" his grandfather shared with Uncle Henry. Similarly, he recalled images of his mother and Rosa working side by side, "cleaning, cooking, and preparing to entertain."[78] While "on the surface southern culture could be characterized as polite, pleasant, and peaceful," Seymour recognized later in life that "there has always been a dark side with the potential for violence lurking just beneath the veneer of societal protocol."[79] His early childhood was shaped by these relationships.

When Seymour graduated from high school, his classmates predicted that he would "either be a preacher or a politician."[80] He pursued the former. Rather than attend Furman University, the Southern Baptist institution in nearby Greenville, followed by Southern Baptist Theological Seminary, the flagship SBC seminary in Louisville, Seymour took a different path to his theological education. With America in the midst of World War II, Seymour delayed enlistment for a year, enrolling at The Citadel, a military institution that would prepare him for military service. His experience at the school could not have been more unpleasant. Before the conclusion of his freshman year, Seymour enlisted in the navy's new V-12 program that was designed to both train officers and sustain the student populations at more than 130 institutions of higher learning across the country. The following year the navy placed Seymour at Newberry College, a Lutheran school in South Carolina, and he later transferred again to Duke University for his senior year.[81]

Upon graduating from Duke, Seymour continued his education through the navy to become a military chaplain. This path led him to Yale Divinity School, where he studied with many of the same faculty who trained Olin Binkley a little more than a decade earlier. Seymour and Binkley were not the only two progressive Southern Baptists that Yale trained during this period. Will Campbell, a self-described "bootleg preacher" and author of the well-known memoir *Brother to a Dragonfly*, attended Yale Divinity School before becoming the chaplain of the University of Mississippi and later a civil rights leader with the National Council of Churches.[82] All three shared the experience of learning theology outside Southern Baptist circles, and this experience shaped each of them as they became progressive voices for white Baptists upon returning to the South.

Seymour later described living outside the South as a life-changing experience. Living in New Haven, Connecticut, provided him the first opportunity to see "[B]lacks and whites living together as equals."[83] He described the impact of living with Black peers as "something akin to a religious conversion."[84] As a rare

Southern Baptist at Yale, Seymour challenged the southern caricatures many of his classmates had developed while living above the Mason-Dixon line. Seymour, too, came to reflect upon his southern identity. Over the course of his studies, his theological conservatism evolved to accommodate theological perspectives from liberal Protestant movements like the Social Gospel and Neo-Orthodoxy. Much like Binkley, Seymour too studied both movements simultaneously and adopted elements of both perspectives despite Neo-Orthodox critiques of the Social Gospel. Seymour's parents, and particularly his father, struggled to understand this evolution. Years after his graduation, he overheard his father say to an acquaintance, "I lost my son at Yale."[85] Such tension reveals the weight and challenge progressive Southern Baptists faced from the communities that raised them as their faith and theology changed.

Instead of going straight into the ministry, Seymour pursued further studies at the University of Edinburgh following his time at Yale. He thought that he could use some time away from the United States. Much like Yale gave Seymour perspective on his "southernness," Edinburgh gave him perspective on his Americanness. He wrote his dissertation on the eighteenth-century Baptist theologian John Gill. According to Seymour's research, Gill was a hyper-Calvinist minister who had a "withering effect" upon the growth of English Baptists. Gill's theological perspective provided ministers "no prerogative to offer Christ and His salvation to sinners lest they interfere with the work of God who will save whom He will." Such a perspective rubbed against Seymour's more progressive theology. At the same time, Seymour recognized the Baptist elements of Gill's theological orientation—from his "interpretation of Baptism" to "his insistence upon the Bible as the sole rule of faith and practice" as well as "his understanding of church organization."[86] Seymour began his dissertation, but after one year decided to put off writing the project until a later time and entered full-time ministry.

Seymour's northern and international educational experiences provided a particular challenge in finding a pastoral call in a Southern Baptist congregation. Southerners, like Seymour's father, looked upon northern education and liberalism with much skepticism. Seymour managed to return to the American South, however, through an associate ministry position at Myers Park Baptist Church in Charlotte, North Carolina. Myers Park was established in the early 1940s across the street from Queens College and grew quickly after its founding. The church's first pastor, George Heaton, recalled that the congregation's early membership desired to create a church that was nothing like the congregations in which they had grown up. While southern religion was often understood to be emotional and ignorant,

Myers Park sought to be intelligent and thoughtful.[87] It was perhaps the perfect first vocational call for a young Seymour.

While Seymour did not recall race being a subject of controversy at Myers Park, he was formed by the congregation's admittance of non-Baptist members. For Baptist congregations of the period, membership was predicated upon whether individuals had received adult baptism. Myers Park became divided on this issue, with some members believing baptism to be necessary and others much more amenable to an open-membership policy that would welcome and admit individuals who had received baptism as infants within other denominations. Such a debate within a Southern Baptist congregation was quite novel, and it shaped Seymour's ecumenism.[88] As a young minister, Seymour took his experience of this division over membership and allowed it to shape how he conceptualized congregational membership more broadly—with regard to the question of Black membership in a predominately white congregation.

After a short year at Myers Park, Seymour took his first senior pastorate at First Baptist Church of Warrenton, a racially divided, rural community just south of the Virginia border in North Carolina. Seymour was far more progressive in his theology and politics than either the residents of Warrenton or his congregation. He raised eyebrows in the community through the relationships he formed with local American Indian and Black residents. Seymour desired to make racial justice part of his ministry at Warrenton, but the congregation was resistant.[89] When the church's deacons confronted him about his activity in the local community, Seymour explained that his objective was "not to start a revolution" nor "to stir up antagonisms." He instead explained that "God is no respecter of persons" and he merely sought to bridge divides and live into what he believed was a Christian calling.[90]

Seymour recounted learning much from his time at Warrenton. He learned that despite his best efforts to preach against racial segregation from the pulpit, numerous well-prepared and thoughtful sermons paled in comparison to holding interracial meetings. Seymour identified local community issues that affected both Black and white residents of Warrenton and used these issues strategically to bring people together. He also found that he relied more heavily upon scripture as his first line of defense against critics of his more progressive stances. Pointing to the Bible was an effective mode of argumentation. Despite learning a great deal from pastoring this more conservative congregation, after two years of living in Warrenton, Seymour discovered the town seemed to be becoming more resistant to racial change. Reading the signs of the times, he resigned from his position as pastor in 1953, returning to work on his dissertation.[91]

After two years of work, Seymour completed his PhD and took advantage of an opportunity to return to full-time ministry in 1955 at Mars Hill College in Mars Hill, North Carolina. The school was one of several Baptist institutions of higher learning in the state. While members of the Baptist State Convention warned the congregation of Seymour's liberalism, the church hired him anyway. Seymour thrived in this congregation. College students flocked to hear the young preacher who did not proclaim a fundamentalist ideology like many were accustomed to hearing in their home congregations. On Sunday mornings, college students crowded together in the church's balcony to hear the week's sermon. Numerous faculty members, administrators, and other ordained ministers also counted themselves among the active membership of the church.

From the beginning of his tenure at Mars Hill, Seymour was deliberate in stating his opinions on the issue of race. In one of his first sermons, Seymour preached on John 1:46, in which the disciple Nathanael asks whether anything good can come from Nazareth. Seymour drew the parallel between discrimination against those from Nazareth in the first century and the discrimination experienced by Black Americans in 1950s America. In the mountains of Western North Carolina, where there were fewer Black Americans, Seymour's message was more positively received than in rural Warrenton. He became a prominent speaker among Baptist college students at denominational meetings across the state. After the passage of *Brown v. Board of Education* (1954), Seymour began slowly pushing Mars Hill faculty and administrators to begin accepting Black students. While the school refused to do so until 1961, long after Seymour had left, he laid a foundation for this change through his tenure as pastor at Mars Hill Baptist Church.[92]

Seymour's time at Mars Hill was significant for personal reasons as well. While pastoring the congregation, he also secretly began dating and subsequently married Pearl Francis, who served as the church's organist. Pearl was from LaFollette, Tennessee, and in addition to her responsibilities as organist, she also taught music at the college. They announced their engagement to the congregation at an open house on April Fool's Day, much to the surprise and delight of many congregants. After their wedding, the Seymour family grew to include their two children—Robert and Frances.[93]

Pearl and Bob were happy at Mars Hill, and Bob's success in the wider denomination drew attention. In particular, he drew attention from the members of the newly formed Binkley Memorial Baptist Church. Seymour's success in a college town, communicating with students and faculty alike, made him the perfect candidate for the new congregation. His stance on racial justice was also appealing to

Bob and Pearl Seymour. Photo made available thanks to the Seymour family.

the membership of Binkley. Because of Seymour's reputation within Baptist life in North Carolina, his call to serve as the first pastor of the church, more so perhaps than the founding documents, signaled Binkley's commitment to racial justice and inclusion in their church community.

For Seymour, leaving Mars Hill to start a new congregation in Chapel Hill was a bold and interesting decision. As he remembered, however, it offered a "unique opportunity to bring into being a new Baptist Church in a University community."[94] On January 13, 1959, he wrote to founding member Bill Moffitt, "After much prayer and most careful consideration, I have decided to accept your Call."[95] Both Dr. Binkley and the church's interim pastor John Wayland congratulated Seymour, explaining the congregation's need for a "vital relation to the University" and need for a "liberal witness," respectively.[96] Other clergy in the area also congratulated Seymour and described his willingness to leave Mars Hill to accept a position offering sixty dollars a week as an "admirable act of 'Christian devotion.'"[97] Rev. Charles M. Jones, a white, activist pastor in Chapel Hill who was accused of heresy by the local Presbytery in the late 1940s, congratulated Seymour and looked forward to "inter-church fellowship opportunities" with the recently founded Community Church—a Unitarian Universalist congregation he led.[98] For both Seymour and those who congratulated him, Olin T. Binkley Memorial Baptist Church presented an opportunity to establish a liberal congregation that could respond to the needs of this rapidly changing college town.

The Challenge of Being a College-Town Church

Operating within a college-town, Binkley quickly set itself apart from other Baptist churches in North Carolina through its approach to membership. Not only was the predominately white congregation accepting of Black members, but the church's ecumenism also signaled a willingness to accept non-Baptists as members. Southern Baptists for much of the twentieth century had been reluctant if not adamantly opposed to participating in ecumenical organizations like the National Council of Churches. While individuals and certain congregations were more amenable to interdenominational cooperation, like Myers Park in Charlotte, the denomination as a whole often worked independently. Binkley's membership, however, was more interested in interdenominational partnership than the larger SBC. The church overtly signaled their ecumenical orientation through a novel membership policy. Although at the congregation's inaugural service of organization, those gathered to constitute the new church affirmed a belief that "baptism by immersion is a prerequisite to full membership in a Baptist Church," the church decided to not follow such a statement. Baptism by immersion would not be the only prerequisite in *this* Baptist church.[99] Deviating from this norm later cost Binkley their partnership and cooperation with their local Baptist association.

Within the church's constitution, the founders provided a means for individuals who had not received adult baptism by immersion to become members. The document explained that "Those who are active members of other churches in the evangelical tradition may be received either after transfer of their letter or after baptism by immersion at their request."[100] Such a statement was quite radical for a Southern Baptist congregation, as it meant that individuals raised as Methodists or Presbyterians could become members of Binkley through a transfer of letter without receiving baptism by immersion. It also meant that the church would recognize infant baptisms. Later in the congregation's history, it removed the phrase "in the evangelical tradition," further broadening the membership policy to welcome individuals raised in non-evangelical traditions. Even the progressive Myers Park Baptist Church, where Seymour first served, struggled to make such a definitive stance a few years earlier. As a church operating within a transient college town, such a policy opened the door for students outside the Baptist fold to join and participate in the life of the congregation during their short time in college.

Binkley's ecumenical position, however, raised problems for the congregation's participation in the local Yates Baptist Association, a regional body within the Southern Baptist Convention. From early in the process of drafting their covenant and constitution, the founding members anticipated apprehension from other Baptist groups about how far they could push their desire to be ecumenical. Fred Ellis wrote to Olin Binkley a month before the congregation's formal founding to explain this apprehension. "One of our particular concerns," he wrote, "is the matter of just how strongly we can state our conviction in regard to the ecumenical brotherhood and still retain our Baptist identity and effective relationship with the organizations of our denomination."[101] Before any official ruling on the congregation's membership in the local association, Binkley was "received under the watchcare of the Association for a period of one year."[102] The status of watchcare served as a trial period, delaying a more permanent decision. Ellis hoped he could mount a satisfactory defense of the membership policy before the association made an official ruling. Since Baptists practice a type of congregational polity, Binkley had the power to chart its own course, but at the same time, local networks and associations of Baptist churches too had the power to refuse cooperation with Binkley.

The following year, however, the local association delayed any ruling on the congregation's membership, extending the church's period "under watchcare."[103] While the minutes from the Yates Associational meeting do not indicate why Binkley's membership was delayed, one of the chief reasons was undoubtedly the church's membership policy. Pastor Bob Seymour wrote to Olin Binkley prior to the association's delayed ruling to explain that the church was "contemplating becoming an 'open membership' church." Seymour contended that such a position "can be defended both theologically and historically," but the church did not want to "make any move that could in any way be embarrassing to" its namesake.[104] The congregation experienced the first of many challenges that accompanied being an open-minded and progressive church: their practices and beliefs would affect their ability to partner with other congregations.

Dr. Binkley responded by clarifying that he had "no desire to obstruct in any way the progress of the church or to influence unduly the formation of any policy" the congregation may make. As a Baptist, he respected the autonomy of the local church and wanted the congregation to make its own decision. Dr. Binkley further stated, however, that the constitution's article allowing for open membership "deserves further study and clarification." He humbly claimed that he did not have scholarly "competence as a theologian or historian," but believed that "personal faith in Jesus Christ and baptism by immersion are in harmony with the teaching of the New Testament and our Baptist heritage.'"[105] While he was less than enthusiastic about the congregation's open membership policy, he wanted to allow the church to forge its own path. In a memo he wrote to Fred Ellis and other members

of the church leadership, Dr. Binkley expressed "serious reservations" and "anticipated controversy" over the policy. He was not willing to be quoted in public further than these generalizations.[106]

Dr. Binkley's anticipation of controversy proved correct. The Yates Baptist
Association appointed a Special Study Committee to review the case of Binkley
Memorial Baptist Church. In October 1960, this special committee recommended
the association not approve the church's application for fellowship. They qualified
their decision stating that they would welcome another application "if at any time
the church subscribes to and practices baptism of believers by immersion for all who
seek membership."[107] Despite not offering fellowship to the new congregation, at
the same meeting the Yates Association also fulfilled their agreement with Binkley
by deeding the congregation the plot of land that would eventually become the site
of its permanent church building.

A few days after the association's decision, Olin Binkley sent a short statement
to Southern Baptist leadership in Nashville, Tennessee. He explained the origin of
the congregation and that they had selected him to be the congregation's namesake.
Dr. Binkley explained, "I do not have any official connection with the church. At
one time I was invited to serve as interim pastor but declined."[108] He likely wanted
to quell any rumors that he, as dean of Southeastern Baptist Theological Seminary,
espoused support for open-membership policies in Southern Baptist churches.
Seymour wrote to Dr. Binkley, hoping that the use of his name had not "become a
liability" for him or that the church's position had proven "embarrassing." Seymour
also requested a "personal visit" with Dr. Binkley in order to discuss in detail the
"course of events" at the Yates Association meeting.[109] While Dr. Binkley publicly
presented a neutral position toward the congregation and likely disagreed with the
open membership policy, in private he valued what this small college-town church
was trying to accomplish. He continued to send the congregation small financial
contributions, and he expressed appreciation for the church's "effort to explore at a
deep level the relation of a Baptist Church in a university community to the whole
Church of the living God."[110] There was something unique about a church in a university setting, and Dr. Binkley wanted the congregation to succeed.

Navigating the repercussions of their open-membership policy revealed some
of the difficulties that Binkley Memorial Baptist Church faced because of their
progressive policies. While the Yates Baptist Association refused to accept Binkley
into their fellowship, the congregation instead chose to join the North Carolina
Council of Churches, a state branch of the larger ecumenical National Council of
Churches.[111] The implementation of the policy also revealed one of the challenges

of having a living namesake. The fear that their actions might embarrass Dr. Binkley loomed over the congregation's decision-making process. Dr. Binkley's determination, however, to allow the congregation to forge its own path and identity free from his personal beliefs provided the congregation assurances for future stances it chose to take.

From its founding, Olin T. Binkley Memorial Baptist Church chose to identify itself as an evangelical, Southern Baptist congregation. More importantly, however, the membership chose to shape their religious community as a college-town church committed to the UNC brand of southern progressivism. The University of North Carolina had cultivated a reputation over the course of the early twentieth century of supporting progressive causes and fostering intellectual community rooted in academic freedom and open inquiry. Chapel Hill became a community where Communists and Baptist ministers could debate and argue and engage one another as friends. Binkley became a congregation that wedded this UNC brand with a particular strain of Southern Baptist ideology. From its namesake, Olin Binkley, to its first pastor, Robert Seymour, this new Baptist congregation was the product of a uniquely Baptist interpretation of twentieth-century liberal theology. It was a Baptist tradition that celebrated the Social Gospel but recognized its limitations. Through this unique theological amalgamation, Binkley was a truly novel congregation intellectually and geographically.

Drawing upon their unique theological mixture and their college-town brand, Binkley charted a new path for itself particularly with respect to membership. While other Southern Baptist churches remained committed to the policies of separate but equal, Binkley sought to be a welcoming and interracial congregation. While other Southern Baptist churches held closed membership policies and would only admit other Baptists into their congregations, Binkley charted an ecumenical, open-membership policy. College towns are transient places, and Binkley sought to make itself open and accessible to this transient population regardless of their skin color or denominational affiliation. Demonstrating even more Binkley's commitment to be a college-town church, the year Binkley opened its doors, the other local Baptist church—Chapel Hill Baptist Church—changed its name. Perhaps concerned that Binkley was encroaching upon its ministry to college students, Chapel Hill Baptist Church changed its name to University Baptist Church. Binkley's organization clearly sought to engage the local college community, and the older, more established Baptist congregation sought to gently stake out its own territory and authority.

The growth of Chapel Hill in the 1960s determined that there was room for both Binkley Baptist and University Baptist in this southern college town. Binkley, however, would emerge as the progressive voice among these two Baptist congregations during the civil rights period. Under the leadership of Seymour, Binkley became an active congregation in every facet of life in Chapel Hill. With a supportive pastoral leader, a congregation composed of Black and white members, and a commitment to the success and well-being of Chapel Hill, Binkley greeted the 1960s with force.

2

Town and Gown: Binkley and the 1960s

BINKLEY ENTERED THE 1960s with creativity and energy. Under the leadership of Bob Seymour, the congregation grew to become a thriving and active religious community eager to address the needs of Chapel Hill. The church quickly organized, creating standing committees on worship, education, missions and ecumenism, fellowship and recreation, membership, student affairs, building and grounds, and finance—all of which, except for finance, had regular monthly meetings.[1] Like many Baptist congregations in the South, Binkley met on Sunday mornings for Sunday school and worship as well as on Sunday and Wednesday evenings for additional educational programming. Binkley's creativity and energy were born out of necessity. Unlike many white Baptist churches in the South, Binkley accepted Black members, which, in an era when much of the South remained segregated, meant that Binkley had to consider things like which retreat centers were integrated when planning congregational activities and retreats.[2] Without the same financial resources and facilities as an established congregation with multiple staff members, Binkley had to be flexible and rely upon the engagement of its membership if the church was going to have any influence on the surrounding community. For much of the 1960s, the congregation channeled their energy and creativity into combatting segregation and supporting the civil rights movement.

Understanding the role religion played within the movement for civil rights is complicated. From within the movement, scholars have studied the role of religion generally, and Christianity specifically, in providing an intellectual framework for Black Americans to resist the Jim Crow South and fight for their rights.[3] Many of the leaders of the movement were pastors, whereas others were deeply committed Christians. Institutionally, the Black Church, as has been the case since the nineteenth century, was crucial for helping to organize and sustain Black political engagement. During the civil rights movement, Martin Luther King Jr.'s narration of the Montgomery bus boycott illustrates this institutional organization well. Black churches not only provided meeting locations, but they also helped in organizing the transportation of workers no longer taking public transportation. Churches were essential in this work.[4]

Other scholars have focused on the response of predominately white congregations to the civil rights movement. One prominent interpretation built upon the work of historian John Lee Eighmy argues that white churches in the early and mid-twentieth century were held in "cultural captivity" to the broader systems of racism and white supremacy—in essence white southern congregations were at their core good, but the broader culture had corrupted and led them astray.[5] Critics of this interpretation argue that Christian churches were not merely the captives of this culture of white supremacy but creators of it. Certainly, the Ku Klux Klan wedded Christianity to a white supremacist ideology, but average congregations also perpetuated and undergirded racist systems, refusing to admit Black members.[6] Much of this scholarship compellingly shows that white Christians sought to frame racism as an individual sin, relieving their institutions of the social and corporate sin of constructing and upholding larger systems of racial injustice.

Few scholars have addressed the role of white congregations who participated in and raised their collective voice in supporting the civil rights movement. By the 1960s, historian Mark Newman argues, many Southern Baptists engaged in the larger denominational structures of the Southern Baptist Convention began to re-assess their stance of segregation. He suggests that Southern Baptist progressives followed larger federal policy, pushing for equality when "separate but equal" was the law of the land, later endorsing obedience to *Brown v. Board of Education,* and finally pushing for civil rights by 1964.[7] This may have been the trend among progressive Southern Baptists operating within the larger denominational atmosphere, but such a trend misses what a progressive Southern Baptist identity looked like on a congregational level.

Similarly, national politics were in the middle of a drastic transition as white southerners left the Democratic Party to vote for Republican candidates like Barry Goldwater and Richard Nixon. Binkley certainly welcomed members from both political parties, but its commitments to racial inclusiveness and combatting poverty aligned the community more with the policies of President John F. Kennedy, Lyndon B. Johnson, and the Democratic Party.[8] As a Baptist congregation, Binkley respected the separation of church and state and refrained from overt partisanship. Very early into Binkley's history, however, individual members participated in local electoral politics. These members, as a result, inadvertently promoted the small, young congregation through their public service, and in turn helped attract new members with similar political ideologies. This dynamic reinforced Binkley's progressive spirit that resonated with the Democratic Party of the 1960s.

Binkley Memorial Baptist Church provides a case study for understanding how a young, progressive Southern Baptist congregation approached their support for the civil rights movement. Without a physical church building until 1964 or any institutional memory to guide and dictate how the congregation ought to advocate for societal change, Binkley's newness gave the church a more radical edge to its ministry in the surrounding community. Without significant financial resources or institutional clout, Binkley found its voice in different ways—often through the passions and vocations of its membership. As the congregation grew over the course of the 1960s, the church worked to balance its commitments between both "town and gown." As the decade progressed, the congregation grew quickly and began to realize the difficulty of balancing both commitments. When Binkley constructed its first permanent building at the 15–501 intersection just north of the UNC campus, it helped to attract more young families. Shifting the congregational meeting location affected the congregation's demographics. The story of Binkley in the 1960s is the story of a young and energic congregation transitioning from niche and nimble origins to an established progressive fixture of the Chapel Hill community.

Chronicling this transition serves as a daunting task, as Dr. Seymour and Binkley's members were involved in many aspects of community change in Chapel Hill. Without established forms of institutional record keeping, demarcating the work of the church from the work of individuals who attended Binkley remains tricky. In many ways, the work of Binkley Church became the work of its individual membership. This chapter provides a few snapshots and snippets of the evolution of the young congregation's identity throughout the 1960s as the congregation gained a reputation around Chapel Hill for its activism and involvement within the community. As a progressive congregation, Binkley sought to help bring about the kingdom of God on earth as it is in heaven, and they did so by strategically supporting individuals in both political and professional positions who could effectively bring about social change. This chapter addresses in detail how the church supported Fred Ellis's work on the Chapel Hill School Board putting an end to the segregated public school system, Dean Smith's work integrating the UNC men's basketball team, and Howard Lee's historic victory in the 1969 Chapel Hill mayoral election.

There was an energy that enlivened the Binkley congregation in these early years. Members held neither a preconceived reputation that the church had to live up to nor a legacy that the congregation needed to protect. Instead, there was a calling to be something new—to be something different. As a result, the church's history during this decade is rather chaotic as the congregation worked to find its voice in the community. By the end of the decade, however, Binkley Memorial Baptist Church's voice would become a clear and distinct fixture of Chapel Hill's religious landscape.

Binkley among the "Gown"

From its founding, Binkley held a close relationship with UNC as it gathered on campus in Gerrard Hall. At the time, university chancellor Bill Aycock recognized that the growth of the school necessitated the formation of additional congregations within the community to serve the student population, and he "assisted them by making available temporary facilities until they were strong enough to make the transition to a building elsewhere."[9] Binkley charter member Don Freeman remembered that Gerrard Hall was an "ideal place to worship and certainly the 'price was right,'" as the church paid no rental fee. He also remembered the congregation's close relationship with the university. Even UNC president William "Bill" Friday, Freeman explained, sought to "assist Binkley Church in its formative years." President Friday even thought about making some of the school's property available for the congregation to build upon once it had grown financially strong enough to construct its own building. Having such powerful university figures in the congregation's corner allowed Binkley to focus on shaping its identity rather than paying for meeting space.[10]

Meeting in Gerrard Hall across the street from the Old Well on the UNC campus meant that Binkley's early years were integrally connected to campus life. On Sunday mornings, congregants gathered for Sunday school at a nearby house they had purchased for educational meeting space and then strolled over to Gerrard Hall for worship. Founding member Michael Berkut remembered members walking to worship in "discontinuous columns, across Graham Court, passing the Old Well" to get to worship. "It did not matter whether it was freezing, snowing or raining," he recalled, "Sunday School was always well-attended."[11] The location was convenient for students who could sleep in a few extra minutes on Sunday mornings, knowing church was a short walk away. The *Daily Tar Heel*, an independent student newspaper, regularly advertised the congregation's Sunday services in their "Covering the Campus" section. Nestled between information about a "Free Flick" and the "Grad Club," Binkley's Sunday service advertisements, including the sermon title, regularly appeared in the student paper's publicized events.[12]

The congregation also utilized the *Daily Tar Heel* to advertise special events and lecture series, like a three-day series on "The Ethics of Redemption" in 1960 by Dr. Guy Ransom, a professor of Christian ethics at Duke University.[13] Because the church lacked a permanent structure that was their own, events like this often took place at various venues around both the Campus and Chapel Hill. One Sunday evening "supper-seminar" took place at the nearby Institute of Pharmacy, and the congregation advertised a pick-up location for students interested in attending.[14] While at times not having a building caused problems when congregational programming struggled to find a venue, it also gave the church flexibility to schedule programming at a variety of venues to reach out to students at various points in their collegiate careers.

Binkley enthusiastically welcomed the wealth of expertise and knowledge found within the UNC faculty. In the fall of 1960, Pastor Seymour led a "Sunday Evening Seminar" to welcome students back to campus entitled "The Role of Religion and the University."[15] Seymour's background in higher education helped the congregation envision a close relationship between the new young church and its collegiate context. Educational programming regularly reached out to professors across a variety of departments and disciplines. From the departments of religion, political science, and social studies to the School of Medicine, Binkley heard from faculty regularly, many of whom came to call Binkley their spiritual home.[16] During the 1968 election, the congregation planned a multi-week series leading up to and following the national election entitled "Christian Decision Making and American Politics." The series welcomed numerous scholars and political scientists from across the university.[17] Through its location in Chapel Hill, the congregation developed a passion for and commitment to education and learning.

In addition to drawing upon the resources of faculty members, the congregation also developed a close relationship with the Baptist Student Union (BSU) at the university. The former director of the BSU, Julius Herrin, cultivated a progressive culture among Baptists at UNC that indirectly animated Binkley's founding. Herrin's successor, James "Jim" Cansler, continued Herrin's work. The year of Binkley's founding, Cansler explained in an interview with the *Daily Tar Heel* that "the role of the Baptist Student Union is that of tie between the home church and the campus."[18] The BSU worked closely with both Binkley and recently renamed University Baptist Church (formerly Chapel Hill Baptist Church), but Cansler chose to worship at Binkley, which undoubtedly influenced some students to attend as well. In rebranding itself University Baptist Church, the older congregation sought to reaffirm its collegiate context. It met just off the campus of UNC and

served as a known religious community with the advantage of serving as the primary meeting location for the BSU. Binkley, on the other hand, had the advantage
of representing a new and exciting possibility with commitments to ecumenism and
integration, meeting in the heart of campus. Seymour and the congregation recognized this and worked closely with the BSU. Built into the church's constitution,
Binkley included a position of Baptist Student Union representative that served
"on the student affairs committee" and represented "student members on Church
Council."[19] Having a student representative involved in congregational decision
making helped to bolster the relationship between Baptist students at UNC and
the newly founded Binkley.

Alfreida Hammett served in the role of BSU representative at Binkley in the
early 1960s and relayed information back and forth between students and the
congregation. When Baptist student unions at different colleges and universities
around the state of North Carolina began planning a mission trip to South Korea,
Hammett contacted Binkley for help raising money to fund a couple of students to
participate. Binkley also worked to incorporate students into congregational life,
creating opportunities for students to lead. In 1964, the church worked to identify
and pair international students with host families.[20] That same year, the congregation identified and recruited "student 'ministers' who would be interested in"
leading a children's church service on Sunday mornings.[21] Incorporating the college
community into the life of the church was a congregational priority. The collegiate
community inspired ministry opportunities as well as shaped spiritual and educational programming.

The civil rights movement also provided an opportunity for Binkley to forge
strong partnerships with the collegiate community. In July 1960, a short drive down
Interstate 40 in Greensboro, North Carolina, four students from North Carolina
Agricultural and Technical State University staged a series of nonviolent protests
at the local Woolworth department store. The next day more students joined their
ranks, and within a few days, hundreds of students both men and women, Black and
white were participating in similar protests throughout the Greensboro business
district.[22] The actions of these students helped lead to the formation of the Student
Nonviolent Coordinating Committee (SNCC) founded at Shaw University in
nearby Raleigh, North Carolina. Many colleges and universities harbored the
south's more liberal and progressive individuals who supported civil rights, and
UNC-Chapel Hill was no different. The small college town, however, was "a split-
personality town," as one Binkley congregant remembered years later. While the
university community supported the town's liberals, the more conservative political

leaders and businesspeople retained the power. Binkley joined students and faculty to help disrupt and change this dynamic.[23]

The same year students staged protests at Woolworth's in Greensboro, Dr. Martin Luther King Jr. came to Chapel Hill to speak at a luncheon of clergy, and later that evening he addressed members of the student population. Seymour was sure to attend both events. When King addressed the student population on "The Struggle for Racial Justice," Seymour worried that the overflowing crowd might be harboring hecklers.[24] If there were, King quickly disarmed them. "Before the evening was over," Seymour wrote in his memoir, King "had everyone listening intently and succeeded in disarming even the more belligerent questioners."[25] King even met with the campus BSU at the University Baptist Church, but because of the church's policy about Black individuals on the premises, he had to speak with students in the basement.[26] The deacons were adamant that King not be allowed to speak from the pulpit.[27] University Baptist's policy on interracial gatherings dated back to the 1950s, when Herrin led the BSU. Their unwillingness to accommodate King's visit served as another reason the more progressive Baptist student body gravitated toward Binkley in its early years.

In 1961, Binkley joined with UNC students in support of members of Chapel Hill's Black community who sought to attend showings of *Porgy and Bess* at the local Carolina Theatre. The movie theatre was segregated, and when members of the local Black community requested special showings of the opera's film adaptation, they were denied. Members of the faculty and staff at UNC joined together in picketing the theatre, and numerous local clergy issued a collective statement outlining their concerns over the theatre's decision, explaining their own decision to withhold patronage from the establishment. Seymour was among this group of clergy.[28] When he brought the issue of desegregating the movie theatre up with the congregation, their discussion "resulted in no concrete plan of action at the moment except to boycott the movies."[29] It remains unclear what else the church thought it might do, but supporting the local boycott was a significant departure from the approach University Baptist had taken by refusing to welcome Black individuals into their sanctuary.

Echoing what she heard in church on Sunday mornings, Binkley's BSU representative, Alfrieda Hammett, also pushed for a progressive stance on race relations in the larger state Baptist student union. After the bombing of the Sixteenth Street Baptist Church in Birmingham, Alabama, Hammett organized an offering to be sent to the congregation from the BSU at UNC.[30] The following month, she and several other students proposed a resolution at the state BSU convention to be sent to the Alabama BSU convention "expressing Christian concern over our role in the racial crisis." While the UNC resolution was defeated, another resolution from students at Mars Hill college passed and was sent to all state Baptist student unions across the country.[31] Binkley too included line items in their budget for the historically Black "General Baptist Convention" as well as "Burned Churches in the South."[32] The young church's desire to be a Baptist congregation that welcomed Black congregants resonated with UNC students like Hammett. With a desire to learn and hear from the expertise of scholars, Binkley fit into the collegiate community well. Amid the numerous campus lectures and student organizations, Binkley made itself at home, participating in and contributing to campus life.

James Forbes and Binkley's Summer of Interracial Ministry

As a recently founded church, Seymour was the only staff member for the first few years of Binkley's existence. Stretched thin, the church began to wonder if he was "adequately compensated for his excellent leadership."[33] In the spring of 1962, however, Seymour received a phone call offering Binkley the opportunity to welcome an intern for the summer who might help lighten some of the pastor's responsibility. The call was from Union Theological Seminary in New York City, inquiring to see if Binkley Memorial Baptist Church would be interested in participating in the newly formed Student Interracial Ministry (SIM) program. They wanted to see whether Binkley would be willing to host a recent Black seminary graduate to serve as a ministerial intern in the predominately white congregation.

Only two years old, SIM formed when a group of Union Theological Seminary students attended the founding meeting of SNCC. These seminarians thought that they might have a unique role to fill alongside the work undergraduate students were doing through SNCC. They developed SIM as an organization committed to the idea that the church should be "playing a role of leadership and conciliation in the struggle for social justice." Raising funds from various religious organizations, including the National Council of Churches, SIM sought to place Black seminarians in white congregations as ministerial interns and vice versa.[34] Seymour thought the placement of a Black seminarian at Binkley would provide "a way to put to the test our professed racial convictions and to ferret out those last vestiges of prejudice that still remained."[35] After clearing the idea with the diaconate, Binkley welcomed James Forbes to the congregation for the summer of 1962.

Forbes grew up near Chapel Hill in Raleigh, North Carolina, and was the son of a Pentecostal preacher. He attended Howard University for his bachelor's degree, and after being rejected from Duke Divinity School on account of race, he decided to attend Union Theological Seminary in New York City. After completing his master of divinity in May, Forbes arrived in Chapel Hill in early June, ready for his summer in the predominately white Binkley Memorial Baptist Church. He first met with the Christian Education Committee to discuss his role for the summer. As a young minister, the committee asked Forbes to "assist with the outdoor recreational activities of Vacation Bible School."[36] Binkley often tried to create educational opportunities for children led by people of color, typically men. When Binkley invited Wake Forest University professor George McLeod "Mac" Bryan to come and speak earlier that year, Seymour inquired if Edward Reynolds, one of Bryan's Black students, could come with him and help with the children's program.[37] By creating these types of educational opportunities for children, Binkley sought to combat the societal racism that children observed in the world around them. As Seymour remembered of Forbes's time at the church, "The children fell in love with him immediately."[38]

Forbes also served as a liaison between the BSU and the congregation, helping to lead the student Sunday school class for college-aged students who stayed in the area over the summer months.[39] Beyond these specific roles he filled throughout his summer with Binkley, Forbes participated in all aspects of church life. He reported back to the SIM program that "nearly every afternoon I am invited for dinner at the homes of members of the Church." He also explained that he "spent a great deal of time doing pastoral calling, attending Church committee meetings, and civic activities." Describing the benefits of his summer at Binkley, Forbes wrote that he had the opportunity to approach his work from a different perspective and that he had been able to understand "more fully some of the problems of the white community during this period of social change."[40] Seymour likewise found the summer to be quite fruitful, describing Forbes as a "God-send" with "magnetic charisma." The two men conducted congregational visits together as well as planned worship together. On the first Sunday of July, Seymour recounted in his memoir, "Forbes and I stood behind the Communion table together to celebrate the Lord's Supper." Observing a Black minister and a white minister stand side by side to perform the ritual of communion was a powerful and moving experience for many in the congregation in 1962. By the end of the summer, Seymour went on vacation, leaving Forbes in charge of a Sunday service.[41]

The SIM program and Forbes's time at Binkley was particularly meaningful to the church's membership, but it was not without challenges. At the time, Bert and

Diane Adams were members of the church and expecting a newborn. After the birth of their child, Forbes arrived at the hospital to pay them a visit. He told the desk clerk that he was their pastor and asked for the room number. As the couple recalled years later, a "scene" ensued as the "clerk insisted" that Forbes could not be their pastor because he was Black "and refused him entry to the hospital." The couple remained unaware of the event until the following day as they planned to bring their newborn home. They remembered their frustration with the hospital and "almost refused to pay the bill!" Forbes's presence at Binkley allowed their congregants to think about and understand in a new way the types of discrimination facing Black citizens in 1962 Chapel Hill.[42]

Binkley and Forbes both came to value their participation in the SIM program. Two years following the internship, the Christian Education Committee recommended that the Church Council consider hiring another Black summer intern for the congregation.[43] For Forbes, his time at Binkley marked the beginning of a storied career. He later received his doctor of ministry from Colgate Rochester Divinity School before coming to serve as a professor of homiletics at his alma mater, Union Theological Seminary. In 1989, he succeeded William Sloane Coffin as the first Black senior minister of Riverside Church in New York City, one of the most prominent multicultural and liberal Protestant congregations in the United States. Forbes served in this position for eighteen years. Looking back on his experience, he contended that his summer at Binkley "opened up the world of interracial activity, making it a norm. For me, my world became not an isolated [B]lack existence but a world in which [B]lack and white had commerce together on many levels. . . . Binkley was a boot camp for the extended interracial ministry that I would experience."[44]

As a young congregation with limited resources and a progressive outlook, Binkley happily participated in the SIM program. While a more established white, southern congregation may have been hesitant to welcome a Black ministerial intern, Binkley welcomed the many ways the opportunity would shape their new ministry. Forbes was accustomed to southern segregation having grown up in nearby Raleigh, but he welcomed the new experience of having a community of white Christians supporting him. Forbes's summer was a formative moment in the history of the young congregation, but also in the life of Bob Seymour, as the two became lifelong friends. In taking the risk of welcoming a Black seminarian for the summer, both Seymour and Binkley were challenged to put their progressive ideals to work.

Becoming More than Southern Baptist

The newness of Binkley provided opportunities to rethink community partnerships and take risks. From forging close relationships with UNC students and faculty to welcoming a Black ministerial intern, Binkley took advantage of opportunities where they were able. They were quite a different Southern Baptist church from the established University Baptist Church. In many ways, Binkley was never a typical Southern Baptist congregation. Despite being atypical, however, it was still Southern Baptist. The church's namesake, Dr. Olin T. Binkley, was a prominent Southern Baptist educator, and its pastor, Robert Seymour, was also a lifelong Southern Baptist.

At the same time, the congregation was not like other Southern Baptist congregations. As mentioned in the previous chapter, the decision to have an open-membership policy resulted in the congregation's rejection for membership in the regional Yates Baptist Association. For a more typical Southern Baptist church, a congregation would have standing in a regional association that was part of a larger state convention or association that subsequently participated in the national SBC. A typical SBC church would have these three affiliations: regional, state, and national. Binkley participated in Southern Baptist life at both the national and state level, but because Baptist polity and governance stresses autonomy, the local association barred the congregation from participation at the local level.

In the early 1960s, at the prompting of Sam Hill, a member of Binkley and professor of southern religion at UNC, the church began to explore the possibility of expanding its denominational affiliations. Hill was a relatively unknown and young professor at the time with a keen interest in religion in the American south. From his position inside the congregation, Hill encouraged Binkley to consider what is colloquially known as "dual affiliation" with both the Southern Baptist Convention and the American Baptist Convention (ABC). American Baptists traced their history to the 1812 Triennial Convention of Baptists. The SBC broke away from this body in 1845 over a dispute regarding the appointment of two enslavers to serve as missionaries. There was no reunion between the two groups following the Civil War as there was with other denominational groups who split over slavery. While attending Binkley, Hill was working with an American Baptist scholar in Kansas City, Robert Torbet, on a co-authored book, *Baptists North and South,* that outlined what kept these two major denominational bodies separate and offered a method for approaching a united witness.[45] The publication of this work preceded a gathering of seven Baptist groups in Atlantic City to "celebrate the one hundred and fiftieth anniversary of the beginnings of Baptist overseas missions from American shores."[46] Utilizing his position as a professor of religion, Hill strove to lead a national conversation among Baptists regarding reunion between American and Southern Baptists.

In the 1960s, however, repairing this fracture in Baptist life remained an uphill battle, one that Hill and others sought to tackle by advocating for a more cooperative relationship. The American Baptist Convention, which was more prevalent north of the Mason-Dixon line, had recently appointed Julius Herrin, former BSU director at UNC, as an assistant general secretary for work in the south. A familiar face to Chapel Hill, Herrin's work in the years preceding Binkley's founding helped to pave the way for a progressive Baptist voice in this growing college town.[47] He utilized this new position within the American Baptist Convention as an opportunity to support "activist pastors and congregations isolated by their stand for civil rights." His work also included helping secure scholarships for student leaders in the civil rights movement, and prominent figures like Congressman John Lewis, Sweet Honey in the Rock founder Bernice Johnson Reagon, and Stokely Carmichael benefited from this work. Working out of a small building in Chapel Hill, Herrin also rented office space to Binkley in its early years. His appointment to work for the American Baptist Convention in the south also provided another layer of encouragement for Binkley to begin imagining what affiliating with both conventions would look like.[48]

At the congregational level, Binkley followed Hill's national leadership to consider dual affiliation. In July 1964, a few months after the national Atlantic City gathering, the diaconate met with a representative of the ABC. The congregation's leadership had already been discussing the "advantages and disadvantages of becoming dually aligned," but wanted to hear from a denominational representative before making any final decision.[49] Very few congregations practiced dual affiliation, as it required congregations to split their financial contributions between two larger denominational ministries and missions. Fortunately for Binkley's diaconate, Watts Street Baptist Church in nearby Durham, North Carolina, had also recently sought dual affiliation and served as a helpful point of contact for Binkley's congregational leaders to learn more about the process and logistics of becoming both an SBC and ABC congregation.[50] After finishing their inquiries with both denominational representatives and Watts Street, Binkley set a final vote for the first Sunday of August in 1964. With an affirmative vote, Binkley became both a Southern Baptist and an American Baptist congregation.[51]

While Sam Hill's larger goal of bringing unity to both major Baptist denominational groups never came to fruition, his influence and leadership at Binkley helped the congregation model what such a unity might look like at the local level. Hill later published his well-known work, *Southern Churches in Crisis,* that helped spur the establishment of the academic field of scholarship known as southern religion. The work traced the development of white Protestantism in the south from the colonial period to understand the challenges facing these congregations amid the backdrop of the civil rights era. In a reprinting of the book in 1999, Hill described the text as a "theological treatise from beginning to end" and explained that he "was a man of the church" and had "personal investment" in the subject. Binkley was the congregation that shaped and influenced Hill's spiritual life at the time he composed the work, and it modeled the type of southern religion that Hill believed to be faithful to the Christian Gospel.

Through the influence of Hill, Binkley thought deeply about its place in the American religious landscape. Without a large budget, Binkley did not have the same financial concerns regarding whether a dual affiliation would limit its giving capacity to the SBC. Instead, its willingness to live into a different approach to denominational cooperation signaled the congregation's willingness to rethink the typical southern congregational paradigm. The dual affiliation provided the congregation a denominational structure to grow into as the church grew both its membership and budget. Through the dynamism of its pastor Bob Seymour and the energy of its membership, Binkley soon garnered a reputation in the community for its activism, and that reputation in turn attracted more members.

Binkley among the "Town"

Meeting in the heart of UNC's campus in Gerrard Hall contributed to the fluidity and novelty of the church in its early years. Without a permanent structure to define the community, Binkley had flexibility. It could protest with students and faculty, welcome an intern like James Forbes, and contemplate dual membership in the SBC and ABC. But life among the gown was not meant to last forever. As the community grew, a larger, more permanent structure became necessary. The town beckoned. From before the congregation had been officially conceived, much less named, it owned a plot of land just north of campus that was to become the site of its permanent church building. By 1963, Binkley's membership rolls topped two hundred—a number that would double in another five years.[52] As a result of this growth, the congregation broke ground on a simple, multi-purpose chapel that year. Recognizing the close relationship Binkley had forged with the university, the church intentionally timed its move into the new building in conjunction with the academic year.[53] They planned for a September dedication.

The cost of a new church building was substantial for such a young congregation, but Binkley benefited from Dr. Seymour's close relationship with his former congregation, Myers Park Baptist Church in Charlotte. It was an affluent congregation in one of Charlotte's wealthiest neighborhoods. As mentioned in chapter one, Myers Park was Seymour's first congregation out of divinity school. While he only served as the associate pastor for one year, he maintained a strong enough relationship with the congregation that Myers Park contributed $25,000 to help Binkley construct a permanent building. Dave Brown, Binkley's moderator at the time, and Leo Wagoner, one of the congregation's founding members, sent their sister congregation in Charlotte a letter of deep thanks and gratitude for their generous financial support.[54]

After over a year of planning, on September 27, 1964, Binkley moved out of Gerrard Hall and held a dedication service for its new sanctuary. On the bulletin for the service, the congregation described itself as "A Church for all People" affiliated with the North Carolina Council of Churches, the Southern Baptist Convention, and the American Baptist Convention. As Pearl Seymour played the prelude to open the service, her husband stood outside the closed door to the sanctuary with the choir and other participating clergy members from the community. After the music ended, Rev. Seymour knocked upon the door three times, proclaiming, "Open the gates, that those who keep faith may enter in." The short call and response between Seymour and the congregation concluded, and Seymour opened the door, leading the procession into the chapel as the congregation sang the hymn, "O Thou, Whose Hand Hath Brought Us."[55]

The dedication service included the participation of many local ministers with close ties to Binkley. Henry Turlington of the more conservative University Baptist Church read the scripture lesson, and John Manley of the historically Black First Baptist Church in Chapel Hill led the congregation in the affirmation of faith. Myers Park Baptist Church's pastor, Carlyle Marney, traveled from Charlotte, North Carolina, to deliver the dedication sermon.[56] Marney was a well-known "liberal" in Baptist circles. He was an outspoken advocate for civil rights for much of his career and accepted a call to pastor the Myers Park Baptist Church in the early 1960s after pastoring First Baptist Church of Austin, Texas. While in Austin, he and a couple of other local ministers pressured the local Southern Baptist Association to accept two local Black Baptist churches as member congregations. While Marney had not

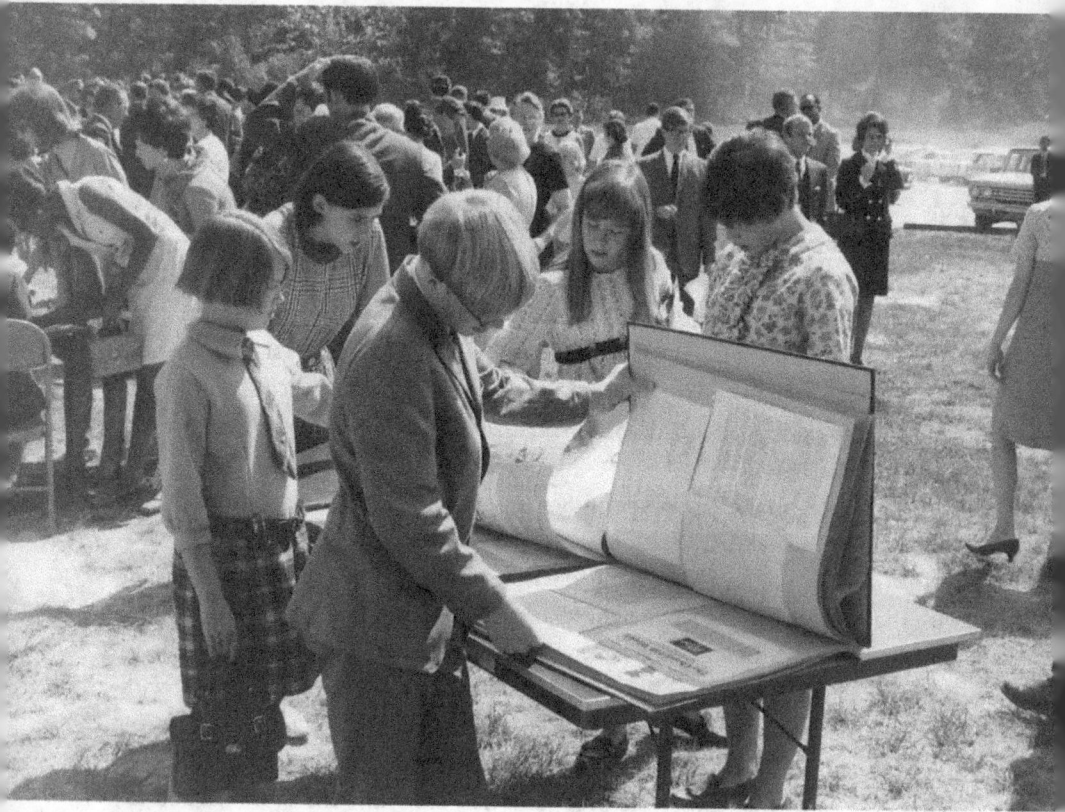

Binkley Members gathering for the dedication of its first sanctuary and permanent building in 1964. From the Robert Seymour Papers (04554), North Carolina Collection Photographic Archives, Louis Round Wilson Special Collections Library, University of North Carolina at Chapel Hill.

been the pastor of Myers Park Baptist during Seymour's brief tenure there, the two occupied the progressive end of the Southern Baptist spectrum.[57]

The new building significantly changed the life and ministry of Binkley Baptist Church. On one level, moving from Gerrard Hall made it more challenging to include college students in the life of the congregation. Binkley's leadership anticipated this challenge. A year before the new building was finished, the congregation began "looking into the involvement of transportation of the students to the new church."[58] Once the new building was in use, advertising in the *Daily Tar Heel* continued, but provided details regarding transportation options to and from the church building. The congregation scheduled a routine pickup from Y-Court, then a central location on campus, and if this location proved inconvenient, the church included a phone number students could call to arrange a personal pickup.[59]

While the new building created challenges for the congregation to remain connected to campus life, it also allowed the church to grow, opening new opportunities for community engagement. Recognizing the quick growth of the congregation, founder and deacon Leo Wagoner reported to the Church Council less than a month after the dedication service that "the crowded classroom situation indicates increased need of education facilities" to accompany their new building.[60] This observation confirmed that Binkley was growing faster than anticipated. It also revealed the congregation's desire to utilize its space to its fullest potential. Before moving into the new building, a small committee had been studying the feasibility of establishing an interracial nursery day school that could utilize the space during the week when it might have otherwise gone unused. Rather than rushing to begin such a program in the fall, the congregation moved into the new space, and the committee recommended delaying the school for a year. Following the committee's recommendation, in 1965 Binkley Preschool opened its doors and continues operating out of the church today as its own 501(c)3 nonprofit.[61]

Binkley and the Civil Rights Movement in Chapel Hill

While Binkley was growing and expanding throughout the 1960s, tensions over the civil rights movement continued to boil across the country. In his memoir, Seymour recalled that in winter of 1964, "all hell broke loose" in Chapel Hill. "The crisis did not come upon us all at once," he wrote. "We eased into it."[62] In the process, Binkley garnered a reputation around town, and as one congregant remembered, the church did not always have the "highest respectable image." The same congregant explained that many of the town's more conservative figures came to realize and expect "that if there was going to be trouble made, it'll happen at Binkley."[63] Congregants, along with the town's more progressive faction, saw an opportunity for Chapel Hill to become the first town in the south to voluntarily pass a public accommodations law, prohibiting businesses from discriminating on the basis of race. Many of the town's business leaders, however, were ready to resist such local legislation.

Since the late 1950s, the call for a public accommodations law had been growing in Chapel Hill. In the summer of 1963, the Mayor's Committee on Integration recommended the law to the Board of Alderman. The law sought to make it "illegal for restaurants, retail stores, theaters and similar establishments doing business with the public to deny service to anyone on the basis of race." Demonstrations with up to 350 Black and white protestors on Chapel Hill's prominent thoroughfare, Franklin Street, had put pressure on local government officials to adopt such measures.[64] These pro-integrationist demonstrations grew in Chapel Hill at the direction of the Congress of Racial Equality (CORE), but little seemed to sway the Board of Alderman in passing any local legislation.[65] By February 1964, the town witnessed the rise of sizable counter demonstrations against integration.[66] The rise of anti-integrationist demonstrations raised concern regarding a few "incidents of violence," but the *Daily Tar Heel* praised the "cool-headed efforts of Police Chief William D. Blake" for not letting things get out of hand.[67]

The tension between those who favored and opposed local integration efforts became difficult terrain for Binkley to navigate under the leadership of Seymour. Before the construction of the new sanctuary and the calling of Rev. Bill Currin as the church's first associate minister, Seymour served as the sole minister on staff. In a small congregation committed to realizing an integrated Christian fellowship, Seymour's time and energy was increasingly never enough. As tensions rose in the early months of 1964, Leo Wagoner proposed that the Church Council go on record giving Seymour their complete support, which the council unanimously approved.[68] A few months later, Binkley approved sending a resolution to the mayor's office expressing the congregation's concerns regarding the local racial crisis and offering support for a public accommodations law. While the church had hoped the resolution might be approved unanimously, seven members dissented for reasons that are unclear in the historical record. With ninety-six votes in favor, however, it still passed overwhelmingly.[69]

The institutional and collective statements and actions of Binkley are important for understanding the identity and values of the congregation. Similarly, the actions of a congregation's leader as well as the actions of individual congregants

Binkley members talking outside the congregation's first church building constructed in 1964.

are illustrative of a church's priorities. Seymour was only one man, and he could only sign on to so many statements, attend so many meetings, and serve on so many panels.[70] Fortunately, congregants also carried the life and ministry of Binkley with them out into the local community. Understanding the life of a congregation through its individual members, however, is difficult not only to conceptualize but also to record. The boundaries between people's personal religious lives and their professional lives are often quite bifurcated, and determining which parts of a congregant's life are relevant to their congregation's collective life can be difficult.

In the early part of Binkley's history, Seymour worked to better utilize the professional lives of his congregants to further the congregation's mission and ministry. From time to time members were informally given assignments from the congregation to advance an integrationist agenda within the community. There was no congregational vote or formal resolution or edict; rather, there was a collective understanding from the community that certain individuals were busy working on something in their professional lives that intersected with the work of Binkley. As one member from the period noted, Seymour was the "driving force" of the congregation's engagement in the community and he kept "Binkley focused."[71] Through his leadership and encouragement, Binkley's members addressed segregation in the public schools as well as within UNC athletics. By the end of the decade, the congregation also found its influence reaching the local mayor's office.

FRED ELLIS AND INTEGRATING THE PUBLIC SCHOOLS

While the University of North Carolina may have integrated shortly after the ruling of *Brown v. Board of Education,* the public school system in Chapel Hill remained segregated into the 1960s. Like many school systems in the United States, Chapel Hill took a liberal interpretation of the Supreme Court's mandate to integrate "with all deliberate speed." The State of North Carolina's Pearsall Plan sought to allocate educational control to local communities, which led many North Carolina counties to refuse integrating their school systems. As a small, southern town, Chapel Hill embraced the Pearsall Plan and delayed integrating its two public high schools— Lincoln High, which educated the local Black population, and Chapel Hill High, which educated the white population. John Manley, the pastor of the historically Black First Baptist Church of Chapel Hill, joined the school board in 1959 with hopes of strengthening the educational opportunities for the town's Black students. Manley was a respected voice on the school board, but his one voice was not enough to affect policy.[72]

Binkley had several young families with school-aged children, including Pastor Seymour, whose neighbor once asked him to sign a petition to block integration efforts in the public school system. Despite these anti-integrationist efforts within the community, however, Binkley's welcome of Black members extended to the congregation's overwhelming support of efforts to integrate the public schools. With the school board unwilling to act, Seymour approached Fred Ellis, a member of the congregation and professor in the UNC medical school, to run for school board. Ellis was invested in the issue as a parent. He had four daughters who attended every level of the local school system. Seymour asked Ellis to run for school board as his "church assignment," and the congregation supported such an effort. Seymour and the congregation vowed that Ellis would not be asked to join any congregational committees or serve in any congregational leadership positions that might distract him from the campaign or his subsequent service on the school board. Helping to integrate the public school system would be Ellis's "church work."[73]

After a short and successful local election, in May 1961, Fred Ellis was inaugurated as a member of the Chapel Hill City Board of Education, joining Pastor John Manley.[74] That same year, the school board began the slow work of making quality public education more accessible to the town's Black residents. The first steps the school board took toward integration entailed passing a ruling to allow first-grade students to attend "the school nearest them regardless of race."[75] After beginning with elementary-school-aged children, Ellis and Manley turned toward the longer task of fully integrating the school system. It took five years. In 1966, the all-Black Lincoln High School was closed, and Black students were permitted to attend the all-white Chapel Hill High School.[76]

Ellis's work on the Chapel Hill Board of Education functioned as an extension of the work of Binkley Memorial Baptist Church out in the wider community. The congregation as a collective was not deeply or formally involved in the work beyond supporting Ellis and his family, yet it is precisely this support that enabled Binkley to celebrate and view Ellis's work as part of their larger collective work. Seymour and the congregation found this model of ministering to the community to be effective. It required, however, identifying congregants who could leverage their positions in the community to effect social change. Ellis had the capacity and clout in the community not only to run for a position on the school board but also to secure the position. His work on issues of local public education resulted in tangible change within the local community, but he served in a relatively low-profile elected position. His influence provided an example for the rest of the congregation who likewise remained interested in effecting change within Chapel Hill. For some of Binkley's members, pursuing this change would place them much more prominently in the public eye.

DEAN SMITH AND INTEGRATING THE TAR HEELS

When Dean Smith first visited Binkley Memorial Baptist Church in 1959, he was simply the new assistant coach for the Tar Heels men's basketball team. When Binkley hosted his funeral in February 2015, he was a two-time NCAA Championship-winning basketball coaching legend. Over the span of an illustrious coaching career, Smith found religious community and support at Binkley. His attraction to the young congregation upon arriving to Chapel Hill centered on the church's emphasis to foster "integration at many levels" of the community.[77] Just as Seymour and the congregation encouraged Fred Ellis to advocate for change in the public school system, they encouraged Smith to advocate for change from his position as assistant and ultimately head coach of the Tar Heels.

A native of Kansas, both of Smith's parents were high school teachers at the local Emporia High School. When his mother gave up teaching to raise both he and his sister Joan, she worked as the organist and Bible school coordinator at the Baptist church their family attended. His father, meanwhile, also coached many of the school's sports teams, and in 1934, he won the state championship in men's basketball with an integrated roster that included a young Black student named Paul Terry, the son of the school's janitor. Shaped by the influence of his parents and his Baptist upbringing, Smith was raised to value everyone regardless of race.[78] Both his mother and father instilled within him many of the values that resonated with the membership of Binkley.

In 1958, after serving as an assistant coach at the Air Force Academy, Smith moved to Chapel Hill with his wife, Ann, and their three children to serve as assistant coach under Tar Heels head coach Frank McGuire. As Smith remembered, he fell in love with Chapel Hill at first sight. At the same time, as a Kansan who had never lived in the south, he worried about how he might adjust to the overtly segregated culture of this southern, college town. While he recognized that racism affected the whole country, Smith recalled feeling "shocked" when he first saw a set of "dual drinking fountains."[79] Southern segregation rubbed against the values his parents had instilled in him to treat everyone with dignity and respect. Fitting into the new southern culture in which he found himself proved a challenge.

To ease their transition, Smith and his family made finding a church one of their "first orders of business." Smith grew up in a more mainline American Baptist church, which meant that Southern Baptist congregations were a different and unfamiliar experience. After the Smiths visited a few churches outside the Baptist tradition, Jim Cansler, the Baptist campus minister, invited them to attend Binkley, which at the time had yet to become dually affiliated with both the Southern Baptists and American Baptists. In his autobiography, Smith recalled "so vividly [the family's] first visit to the Olin T. Binkley Memorial Baptist Church." He was particularly enthralled by Bob Seymour, who was delivering his "initial sermon." Smith and Seymour quickly became good friends, perhaps in part because Seymour had "little interest in basketball" and saw beyond Smith's profession. Seymour's wife, Pearl, however, balanced out her husband and became one of the Tar Heels' and Smith's most avid fans.[80]

Smith and his family became active members in the young congregation. From teaching Sunday school to serving in the nursery to joining various congregational committees, Smith and Ann contributed widely to congregational life.[81] Seymour recognized the importance of Smith's position in the community even as an assistant coach and sought to employ Smith in the work of the congregation's mission to foster integration in the wider Chapel Hill community. Smith was happy to oblige.

Before he had been at the congregation a year, Seymour asked Smith to accompany him to lunch with a Black theology student at The Pines, a well-known segregated restaurant that often catered pregame meals for the basketball team. Although the twenty-eight-year-old Smith was just an assistant coach, he was familiar enough with the restaurant management. The three men were seated and enjoyed their meal without any trouble.[82]

Accounts of this story vary widely. A variation of the tale was included in the November 1982 edition of *Sports Illustrated* that also included a photo of Seymour as Smith's pastor.[83] Smith and Seymour remember different details, but both remark in later writings that the story was embellished. While the men certainly did not single-handedly integrate Chapel Hill, or even The Pines for that matter as some accounts chronicle, their act of defiance toward the policies of segregation was significant in shaping the community at Binkley. The congregation encouraged its membership to advance their understanding of God's kingdom through their own spheres of influence—for Dean Smith, that was basketball.[84]

When Smith became the head coach of the Tar Heels in 1961, Seymour and Binkley had plans for him in his new role. On the day the school made the announcement, Seymour called to congratulate Smith and asked him about "recruiting a [B]lack player." As Smith recalled the conversation, Seymour explained, "Now that you are head coach your primary church work is the opportunity afforded by your vocation. Go find a [B]lack basketball player for the university."[85] Smith's recollection of this conversation with Seymour reveals how Binkley encouraged its membership to use their "day-to-day" activities to serve as congregational work. Individuals with higher profiles in the community, like Smith, while certainly not more important than any other congregant, provided the congregation a wider range of influence and more opportunities to effect change.

Smith's early head-coaching days in Chapel Hill were not smooth sailing, however, and despite being a high-profile community member, he did not always enjoy the town's support. In 1964, the men's basketball team opened the season as a nationally ranked team to the delight and enthusiasm of fans. After a few games into the season, however, the Tar Heels dropped from the rankings. Following a four-game losing streak and a twenty-two-point road loss to Wake Forest, Smith and his team returned to Chapel Hill to see an effigy of Smith hanged from a tree outside the Woollen Gymnasium. He called his sister Joan as well as Seymour questioning whether he was meant to be a head coach. Later that season another effigy was hanged after a loss to North Carolina State University.[86] This was one of the lowest points in Smith's career, but coaching success was only a few seasons away.

Coupled with his coaching struggles, tensions over civil rights in Chapel Hill were rising, which made the prospect of recruiting a Black player even more difficult. Binkley, however, was ready to support Smith. In 1966, after a loss to the University of Virginia, Smith heard a high school scouting report about Charlie Scott, a talented Black player at a school in Laurinburg, South Carolina. Upon investigating Scott further, Smith and his team of coaches concluded that Scott could be a potential candidate to integrate the basketball team. They began the recruitment process to entice him to come to Carolina. The weekend that Scott visited Chapel Hill, Smith made sure the young Scott spent a significant amount of time getting to know the players who would be his teammates. Smith spent very little time with Scott that weekend, but when Sunday arrived, he invited Scott to attend Binkley with him. Scott obliged.[87]

Determining how significant that Sunday morning service was to Scott's ultimate decision to attend Binkley would be difficult to evaluate. Scott later acknowledged that he had not been invited to attend church with any other coach who courted him to their schools. Sports historian Art Chansky has argued that inviting Scott to a mixed-race church service was part of Smith's "cutting edge" recruitment "tactics."[88] Perhaps one of the reasons Smith was so cutting-edge was that his Sunday invitation was less of a tactic and more of a means of living out the work of Binkley Baptist Church. That Sunday, Scott heard a sermon by Seymour about racial equality and was introduced to members of the congregation. Smith knew that Scott was interested in pursuing a pre-medical degree, so he reintroduced him to Thal Elliott, a Binkley member and Black medical student who had previously met Scott on a recruitment visit to Laurinburg. Smith also introduced Scott to Howard and Lillian Lee, a young Black couple who attended Binkley. The Lees continued to foster close relationships with many UNC student athletes throughout Smith's career.[89] Many former Tar Heels turned professional basketball players returned to Chapel Hill for alumni gatherings and asked Lillian if she could make them a carrot cake.[90]

Following his weekend visit, Scott elected to attend UNC as the first Black scholarship athlete, and while Dean Smith should receive much of the credit for integrating the school's athletics, the faith community supporting Smith played a significant role as well. Historians who look back on the role of religion in integrating American sports often highlight the personal piety of the coach or manager who made the final decision. For instance, Branch Rickey, a known Methodist, signed Jackie Robinson to the Brooklyn Dodgers and was hailed as a "progressive hero." Rarely do these histories look to the communities that shaped and sustained the "progressive ideologies" of these coaches and managers. Smith was not a lone Christian; he was rooted in the community of Binkley Baptist Church.[91]

Binkley provided a spiritual home for Smith and his family for the remainder of his life. As basketball took up more of his time, it put stress on Smith's marriage, and in 1973 he and his wife divorced. Binkley and Seymour remained present for both Dean and Ann during such a difficult time, and they both remained active members in the congregation for many years following. Dean remarried in 1976 to Linnea Weblemoe, a psychiatrist who had attended medical school at UNC. The couple had two daughters who grew up attending Binkley. His involvement and participation in the inner workings of congregational life would ebb and flow as his national reputation grew, winning National Championships in 1982 and 1993. He remained throughout his life, however, a faithful Binkley member.[92] His early and active participation at Binkley reveals how the congregation encouraged its members to live out its mission in their daily lives. Like Ellis, he became another model for Binkley's membership to look toward as they sought to shape Chapel Hill into a more equitable and inclusive community.

HOWARD LEE AND INTEGRATING CHAPEL HILL

Shortly after helping Smith recruit Charlie Scott to play for the Tar Heels, Binkley members Howard and Lillian Lee began their own journey fighting for change in Chapel Hill. In 1969 Howard successfully ran for mayor of Chapel Hill, becoming the first Black mayor elected by a majority white electorate in a southern town following Reconstruction. Unlike the work of Fred Ellis or Dean Smith, Lee's pursuit of change through local, public office originated outside the walls of Binkley Church, but much of the church's membership eventually came to enthusiastically support and even help run his campaign. Lee's victory began a long and storied career in North Carolina politics that included serving as mayor of Chapel Hill for three terms, secretary of the North Carolina Department of Natural Resources and Community Development, state senator, and chair of the North Carolina State Board of Education.[93] Through his career in public service, Lee provided Binkley a greater audience as congregants continued to advocate for certain policies and changes in the local community.

Howard and Lillian met in 1961 in Savannah, Georgia, where Howard had been working as a juvenile probation officer and Lillian as a public school teacher. The couple moved to Chapel Hill in 1965 for Howard to attend UNC's School of Social Work. Early in Howard's program, and before Lillian made the move to North Carolina, he visited several local Black churches to become acquainted with the local community. A classmate at UNC, however, invited him to Binkley one Sunday, and Howard obliged. It was the first time he had attended a Sunday service at a predominately white congregation. In his memoir, Howard remembered being "highly impressed" with Rev. Seymour's "thought provoking" message. However, "what impressed me most," he wrote somewhat in jest, "was the length of service, one hour, as opposed to close to two hours at most [B]lack churches."[94]

Howard did not attend Binkley again until Lillian joined him in Chapel Hill. She resisted visiting Binkley, having no interest in joining a predominately white congregation. After some amount of convincing, she eventually agreed to attend. Lillian too was impressed by Rev. Seymour as well as the warm and welcoming atmosphere of the congregation. Howard and Lillian returned and visited Binkley with some frequency over the course of Howard's graduate program. The two officially joined the church after Howard took a position at nearby Duke University and Lillian began a job teaching hospitalized children at North Carolina Memorial Hospital. While Binkley had welcomed Black members since George Grigsby, when the Lees joined in 1965, Howard recalled that they were the only Black couple in the church.[95] Looking back on their decision to join, Lee explained that "Bob Seymour swayed us" into joining; the church was secondary.[96]

Planting roots in Chapel Hill was not without its challenges for the young Black couple. When they sought to buy a home in 1966, they received resistance from the realtor. Fellow congregant and friend Dean Smith helped to calm anxious neighborhood residents and pressure the realtor to sell to the Lees. After purchasing the home, Lee remembered his family received numerous calls threatening his life and the lives his children. One evening, after hearing a "banging noise near the house," Howard "looked out of the window to see a small cross burning" in his yard. The image reminded him of his childhood, growing up in Lithonia, Georgia. A phone tap later revealed that the calls had come from the secretary of the realtor who sold the property, and the police discovered that a group of neighborhood kids was responsible for the cross-burning after they bragged about it in school one day.[97] Howard and Lillian experienced firsthand the racism of this alleged "progressive" Southern town.

While the Lees found support within Binkley, they also witnessed some hesitancy and concern. In the same way that James Forbes provided a test for the young congregation looking to foster an interracial community, Howard and Lillian's membership also tested the congregation. Many of the founders of the church were not "liberals" in every sense of the word. Rather, as Lee remembered, many of Binkley's founders sought for society to be "fair and equitable" and "inclusive." Buying a house in an all-white neighborhood caused considerable local disruption, and Lee discovered that even some of Binkley's founders were "concerned" by his family's decision to purchase the home.[98]

In April 1968, Howard and Lillian along with many Americans were shocked and dismayed to hear of Dr. King's assassination. King's philosophy and approach to civil rights deeply resonated with the couple. The evening of King's assassination, Howard decided that he had to continue pushing for change in Chapel Hill. He wrote in his memoir that "it was not okay for me to live in one part of Chapel Hill when there were [B]lacks in other parts of the town with unpaved streets, rundown houses, and no new construction." When the Board of Aldermen rejected his second request for an open housing ordinance, Howard began thinking about how he could influence change in local politics. He approached his friend Buie Sewell, the pastor of a predominately white, progressive Presbyterian church in town, and encouraged him to run for mayor. After entertaining the idea, Sewell turned the proposition back around to Howard, suggesting that he run for mayor.[99]

Lee initially scoffed at the proposal that he run for mayor, but as he considered the prospect further with Lillian, he warmed to the idea. Lillian had once pressured Howard to promise that he would never run for political office, but she recognized the need for local leadership and became comfortable with the campaign. The Lees enlisted the help of friends and fellow Binkley members Anne and Billy Barnes, who joined Binkley in 1965.[100] Anne was a community organizer and Billy worked for the North Carolina Fund as a part of the country's larger War on Poverty before becoming a freelance photographer for news outlets including *Time* magazine. The two were well connected and active in the local chapter of the Democratic Party. Anne and Billy enthusiastically agreed to attend a small gathering to consider Howard's run for mayor. This small gathering, initially thought to include no more than fifteen individuals, ballooned to fifty. It gave Howard the confidence and confirmation he needed to formally decide that he would enter the race. He asked the Barneses to co-chair his campaign.[101]

The Barnes' membership at Binkley helps reveal the congregation's loose connection to a larger Democratic political network. Billy's work with the North Carolina Fund helped spotlight poverty in the country preceding President Johnson's Great Society. Anne first began her involvement with the Democratic Party through a bake sale, later helping with Hubert Humphrey's 1968 presidential campaign. She later served in the North Carolina House of Representatives. Because the congregation facilitated the gathering of individuals who shared larger societal concerns,

Howard Lee campaigning for mayor in 1969. From the Billy E. Barnes Photographic Collection (P0034), North Carolina Collection Photographic Archives, Louis Round Wilson Special Collections Library, University of North Carolina at Chapel Hill.

it also facilitated connections. The Barnes' decision to manage Lee's campaign was aided by their relationship through Binkley. Anne even taught Sunday school for the Lees' children. The church was not intentionally or even indirectly encouraging congregants to support the Democratic Party, but it did facilitate and nurture relationships between individuals and families who shared similar social concerns that aligned more with the Democratic Party of the 1960s.[102]

In April 1969, a month before election day, the *Raleigh News and Observer* reported "Chapel Hill Negro to Run for Mayor." While the position of mayor in Chapel Hill was largely ceremonial, Lee campaigned on an aspirational platform of starting a public transportation system, improving housing, and strengthening relationships between the university and town. He proposed a "town-gown committee" that would bring together university and community leaders to address challenges arising because of Chapel Hill's massive growth in population.[103] Lee sought to appeal to Chapel Hill's Black and student populations as well as the town's progressive voters. While he was unsure whether he could win, Lee was certain he would raise the issues that were important to him.[104]

While the church fostered relationships that helped get Lee's campaign off the ground, Bob Seymour and some other members of Binkley were initially hesitant about his campaign. Some thought Lee would only further divide the city and possibly hurt the progressive cause. While Binkley as a religious institution was not in the business of formally endorsing political candidates, as the campaign evolved, more and more members of the church became excited and "very active" in supporting Lee's candidacy, including Seymour.[105] Charlie Scott also helped recruit UNC students to campaign for Lee, and Dean Smith, riding three consecutive ACC championships, gave his support and rising notoriety to Lee's bid for mayor. On election day, the *Daily Tar Heel* endorsed Lee, celebrating his call "for greater participation by all residents of Chapel Hill—students and townspeople." The paper claimed that Lee's opponent, Roland Giduz, represented "the past" and not the future.[106] When the votes were tallied later that evening, Lee won by nearly four hundred votes.[107]

Howard Lee's election was pioneering as he became the first Black mayor in a predominately white town after Reconstruction. Through his successful career in public service, the Lees remained active members at Binkley. His campaign promise to inspire greater collaboration between the town and university mirrored Binkley's approach to ministry during this decade, in many ways functioning as an extension of that investment. Through his bold ideas and political initiative, he approached the position of mayor with the intention of improving the conditions of all residents. As a result, Howard Lee forever changed Chapel Hill. His campaign also helped to further connect Binkley to Democratic politics. On one level, Lee's election granted Binkley press coverage and name recognition in the community that it had not been able to generate on its own. On another level, the continued engagement of Howard Lee and Anne Barnes in North Carolina Democratic politics furthered the congregation's connection to the political party. Due to the congregation's core social commitments throughout the 1960s, they attracted members like Lee and Barnes who brought their political convictions along with them.

Binkley and the 1960s in Hindsight

The early history of Binkley Memorial Baptist Church is the history of a young and energetic community committed to making a difference in their local community. The congregation was not bound by walls, quite literally, during its first few years worshipping in Gerrard Hall on the campus of UNC. Binkley lacked the resources or reputation to strategically approach their ministry to the wider community. Instead, they took advantage when opportunities arose and made the most of the connections they fostered institutionally and personally. In many ways the congregation was experimental in orientation. This experimental nature gave this Southern Baptist congregation a radical edge for its time. Much like a college freshman may throw themselves into all of the extracurricular opportunities available to them, Binkley quickly became deeply involved in both the student life at UNC and the community of Chapel Hill more broadly.

Twenty-first-century readers committed to racial justice and civil rights can look back on Binkley's history and find much to celebrate about this congregation that threw themselves into the fight against segregation. Not all approaches to ending segregation, however, reflected equity between the Black and white communities of Chapel Hill. In particular, Binkley's work to desegregate the public school system remained entangled in white supremacist ideas that erased the legacy of Black education in Chapel Hill. As scholar Dwana Leah Waugh notes, "While whites recount desegregation as a narrative of progress, [B]lacks view it more dismally." The all-Black Lincoln High School had a rich legacy that was cast aside and lost when Black students began attending the white Chapel Hill High School. Black teachers and administrators lost jobs, and Black students entered a white school system without the same supportive faculty and programming that existed in their all-Black, segregated school.[108] There was a presumption that white public schooling was better than Black public schooling, and while elements of this may have been true, Black public schooling developed unique and vibrant communities and cultures that were disregarded by integrationists. Rather than equitably integrating the two school communities into one another, Chapel Hill closed Lincoln High and forced Black students to assimilate into the all-white Chapel Hill High School.

Additionally, Binkley's strategy to appoint individuals to fight for social change in the community through their positions of power tended to reinforce systems of stereotypical gender norms. The congregation regularly held workdays and advertised for them in the Binkley Newsletter—"calling all men."[109] As Joe and Eva Clontz remembered of the period, it was a "patriarchal society."[110] Men like Fred Ellis, Dean Smith, and even Howard Lee were able to attain positions of authority to enact social change in large part because of their gender. Seymour's encouragement of congregants to utilize their vocation as opportunities for ministry was largely geared toward privileged men who often held public vocations. Congregants looking back on this period acknowledged that there were "more women at home." At the same time, however, Howard Lee remembered that women "worked hard to prop things up in the background."[111] Eva Clontz acknowledged that during this early period at Binkley, women were still coming to a greater awareness of how things might be different, but that did not mean that women were not present and involved.[112]

Women were active members of Binkley Church during its early history. As scholars have recognized, while individual women may not have held specific positions of authority within Southern Baptist life, their collective strength and numbers fueled the work of both local churches and the larger denomination.[113] Tracing the activity of women at Binkley is difficult and often obscured within the congregation's historical record. Elizabeth Ellis, a founding member of the church, became chairperson of the diaconate in 1967, a significant milestone at a time when many Southern Baptist congregations would not consider allowing women to serve as deacons, much less chair the diaconate.[114] Aside from this noteworthy leadership role, Binkley's women more typically worked together in groups rather than as individuals.[115] Women at Binkley joined with other local women to help found the Inter-Church Council for Social Services, which later became the Interfaith Council for Social Services. The organization sought to address problems of poverty in the community and to "organize, coordinate, channel, support, and direct volunteer efforts to meet these needs." Binkley's relationship with the organization became one of the congregation's longest-standing partnerships, spurred on by the work of the congregation's women.[116]

The congregation also formed a Women's Association—the only church group that met twice a week, gathering on Tuesday evenings and Thursday mornings in order to include women who worked.[117] The meetings of the Women's Association varied in formality and sometimes included lectures from local scholars.[118] Pauline Binkley Cheek, a Binkley member and daughter of the congregation's namesake, remembered reading and studying Betty Friedan's *The Feminine Mystique* shortly after the book's release in one of the weekly meetings.[119] Women also provided congregational leadership by teaching Sunday school and serving on various committees. If men like Fred Ellis, Dean Smith, and Howard Lee were relieved of this type of congregational leadership to pursue congregational goals in their professional lives, women filled these roles within the congregation and in so doing supported this work. It was not until the 1970s that women began to advocate for greater representation and more significant leadership roles within the congregation.

Such critiques should not diminish the radical work that the congregation participated in throughout the 1960s, but it does reveal some unintended consequences of that work. It shows that progressive congregations who sought to instill social change, and indeed bring about the kingdom of God on earth, faced numerous challenges regarding how to enact such work and how to prioritize their commitments. While integration was indeed a progressive cause, implementing such a policy effectively, history shows, proved difficult. With regard to gender equality, as the congregation progressed into the 1970s, this issue would come into better focus. How the congregation channeled their resources and energy was and continued to be a significant challenge as society changed and ideas and theology evolved.

Not all of Binkley's approaches to ministry in the 1960s were remembered with the same success and pride. Toward the end of the decade, the congregation began what was known as the Carr Court Project, located in a predominately Black neighborhood in nearby Carrboro, North Carolina. To get to the neighborhood, one had to "follow a crumbling blacktop road behind a service station, cross rusty railway tracks, and pass an abandoned car."[120] Binkley purchased a home in the neighborhood to establish a community center for the local children. Working with other congregations in the area, Binkley sought community input for the project and began implementing various forms of educational and recreational programming. The Carr Court Project sought to involve both church members as well as local college students, but church documents regularly cited a lack of volunteers.[121]

Seymour remembered in his memoir that the Carr Court Project successfully ran for six years. He suggested that the reasons for its conclusion resulted from a "separatist movement" within the local Black community. White leadership was intentionally phased out of the project, and Binkley continued to provide financial support for a period as Black leadership emerged.[122] Creating a community of shared and equitable leadership proved difficult. Much good certainly came from the project, but the fading of this ministry from the congregation's records coupled with the struggle to find consistent volunteers suggests Binkley may have overextended. It could also be that some members of the congregation assumed that much of the work of racial justice had been accomplished, and this belief among some shifted the gravity of the larger institution to focus on other issues.

As Binkley sought to balance its progressive commitments between both town and gown, the church actively and unquestionably fought for civil rights throughout the sixties. The congregation partnered with students and faculty and took advantage of opportunities to push for integration when and where they were able to effectively enact change. They adopted new ways to be Baptist, affiliating with Southern and American Baptists, and gained a reputation for being a progressive congregation. While Seymour gave voice to the church and provided a public face for its ministry, he also worked to enlist its congregants in unique ways to serve

Binkley Memorial Baptist Church before the addition of the new sanctuary.
From the Billy E. Barnes Photographic Collection (P0034), North Carolina Collection
Photographic Archives, Louis Round Wilson Special Collections Library, University
of North Carolina at Chapel Hill.

the community. Church work entailed everything from teaching Sunday school to coaching basketball to running for public office. Even beyond the nudging of Seymour, Howard Lee's campaign shows how congregants worked among themselves to fight for change in the local community through partisan politics.

Reflecting on this period in the life of the congregation, Kate Wagoner Maynard and Lee Wagoner recalled many memories for which they were grateful. The two had grown up in the congregation as children of founding members Leo and Grace Wagoner. Kate remembered her parents as "authentically [trying] to live their faith, particularly during the turbulent 60s when all was questioned." Lee explained that growing up at Binkley afforded him the opportunity to "challenge and question what it meant to be a believer in God and Christ." He further claimed, "Binkley was where I truly learned that all people were equal in God's eyes, that no one was better than another and that we should all strive to help each other."[123] The 1960s was an exciting time for the congregation, and the memories of these early years carried the congregation forward into its future.

By the end of the decade, Binkley had grown and changed significantly. Beginning as a young and energetic congregation meeting in Gerrard Hall, the church now met in a permanent structure and counted the town's mayor as one of its congregants. Binkley was now a local establishment. The change pushed against some of the congregation's more youthful and energetic characteristics. By 1970 the Church Council reported that the congregation "is currently a church ministering primarily to the married graduate students from the university rather than undergraduate and single students. Efforts to involve more undergraduates have been a failure."[124] Changing the location of the church changed its identity. Binkley would never completely give up the college-town vibe that animated so much of its founding and early identity, but by the 1970s, it had to contend with the challenges of being a well-known, established church with a progressive reputation.

The Rise and Fall of a College-Town Church

"LIKE A BRIDGE over troubled water, I will lay me down," sang the congregation of Binkley Memorial Baptist Church on August 11, 1974. This was not the first time the congregation had heard a song from the popular secular artists Simon and Garfunkel in their Sunday Family Enrichment Hour. The previous week a member of the congregation performed "The Sound of Silence" in American Sign Language. The Family Enrichment Hour began that summer as a part of Bob Seymour's ongoing attempt to explore "experimental worship services" that would increase "the amount of secular music."[1] Services that summer also included Broadway hits like "The Sound of Music" and "The Impossible Dream" from *Man of La Mancha*. These secular songs joined a cadre of protest songs the congregation already regularly sang, from "We Shall Overcome" to "If I had a Hammer"—a Pete Seeger song made famous by the trio Peter, Paul, and Mary. Seeger had originally performed this song at a dinner for leaders of the Communist Party of the United States in 1949. Now it was sung in a Baptist Church.

The period from 1970 to 1988, when Bob Seymour retired, was one of great change within the life of Binkley Memorial Baptist Church. No longer the niche, start-up church plant next door, Binkley was now an established church within the Chapel Hill community. The use of the term "established" here does not seek to convey the idea of a traditional religious establishment in which the state financially supports the church, but rather seeks to illustrate the ways in which this former church plant had taken root in the community. Binkley held a close connection to the University of North Carolina at Chapel Hill, from faculty and staff to Dean Smith, now a growing basketball celebrity. Howard Lee, the town's first Black mayor and Binkley member, solidified the congregation's relationship to the local political establishment. In 1971, Seymour was asked to deliver the commencement address at the local high school.[2] As a result of the congregation's growing notoriety in the community, its membership was also growing. Over the course of the 1970s and early 1980s, this growth would create conflict over Binkley's identity and how to accommodate an increasingly larger church membership. Would the church remain true to the identity of a niche, progressive community, or would the identity of an established, religious institution be more appealing? Could the congregation balance the two?

Binkley faced this larger question of congregational identity during a period of change within American religious history. The importance of particular denominational identity was waning, whereas political division between the "religious right" and the "religious left" across denominational bodies was growing.[3] American religion scholar Benjamin Rolsky suggests that the 1970s witnessed a swift ascendency of the religious left through media and popular culture that served as the prelude to the more well-documented rise of the religious right in the 1980s through groups like Jerry Falwell's Moral Majority.[4] Television shows like Norman Lear's *All in the Family* presented audiences with what Rolsky describes as a "spiritual politics of the Religious Left." Such a politics later served to animate the work of Lear's interfaith nonprofit, People for the American Way.[5] The consequences of this cultural ascendance, however, fueled a sense of superiority among those of the religious left while breeding resentment among those of the religious right who were left behind—caricatured by Lear's infamous character Archie Bunker. Years later, Binkley pastor Bob Seymour described Bunker as a "lovable blue-collar bigot" who "felt superior and was always suspicious of other ethnic groups." The irony of Seymour's characterization, as well as that of many within the religious left, was that he too felt morally superior to Bunker.[6] By the 1980s, Rolsky argues, this resentment motivated the rise of a conservative Christian coalition that would not only shape American politics for decades to come but also eclipse the religious left's cultural power.[7]

Whereas Rolsky examines the broad and national rise and fall of the religious left during the 1970s, this chapter examines a narrow and localized congregation in Binkley Memorial Baptist Church. Much like the religious left on the national stage, Binkley knew that it was on the right side of history with regard to civil rights, and that fueled its sense of moral superiority. Once Binkley had a brick-and-mortar building coupled with some cultural and political standing within the Chapel Hill community, the congregation faced the question of how to wield this cultural standing. For some congregants this entailed reinvesting into the niche, social justice-oriented communal identity that birthed the church. For other congregants, however, this entailed a continued investment into the institution's growing cultural standing to ensure the church would outlast both its founders as well as Binkley's charismatic pastor, Bob Seymour. Such a division was not easily remedied. By the time Binkley was forced to evaluate its building needs in the late 1970s, this division generated a heated and contentious congregational conflict between those who advocated for the construction of a new sanctuary and those who advocated for investing the congregation's money in different ministry-oriented ways. This chapter argues that the religious left's cultural rise and fall was not only the product of politics, television, and popular culture as seen on the national stage, but also a product of brick-and-mortar congregational politics.

Binkley's membership was certainly ensconced within the broader cultural moment, but the congregation's experience of the ascendancy of the religious left's spiritual politics was coupled with more mundane decisions of congregational politics. Instead of experiencing the national celebrity of individuals like Norman Lear, Binkley experienced the local celebrity of Dean Smith, Howard Lee, and increasingly Pastor Bob Seymour. Seymour entered the second and third decade of his pastorate serving as the public face of the church. His authority shaped congregational decisions regarding Binkley's denominational affiliation, theological perspective, and, perhaps most importantly, facilities. Through his leadership, the congregation became an increasingly outspoken progressive voice within the Chapel Hill religious community. At the same time, as Binkley grew, it lost some of its earlier spirit and energy. The period marked an era of maturing for the congregation.

In examining this era of maturing, this chapter presents a unique challenge to the categories of "evangelical" and "mainline" Christianity. As both a Southern Baptist (traditionally considered evangelical) and American Baptist (traditionally considered mainline) church, Binkley muddled these categories further throughout the 1970s and 80s. The church was not simply a more liberal or left-leaning evangelical congregation nor was it a traditional mainline cultural stalwart. Instead, the 1970s and 1980s show Binkley's identity in flux. The congregation intentionally moved away from some of its more evangelical tendencies and toward a more mainline identity, but such a transition was neither totalizing nor definitive.[8] The congregation was not following a prescribed denominational path. Without a clear institutional apparatus to support its identity and work within the local community, Binkley had previously formed a patchwork network of support through a variety of denominational and para-denominational entities. By the 1970s and 80s, however, Binkley turned its attention toward institution building, showcasing the limits of "evangelical" and "mainline" categories.

Binkley as Institution Builder

Local congregations within the Baptist tradition can showcase a range of participation within wider denominational life. Some churches may be active in their
regional or state denominational affiliations, whereas others may focus more on national participation. Much of this activity is fueled by the interest and investment
of pastors and engaged congregants, without which such activity is often lacking.
Binkley had been an active congregation throughout the 1960s as an institutional
advocate for the civil rights movement. Through this work, the congregation had
cultivated a clearer sense of what it both wanted and needed in terms of denominational support as the church developed and sustained new ministries within the
local community. By the 1970s, Binkley had turned its attention toward shaping
and building the institutions with which it hoped to collaborate.

Binkley's early engagement with denominational bodies illustrates a young and
energetic congregation interested in rethinking denominational commitments.
This young, college-town church, much like many college students, was still in a
process of finding itself. While yes, Binkley was in fact a Southern Baptist church,
it did not exclusively identify with the SBC. Instead, Binkley joined the American
Baptist Convention (ABC) as well as the North Carolina Council of Churches,
a state body of the larger, ecumenical National Council of Churches. In those
early years, Binkley sought to align itself with these various denominational bodies that matched its general progressive and ecumenical outlook. The 1970s presented Binkley with a new perspective on its relationship with denominational
institutions. No longer a young and energetic congregation eager to partner with
existing structures, Binkley was now an established congregation in Chapel Hill.
The church's reputation changed from one of institutional joiner to institutional
builder.

In May 1970, Rev. Seymour gave an update to Binkley's Church Council on
the congregation's participation in the creation of a new regional body within the
American Baptist Convention—the American Baptist Churches of the Southeast
(ABCOTS). While the SBC had a clear national, state, and regional hierarchy,
the polity and governance of the ABC remained less centralized with diverse regional bodies and associations. Due to the division of these two denominational
groups over slavery in 1845, American Baptist congregations in the south tended
to be historically Black and date themselves to the period following the Civil War.
The new regional body sought to represent this congregational constituency within
American Baptist life. Binkley joined several other predominately white, liberal

congregations in the founding of ABCOTS, which desired to work with and alongside these historically Black American Baptist congregations in the south to establish an interracial Baptist denominational body. Binkley became a founding member of this new group along with fellow North Carolina Triangle-area congregations, Pullen Memorial Baptist Church and Watts Street Baptist Church in Raleigh and Durham, respectively.[9] Binkley was active in the early years of the regional body, and in 1974, Rev. Seymour was "invited to serve a two-year term as a Member at Large in the Southern Region of the American Baptist Convention."[10] Members of the congregational leadership also routinely attended gatherings of this body that they had helped to found.[11]

Binkley's involvement with the founding of this regional body in the ABC marked their evolution into a congregation invested in institution building. American religious life was shifting from an emphasis on denominational identities to more issue-based and theological identities.[12] Binkley's effort to establish and create denominational affiliations that resonated with their more open and ecumenical theology served as a response to this trend. After members of the diaconate attended a Billy Graham rally in the early 1970s, they returned to the church expressing a consensus "that the religion expounded by Dr. Graham is somewhat inconsistent with Binkley theology."[13] While Graham may have been particularly adept at shaping his message for the wider American evangelical culture, Binkley increasingly found its community outside that culture.[14]

Shortly following the diaconate's trip to see Billy Graham, a few individuals pushed the congregation to "seek a closer relationship with the ABC." These deacons did not express a desire to completely abandon Southern Baptist life, but they expressed a desire to merely limit the congregation's exposure "to the good areas of the SBC."[15] Under Seymour's leadership, Binkley worked to create a new regional body within American Baptist life that aligned with the congregation's outlook on issues of race. The congregation's relationship with the SBC was primarily cultural, and this relationship only continued to strain in the years to follow. North Carolina's *Biblical Recorder* reminded Binkley's leadership of the congregation's differences from typical SBC congregations when the paper published an exposé on the few Southern Baptist congregations in North Carolina with open-membership policies.[16] The newspaper's analysis led Binkley to reexamine its policy, but little changed and the church continued to welcome Christians who had received infant baptism as members.[17] Since its founding, the policy had significantly shaped the congregation's identity, becoming one of the explicit reasons the regional SBC association denied Binkley membership in the group.

The Southern Baptist Convention and Binkley continued to drift further and further apart. By 1980, a group of more conservative congregations and pastors within the SBC launched a ten-year campaign to reshape the denomination by electing denominational presidents with conservative or fundamentalist beliefs. Depending on which side of history one subscribes to, this campaign may be termed the "Fundamentalist Take-Over" or the "Conservative Resurgence."[18] While this campaign drastically reshaped the denomination, Binkley had already long felt at odds within the SBC before this influx of more conservative theological perspectives into the denomination's leadership. The church issued statements condemning certain actions of the convention over the course of this decade, but such statements were less about fighting over the SBC and more about preserving Binkley's theological integrity.[19]

Binkley was not alone in their frustrations with the SBC. The denominational politics of the 1980s pushed Binkley and other like-minded congregations to imagine an alternative. In 1987, this community of churches who, like Binkley, had never identified completely with the SBC decided to stop investing in Southern Baptist politics and instead founded a new organization—the Southern Baptist Alliance.[20] Binkley members initially questioned the need for affiliating with "another association of Baptists," considering their congregation's relationship with the ABC. The idea of only affiliating with the American Baptists, however, troubled some members whose cultural roots in Southern Baptist life ran deep.[21] The less hierarchical American Baptist Convention presented a different polity structure that was unfamiliar to Southern Baptist members.

Binkley chose to join and help shape the Southern Baptist Alliance (later known as the Alliance of Baptists). This small denominational group valued ecumenism and participation in the "larger body of Christ" as well as the pursuit of "social and economic justice." Such commitments resonated with Binkley and its membership. While initially a reactionary group founded against the theological changes taking place within the Southern Baptist Convention, the Alliance grew and evolved beyond this reactionary identity in subsequent years, thanks in part to the leadership of congregations like Binkley that worked to shape this new denominational entity around issues of common concern. By the twenty-first century, the Alliance of Baptists became one of the congregation's primary denominational affiliations.

Because of Binkley's commitment to founding and shaping denominational institutions like ABCOTS and the Southern Baptist Alliance, the congregation served as a fertile training ground for future ministerial and religious leaders. Between 1971 and 1985, the congregation ordained fourteen individuals to the Christian ministry.[22] As discussed in the previous chapter, the Student Interracial Ministry program's placement of Rev. James Forbes at Binkley was a formative experience for the congregation on many levels. Beyond experiencing the leadership of a Black minister during the era of segregation in Chapel Hill, Binkley gained an understanding of the benefits of welcoming young ministers into the life of the church. By the 1970s, Binkley became a regular placement congregation for divinity students fulfilling their field education at the nearby Duke Divinity School and Southeastern Baptist Theological Seminary.[23] Through these field education placements, Binkley welcomed and nurtured ministerial students who in turn helped sustain and contribute leadership to Binkley's educational programming. These ministerial interns later pursued other vocational opportunities, carrying with them their experiences at Binkley.

The congregation also witnessed two children of Binkley's founding members answer calls to ministerial service during this period. Kate Wagoner, the daughter of founding members Leo and Grace Wagoner, served as a resident teacher at the Hopital le Bon Samaritain in Haiti through a partnership Binkley formed with American Baptist missionaries, William and Joanna Hodges. While Binkley had previously sent congregants to work with the Hodgeses on a more short-term basis, Wagoner's request to serve over the course of a year was enthusiastically welcomed by the congregation. She remembered that her trip was funded "seemingly within minutes of my request!"[24] Similarly, Matthew Moffitt, the son of founding members Bill and Hilda Moffitt, began serving as a student intern at Binkley in the late 1970s and later received ordination from the congregation.[25] After Moffitt led Binkley in a communion meditation in February 1978, Rev. Seymour wrote to Matthew explaining how moved he was watching him lead the congregation. "It was an emotionally difficult moment for me as I remembered the years of your growing up in our congregation," he wrote.[26] In a separate letter to Matthew's parents, Seymour declared that "he represented the past twenty years of our church!"[27]

For Seymour, who had been called to serve as the congregation's founding pastor, Wagoner's and Moffitt's decisions marked a milestone in Binkley's history. He watched them grow up in the congregation just as he had watched the congregation itself mature. While many other Binkley members brought with them experiences and theologies shaped by experiences in other congregations and denominational backgrounds, Wagoner and Moffitt were uniquely the theological products of Binkley Baptist Church. Through shaping both denominational institutions as well as future congregational leaders who would one day inherit those institutions, Binkley had become an established church. Whereas questions of reputation and legacy were nonsensical for the young congregation meeting in Gerrard Hall in the early 1960s, they had become important questions worth asking and considering over a decade later.

Engaging Protestant Liberalism

Like all congregations and religious institutions, members at Binkley held a wide range of theological beliefs. People rarely attend and join religious congregations solely based on theological similarity. As an institution, however, Binkley had a reputation for engaging a theological progressivism that pushed the theological boundaries of what would have been considered typical within Southern Baptist churches. At the same time, Binkley identified, for much of its history, as an SBC congregation. During the 1970s, the SBC had yet to evolve into the more consistently conservative and even at times fundamentalist denominational body known to the early twenty-first century. The convention's decisions were erratic and contingent upon who held power and was willing to make their voices known. In 1971, prior to the Supreme Court's decision in *Roe v. Wade,* the SBC passed a rather progressive resolution allowing for the "possibility of abortion" in a wide variety of cases, including the "likelihood of damage to the emotional, mental, or physical health of the mother."[28] Just a decade prior to this decision, however, conservatives within the SBC fomented controversy within the denomination over the literal historicity of the book of Genesis and the use of historical-critical methods in seminary classrooms.[29] Binkley remained Southern Baptist due to the denomination's moments of progressivism, but it was often on the margins of the denomination theologically, accepting things like historical-critical methods as anything but controversial.

Much of Binkley's progressivism resulted from Seymour's leadership in shaping the congregation. His theological education from Yale Divinity School and doctoral work from Edinburgh provided him with perspectives few Southern Baptist ministers received in their vocational training. At the same time, Seymour saw himself as remaining steadfastly orthodox in his theological beliefs, and he was not afraid to push back or resist theological ideas that he thought strayed from Christian orthodoxy. Seymour did not wholeheartedly embrace liberal theological trends, but he did engage consistently with these theologies. As a result, Binkley established liberal Protestant thinkers as the congregation's theological conversation partners. By shifting their theological conversations away from conservative, evangelical thinkers, the congregation's engagement with liberal Protestant thinkers slowly evolved into the congregation's overall embrace of much of the movement.

The early 1970s ushered in a period of tremendous theological innovation within liberal Protestant circles, and while Seymour remained cautious to accept this innovation, he exposed Binkley to many of these new ideas. However cautious he may have been, Seymour found the changing theological landscape intriguing. Numerous Christian theologians from within academic circles were beginning to articulate socially contextualized theologies that emphasized the importance of human liberation. These liberation theologies contended that God sided with the poor and the oppressed, and they embraced Marxist, feminist, and Black critiques of systematic, universal theologies that centered white men as the normative subject. From Gustavo Gutiérrez's *A Theology of Liberation* (1971) to James Cone's *A Black Theology of Liberation* (1970) and Mary Daly's *Beyond God the Father: Toward a Philosophy of Women's Liberation* (1973), the liberationist movement within theological studies criticized Christianity's lack of attention to economic inequality, racism, and sexism. As historian Lilian Calles Barger argues, liberationists "were more interested in evoking a particular image of God to spur political action than restating moribund dogma." The liberationist movement's push for political action resonated with Seymour, but at times he remained committed to traditional Church dogma.[30]

While his theological inclination was clearly progressive from within the Southern Baptist context, Seymour tried to "resist the traditional labels, liberal, conservative, fundamentalist, etcetera." At the same time, he also tried to characterize himself "as a fairly orthodox Christian." Despite his self-professed orthodoxy, Seymour encouraged the congregation to engage with liberationist theologians, and through this encouragement, liberationist thinkers became the congregation's conversation partners. In 1974, two members of the diaconate, Barbara Bibb and Svein Toverud, conducted a study of James Cone's *Black Theology and Black Power*—the rising theologian's first work, published in 1969. Rather than take issue with the work at the conclusion of their study, Bibb and Toverud concluded that Binkley needed to seek a "fuller relationship with the [B]lack community."[31] Cone became a congregational conversation partner in thinking about Binkley's approach to racial justice.

Despite the positive response from Bibb and Toverud's study, not everyone in the Binkley community agreed. In fact, Seymour remained hesitant regarding some of the more Marxist tendencies of liberationist theologians. He praised these movements for opening avenues for the church to "come into a larger understanding of the social dimensions of the Gospel." Seymour had long been aware of the "economic dimension" within the New Testament, and in 1968, he preached a sermon encouraging his congregation to consider the merits of a "guaranteed annual income."[32] Liberationists, however, pushed further. This worried Seymour. "I feel there are some dangers," he cautioned, especially where "there are liberation theologians who are ready to push this theological perspective to the point of picking up guns and becoming revolutionaries."[33] Violence was a step too far for Seymour. While he agreed with many of the ideas and sentiments behind liberationist theologies, Seymour struggled with how such ideas might be implemented and adopted within the broader church.

The congregation also revealed its theological diversity when engaging feminist theologians who challenged the use of patriarchal language within Christian communities. Beginning in 1975, the congregation appointed a Committee on Sexism tasked with revising the original church covenant in order to reflect more gender-neutral language.[34] A number of members had begun to raise "dissatisfied rumblings" over the "overwhelming masculinity of church language."[35] As a result, the following year the congregation began to investigate "Sexism in Church Literature."[36] These first steps toward making worship inclusive remained important in pushing the congregation to think about issues of gender, but they did not result in the change many women in the congregation were looking for. In 1978, the congregation called its first woman, Carol Ripley, to serve as associate minister. She and later associate minister, Julie Strope, alongside lay leaders Martha Henderson, Judy Eastman, Jenny Weisz, and Velma Ferrell, pushed Binkley to engage in the challenging work of creating a more inclusive worship experience for both women and men.

In 1980, the congregation revised its covenant to include non-gender-specific language, and three years later, Henderson and Eastman drafted a "Proposal for the Use of Inclusive Language in Worship." Their proposal defined inclusive language as "words that include all people irrespective of age, sex, color, race, or creed." They identified numerous areas of worship that necessitated the use of inclusive language, from corporate statements to the "Word preached from the pulpit."[37] Hymns and scripture, however, provided another challenge. Henderson and Eastman would encourage the use of hymns that incorporated inclusive lyrics as well as alternative or even more modern lyrics. Scriptural translation or paraphrasing, they reasoned, should be left "to the discretion of the reader."[38] These changes sought to make the worship experience at Binkley representative for both men and women in the congregation.

Coupled with Henderson and Eastman's proposal for worship, Jenny Weisz and Velma Ferrell founded the short-lived organization, Southern Baptists for the Family and Equal Rights (SBFER). Organized in 1981, SBFER was headquartered at Binkley and sought to "inform Southern Baptists about women's issues," particularly the Equal Rights Amendment.[39] They were following in the footsteps of former first lady and Southern Baptist, Rosalynn Carter.[40] The organization only operated for five years, but it marked an attempt by Binkley women to change the national dialogue among Southern Baptists on the issue of women. An article entitled "On the Power of Word" in the SBFER newsletter passionately explained why inclusive language is important. "We choke on hymns that speak only of 'men' and 'sons,'" the article read. "We struggle with the deepest soul-stirrings, and are blocked by male-dominated images and language."[41] When the ERA was defeated in North Carolina and the amendment's ratification deadline passed, Weisz and Ferrell turned the organization's attention to supporting women's ordination.[42] The short-lived entity remained committed to a liberationist understanding of women's roles in the church. After the organization dissolved, the remaining funds were turned over to the congregation, and Binkley decided to use the money to financially support the newly formed Southern Baptist Alliance—an organization committed to "the freedom of the local church . . . [to] ordain whom it perceives as gifted for ministry, male or female."[43]

Not everyone at Binkley, however, welcomed such an embrace of feminism and the use of inclusive language from a liberationist perspective. At a meeting of the diaconate in 1984, Associate Pastor Julie Strope reported hearing a few "negative comments about inclusive language," particularly from "older people" in the congregation.[44] Another diaconate meeting reported that one congregational leader, Charles Carver, had "tired of hearing about inclusive language."[45] During her time as associate minister, Carol Ripley remembered that the issue contributed to "strained relationships" and required assistance from the Pastoral Relations Committee to help navigate some "rough patches."[46] Even Seymour was slow to embrace the push from Binkley women and feminist scholars like Mary Daly to both reevaluate and combat masculine language in the Christian tradition. "I think it is well-intended," Seymour said in a 1985 interview, "but I was very disappointed in receiving it, because some of the language, I think, distorts the meaning of scripture." Describing God as "Parent" instead of "Father," he argued, lacked the same "emotional feeling or affection." In that same interview, Seymour confessed that he "was a little bit slow in feeling the full impact of the so-called women's issues." By the mid-1980s he claimed to be "very much committed" to these issues, but his trepidation revealed the congregation's theological diversity.[47] Such diversity, however, emerged in relationship to the congregation's liberal Protestant conversation partners who helped set the boundaries of theological engagement.

The advocacy for inclusive language not only made worship at Binkley more inclusive for women, but it also opened the door to other conversations about inclusivity. Shortly after Binkley began interrogating sexist language within the original church covenant, the congregation began a sign language class. Binkley member Sandra Strokes led the class and soon began "signing the worship services" so that deaf and hard-of-hearing members would be able to better participate.[48] The congregation came to recognize that being inclusive of all people was a greater task than simply changing words like "mankind" to "humankind." It also included ensuring that the congregation was equitably accessible to all individuals. By the twenty-first century much of the deaf and hard-of-hearing membership of the congregation no longer attended and services were no longer fully signed, but Binkley continued to sign the doxology as a way of remembering the now defunct ministry of the congregation. It served as a reminder to the congregation that the work of inclusion took many forms.

Spurred on by the liberationist trend in theological higher education, Binkley came to identify inclusion as a chief theological virtue in the 1970s and 80s. Not all members fully embraced the same understanding of inclusion, but the importance of recognizing theological particularity became an important point of shared conversation among Binkley's members. With liberationists like Cone, Gutiérrez, and Daly as their conversation partners, Binkley's theological orientation continued to become more progressive. As certain congregants engaged in this type of theological thought, their engagement turned increasingly toward embrace. This led the congregation to open a theological space for greater participation from all its members—particularly women. As Binkley opened its theological space by embracing new theological resources, the congregation also had to address pressing questions related to the limitations of its physical space and resources.

Balancing a Budget and a Building

Sustaining the congregation's growth and cultivating the institutional stature of Binkley Memorial Baptist Church required financial investment. The sweat equity that Seymour and congregational leaders invested in the congregation's early years could only get the church so far. By the 1970s, Binkley included many prominent residents of Chapel Hill among its membership, and the congregation had become an active presence in the local community. Even so, the young congregation struggled to solicit the financial resources necessary to fully carry out its imagined identity as a fixture of its community. Driven by its memory of the 1960s, Binkley strove to be a church that served the local community, advocated for more just public policies, and helped alleviate social needs. Financially, however, the church often found itself unable to reach all its lofty goals. American religious history can often be understood through the lives of individuals and their beliefs and practices, but on an organizational level much of American religious history boils down to whether an institution can balance a budget and fund its operation.

As Binkley entered the 1970s, the congregation faced several difficult financial decisions that would set a precedent for the upcoming decade. At the first Church Council meeting of the new decade, church leadership discussed whether the congregation should reduce the total amount of its budget allocated for missions from "14% of the total budget to 10% or 12%" to ensure the church met its financial commitments. Rather than "encourage a slackening of effort," the Church Council decided to keep their 14 percent commitment and hold "special Easter and Christmas offerings" that would offset any budgetary shortfalls.[49] Two months later, however, Binkley recognized the extent of their financial limitations when they called a less experienced associate minister over a more experienced candidate who would have had to take a pay cut. Rationalizing their decision, the congregation called Dale Sessions with the hopes that the younger minister would stay with the congregation for a longer period of time and form deep relationships with the church's membership.[50] Money proved to be a consistent factor in the congregation's decision-making process.

As with most congregations, the summer months posed a challenge to the budget as families took vacations, attendance declined, and giving slackened. Many members had professional lives that followed the collegiate academic calendar, making this challenge perhaps more acute at Binkley. As giving slackened over the summer of 1970, the church had to withdraw $1,200 from savings to meet the payroll in late August.[51] By October the congregation still had overdue bills, and members of the Church Council called for the wider membership to be informed of Binkley's "financial crisis."[52] The rhythms of a congregation's financial year often encourage a rebound in the winter months. The coupling of Christmas giving with year-end giving helped propel Binkley to reach its budget commitments in 1970. By the following spring, the church found itself on "sound financial footing" once more.[53] This cycle of financial crisis to financial stability became familiar to the congregation throughout the early 1970s.

Despite receiving good news about Binkley's financial state after the first few months of 1971, over the proceeding years, many of the minutes from the Church Council reflected a congregation struggling to grasp the membership's giving habits.

By the beginning of summer, Finance Committee member Tony Blackwell reported that the church had over $4,000 "outstanding in past due bills."[54] That number rose to "closer to $6,000" by the end of August.[55] Routinely various committees and staff received requests from church leadership to halt spending "unless absolutely necessary."[56] Church records regularly defined the state of Binkley's financials as "not good."[57] Propelled into the new decade with a vision of what their church might become for the Chapel Hill community, Binkley struggled to finance this vision.

The church sought to offset budgetary shortfalls in a variety of ways—some fortuitous and some intentional. When the congregation hired Rev. Seymour in the late 1950s, they purchased a parsonage, but by the early 1970s Seymour and his family were interested in building a larger home that might continue to house them into retirement. Rather than repurpose the house, Binkley sold the parsonage, using the proceeds to cover emergency maintenance costs on their building.[58] The young associate minister, Dale Sessions, resigned after serving as associate pastor for two years to accept a call to serve as pastor of First Baptist Church of Bloomington, Indiana. Resignations and staff vacancies "left money in the budget" that had been "designated for . . . salary."[59] These sporadic occurrences provided opportunities for the church to catch up on budgetary obligations where it might have otherwise struggled to make ends meet.

Binkley also designed programming and events that could help bring in more money for missions and budget shortfalls. Like many congregations, Binkley had its membership fill out pledge cards in the fall for congregational leadership to better plan the budget for the upcoming year. Cassandra Poole, a member of the Church Council, organized a Christmas bazaar for several years where congregants could set up booths and sell craft goods that raised additional funds for missions.[60] This event served as a precursor to the Binkley yard sale, which first took place in December 1976 and became a regular fundraising opportunity for congregational mission projects. By the 1990s, the congregation revamped the yard sale as a partnership between Binkley and Barbee Chapel Church, a predominately Black congregation in Chapel Hill. Through this partnership, the event would bring in tens of thousands of dollars every two years.[61]

Seeking to be fiscally responsible while also expanding programming and proclaiming the Gospel was a challenge for the young congregation. The building was one of the church's primary assets, and it required the unglamorous task of upkeep. Longtime member John Humber served as the head of the Building and Grounds Committee for numerous years during the 1970s and helped keep the building in working order. A general handyman, Humber constructed built-in bookshelves

Prior to the construction of the mall, Binkley members were able to park their cars in the open lot next to the church. From the Robert Seymour Papers (04554), North Carolina Collection Photographic Archives, Louis Round Wilson Special Collections Library, University of North Carolina at Chapel Hill.

for the pastor's study, fixed playground equipment, fielded questions about use of the church property, and either performed himself or organized building repairs.[62] Claudia Cannady, who served as one of the congregation's earliest secretaries, remembered that Humber "often came in to do maintenance." She recalled that when he needed a break, "he would play the piano," much to the delight of staff members, who opened their doors and windows to hear the music.[63]

In addition to his general handywork, during Humber's time in leadership on the Building and Grounds Committee, he helped arrange the paving of the church parking lot. This laborious project took many years for the congregation to green light. Humber negotiated pricing and worked with both city officials and the developers of a recently opened shopping center next to the church property to get this nearly $20,000 project completed.[64] In the midst of pricing and negotiating the paving of the parking lot, Binkley also received a donation of a Dempster-Dumpster. Few, if any, of Binkley's membership would highlight the congregation receiving a large metal trash receptacle or the paving of the parking lot as a significant moment in the life of the church, but such small developments helped to shape Binkley's appearance toward the broader community. A newly paved parking lot and a dumpster to keep unsightly garbage neatly concealed helped maintain Binkley's respectability within the Chapel Hill community. Much of American religious history generally and local congregational history specifically is not glamorous and includes making mundane decisions related to institutional maintenance. For a congregation seeking to attract new members as well as entice local nonprofit organizations to use its facilities, decisions of institution maintenance and appearance are critical.[65]

Institutional maintenance was particularly important for Binkley specifically because the congregation regularly allowed local nonprofits and organizations to use the church's facilities. In addition to the Binkley Preschool, which met throughout the week, groups like the "Chapel Hill Service League, Audubon Society, Kewanettes and Key Club, Alcoholics Anonymous and Alanon" all held monthly meetings at the church.[66] Binkley also hosted a troop of Boy Scouts.[67] Other organizations scheduled to use the church's facilities on a less regular basis. For four summers beginning in 1971, for instance, Binkley partnered with the Chapel Hill Department of Recreation to offer summer camps for children that utilized congregational facilities.[68] That same year, the congregation also worked with a local organization "on an experimental basis" to host a day care for children with developmental differences. The project successfully operated out of the church until 1978, when it outgrew the available space.[69]

The building usage helped solidify both Binkley's presence in the community as well as the congregation's identity as an established religious institution in the Chapel Hill area. At the same time, however, it also strained the congregation's spatial resources. By one estimate, the congregation welcomed "nearly fifty groups and organizations" to use their facilities.[70] This placed a great deal of strain on Binkley's staff, tasked with scheduling the space. In 1976, the Church Council requested that the Building and Grounds Committee create a matrix "showing all of the organizations currently using Binkley's facilities . . . so that the building's uses may be more readily understood and coordinated."[71] Due to the number of groups using the building, Binkley began to turn away organizations who wanted to use their space. Even the congregation's use of the space on Sundays was strained with all Sunday school classes "filled beyond capacity" and a "need to invest in more folding chairs for the sanctuary."[72]

The crisis of space facing Binkley in the middle of the 1970s pressed heavily on the congregation's leadership. The church needed a solution, and opinions abounded. Binkley's Long-Range Planning Committee (LRPC) slowly began to sift through the church's options regarding its spatial needs with respect to both its growing membership and limited spatial resources. When the Church Council received a proposal in 1977 about partnering with the City to build a 1,700-square-foot teen center on the church's property, the LRPC "responded negatively."[73] Such a proposal would expand Binkley's facilities, but a teen center would not address the reality that Binkley was outgrowing its current worship space. The LRPC sought a more holistic approach to addressing the congregation's spatial needs. Rather than a executing a patchwork of quick fixes, the committee sought to address the problem of space for years to come. They also desired to fulfill a dream long held by many of Binkley's founding members—a new sanctuary.

To Build or Not to Build

In September 1978, the LRPC released a report to the Church Council that threw the congregation into nearly seven years of intense conflict and frustration, resulting in numerous families leaving the church. The ordeal caused aftershocks that, according to some congregational leaders, continued to haunt the congregation well over a decade later. At face value, the LRPC's report included little that could be considered controversial. Committee members weighed numerous factors pressing down upon the twenty-year-old congregation and made their recommendations accordingly. Specifically, the committee looked "at the physical needs of the Church." Everyone acknowledged that the basic problems that plagued Binkley revolved around the utilization of its facilities. "Everyone admits that the church should be used," the LRPC reported, but "the problem was finding a way that the church can provide facilities but also not disservice its own life." Binkley's policy regarding "who could and could not use the church" was "unclear." Additionally, the congregation needed more staff to handle the scheduling and maintenance of its building. Such recommendations were uncontroversial. Where some individuals felt the LRPC overstepped its bounds, however, was in its recommendation for the "construction of a new sanctuary and renovation of the existing Christian Education areas."[74]

The prospect of a new sanctuary enticed many Church Council members, but some individuals thought that the report from the LRPC focused too much on the physical building and not enough on the "spirit of Binkley."[75] Council member Paul Lindsay found that the report "underplayed social action as a component of the church's mission." Several council members questioned a component of the report suggesting the new "sanctuary be exclusively used for worship." These more skeptical council members wondered whether such a stipulation resonated with the "attitudes and priorities of the church as a whole." Similarly, Bob DeJardins "expressed disappointment with the report's section on outreach."[76] Council member Susan Brinn wondered if the proposal might cause the church to "actually lose some of those initially attracted by the church's philosophy." Spending money on a new building would inevitably take resources away from other ministries of the congregation. The LRPC justified their recommendations, suggesting they "arose from an objective appraisal of space needs and projections of future growth." Since the LRPC "did not initially set out to recommend an extensive building program," their "objective appraisal" caught a few members of the Church Council off guard.[77]

The proposal for a new sanctuary did not come as a surprise for many of Binkley's founders, who understood the construction of a larger, more formal sanctuary to be part of a longer journey from the congregation's humble beginnings in Gerrard Hall on the UNC campus. Newer members who had joined the congregation precisely because of these humble beginnings, however, saw the proposal as a retreat from what made Binkley unique. Bob Seymour was certainly not surprised by the recommendation. Earlier that year, he had already assumed that Binkley would begin a significant building project. In a letter to a congregant in January, Seymour wrote, "1978 will be an important year at Binkley Church for we will be celebrating a twentieth anniversary this Fall. We also seem to be gearing-up for a major new extension of our building. It looks as if the time has come to build our sanctuary."[78] For Seymour and many of Binkley's founders, a new sanctuary was a progression of the congregation's narrative. For many newer members, it was a departure from it.

When Binkley constructed its first sanctuary in 1965, the architect had also drafted a sketch for a larger, future sanctuary that Seymour kept in his office.[79] In the late 1970s, this sketch animated the desire to build. Southern Baptist Church planting strategies often included architectural plans for a growing congregation in which the original sanctuary would be converted into educational space, or a fellowship hall and a larger sanctuary would be constructed onto a new wing of the church building. This was the approach many founding members anticipated Binkley would take. Some newer members of the congregation saw an alternative for outgrowing the current worship space that included holding multiple Sunday services—an idea Seymour did not like. While the proposal for multiple services ensured the congregation could continue to accommodate its growing membership, it also created a fractured community and further taxed ministerial staff on Sunday mornings. At the rate Binkley was growing, however, the church faced a fast-approaching and tough decision.

The church had gone through periods of quick growth before, but this growth had been tempered by the rhythms of a college town. During the congregation's early history, Binkley lost a significant number of members each spring as graduation gave way to matriculation within a transient collegiate community. As Binkley became more of an established fixture of the local community, however, this typical yearly turnover decreased. Instead of families leaving town, Binkley's membership continued to grow as families who formerly attended Binkley returned to Chapel Hill for work or to settle into the growing local retirement community. Given such population dynamics, Seymour believed the problem of space "needed to be faced now."[80]

Deciding to construct a new sanctuary, however, was a slow process, and division in the congregation ground this process to a halt. Some members saw a new sanctuary as necessary for growth, whereas other saw it as a distraction from outreach and other ministries. Not even the staff were on the same page about the approach the congregation should take with respect to space. Seymour worried that multiple services would create "separate congregations" within Binkley. Associate Pastor Bruce Page, on the other hand, explained in a church conference meeting that churches tend to "overextend in building." Page attended Binkley while a student at UNC, and he explained how he returned to Binkley as a minister because of its "commitment to the community." His comments reflected a hesitancy to embrace a new building project when the congregation might more easily adapt their current approach to utilizing their existing space.[81]

At an early-April church conference meeting in 1979, those in favor of moving forward with a new building project sought to authorize funds for the LRPC to begin soliciting architectural assistance on the best course of action. Not everyone agreed that the church should move forward. Jim Wilde made a motion that sought to appease both sides by suggesting that the church begin investigating many different options ranging from a new sanctuary to heavier renovations of Binkley's current space. Those who opposed the building of a new sanctuary expressed reservations regarding how quickly the congregation was moving and advocated slowing the process down to consider Binkley's philosophy of outreach. Joe Clontz recognized that the conference meeting lacked a quorum and acknowledged that any decision they made would be subject to challenge. The gathering voted anyway—thirty-nine to eighteen in favor of Wilde's motion to begin investigating all options, including working with architects.[82] Two weeks later, a larger portion of Binkley's membership attended the church conference to voice their opinions regarding the solicitation of an architect. Wilde's motion was presented again, and another vote was taken, this time with a quorum of members. With a vote of ninety-six to fifty, the motion passed.[83]

Almost a year after the initial LRPC report had been submitted to the Church Council, Norma Willhoit expressed to a joint meeting between the Church Council and diaconate that there seemed to be a "lack of cohesion" among Binkley's membership. There are "those who wish to discuss philosophy of the church" she explained, "versus those who are interested in the building." The church was divided. Seymour struggled to position himself within this divide and questioned the role he should play in the decision-making process. He worried whether taking an "aggressive leadership" approach was prudent, but at the same time, his opposition to multiple Sunday services was well known.[84] The congregation's leadership felt that despite the "mood of the church," the "time of decision" was fast approaching.[85]

In December 1979 the congregation voted again, and this time the decision sought to appoint a Building Committee that would carry out the congregation's decision to expand its facilities. Those opposed to the building project mounted little resistance as 78 percent of those present voted in favor of appointing the Building Committee, to be chaired by Nape Baker.[86] Over the course of the following year, the Building Committee, composed of three subcommittees—finance, facility, and statement—began its work. Much of the year was devoted to fundraising and identifying an architect. In August, the Building Committee presented to the Church Council their architectural selection of Joseph L. Nassif, chosen due to both his general experience and previous work with other churches. With the Church Council's approval, Baker and his committee began negotiating architectural fees to later present to the wider congregation for final approval.[87]

It was not until early April 1981 that the Building Committee presented Nassif to the congregation so the membership could authorize the "go ahead with schematic drawings." At the time, Seymour described the congregation's decision to hire Nassif as "a compromise," but he also thought the time had come for those in favor of building "to close ranks and move ahead."[88] Since Baptists practice a democratic polity, the decision to "close ranks" depended on whether a majority of the congregation supported the decision. Seymour had the votes to approve the building process, so he encouraged the congregation to move forward in hopes that a "specific decision" might "generate motivation and enthusiasm" for the new sanctuary.[89] His hope, however, was misplaced. A majority of Binkley's membership may have approved of the decision, but a sizable and vocal minority remained opposed to the process. Seymour's high school yearbook predicted he would either become a politician or a preacher. In his autobiography, he confessed that he discovered at times the terms were "virtually synonymous."[90]

In August, four months after the church made the decision to move ahead with architectural designs, a petition began circulating within the congregation garnering fifty-four signatures. These members sought to offer new instructions to the Building Committee or alter "voting procedures" for approving a building alternative.[91] Congregational records do not provide a detailed account of the ramifications of this petition, but over the subsequent months as the architect continued his work sketching out blueprints, congregational conflict continued to fester. Congregational meeting minutes in general tend to avoid recounting unsavory or tense moments in a particular meeting. Describing the weight that this type of conflict had on a meeting where a significant portion of the congregation opposed a particular decision was certainly difficult for a recording secretary to articulate. When the Building Committee presented drawings for an expanded worship space that fall, a group of longtime and founding members surprised the chair of the committee by presenting an alternative set of drawings for a freestanding sanctuary. In response, the committee chair resigned, and the church appointed John Curry to lead the building project.[92] By June 1982, the diaconate requested the Church Council "stop all action" on the sanctuary building project until January 1983.[93] The pause sought to give the congregation time to mend divisions and disagreements.

At this June meeting, Bill Eastman, a deacon, attempted to articulate the conflict in the congregation through a letter to his fellow deacons and the church staff. "Friends," he began, "Binkley Church is hurting; we are in trouble." Eastman went on to vaguely detail how some members had experienced "pressure" to fall in line with the congregation's decision. Other members, he continued, experienced "implicit and explicit suggestions to leave" the church if they were frustrated by the decision. Eastman described overhearing one person in the church characterize those individuals opposed to the building project as a "group of sore losers." He penned the letter warning the diaconate and staff that Binkley Church was "on the verge of becoming a major embarrassment."[94]

For Eastman, at the center of the congregation's division over the new sanctuary was Bob Seymour and his leadership. He described the church as a church that had matured in recent years and no longer needed "strong, directive leadership." The congregation, he suggested, was more prepared to resist this overbearing type of pastoral control. Binkley desired "to share more influence or power." Eastman worried that the church had confused its loyalty to Binkley with its loyalty to Bob Seymour. He felt that Seymour had not been given all the information he needed to effectively lead the congregation. Much of Eastman's letter highlighted the large and overarching feeling within the congregation rather than detailing wrongdoings or misdeeds. His letter certainly contributed to the diaconate's decision to advocate putting a six-month pause on the building project.

Eastman, however, was not alone. Two weeks later, Fred Schroeder wrote a letter to congregational leadership describing how he struggled coming away from recent meetings with "a knot in [his] stomach over things spoken and unspoken." He recognized that not everything can be fixed in the church, but he felt the congregation needed to do more to try and heal its divisions.[95] At the August diaconate meeting, Furman Hewitt, a deacon and professor of Christian ethics at Southeastern Seminary, "distributed copies of 'Foundations for Ministry' from *Resolving Church Conflicts*" and planned to lead "another session dealing with conflict" at the following month's meeting.[96]

Over the next few months, the minutes from Church Council and diaconate meetings rarely addressed the building project. Rather than openly addressing concerns, Binkley's conflict remained unspoken and relegated to unrecorded private conversations. In August 1983, seven months after the diaconate had proposed to resume the Building Committee's work, Bill Harris, the church moderator, reported that the congregation had been approved for a loan "for up to $550,000" to begin construction.[97] The gaps in the congregation's records are glaring, but little indicates that the conflict had been adequately addressed.

Because the congregation had seemingly continued to avoid addressing the conflict openly, the start of construction did very little to defuse the looming tension. Members of the diaconate began to realize the toll this tension was taking on members of the staff, who they described as "lonely."[98] When Associate Minister Ed Huggins resigned in December, it took many in the church by surprise. Bill Eastman penned another letter to members of the diaconate and staff, saying, "Silence breeds more infection, not healing." He relayed information about another "vigorous and loyal" family at Binkley that would be leaving the church "because they no longer can sustain hope that Binkley can be open and confessional enough to heal itself."[99] The family Eastman referred to was the Geissinger family—Ladnor, Shirley, and their three children. Meeting minutes suggest that their departure from the congregation had a "greater impact" upon the diaconate than Eastman's letters, but many of the deacons were also divided on the best way to address the church's division. One voice on the diaconate reminded the group that "Binkley can't be all things to all people," whereas another explained that this was a "larger issue of how do we care about each other with our differences."[100]

The departure of the Geissingers indeed spurred a larger conversation during the January 1984 diaconate meeting regarding the congregation's ministerial staff. The past three associate pastors, Ed Huggins, Carol Ripley, and Bruce Page, had reportedly left the congregation "feeling that they had contributed less than they had." Huggins's resignation in particular raised questions about how well the staff communicated with one another. Whereas Huggins's representative on the diaconate said Huggins resigned both "frustrated and angry," Bob Seymour had a different impression. Members of the diaconate openly expressed dissatisfaction with Seymour's tendencies toward "autocratic leadership" and accused him of not trusting "the democratic process." The current associate minister, Julie Strope, expressed that she struggled with "being upfront" and that she was "working on a technique for being upfront with Robert S." The minutes themselves reveal some of the congregational tension. Throughout much of the congregation's history, Seymour is recorded in the minutes colloquially as "Bob." Throughout this 1984 meeting, he is recognized more formally as Robert S.[101]

Seymour himself did not believe that Binkley was a "strife-ridden, fragmented, torn congregation." At the same time, he admitted that he had difficulty in identifying the problem. He expressed disappointment at hearing personnel reports that identified him as the congregation's primary problem. "The message is that I've been here too long," Seymour lamented, "and that is very very painful." He worried that he could not leave the church at the present time amid a building project. The diaconate overwhelmingly responded to assure Seymour that his long tenure as pastor of the congregation was not the problem. The minutes recounted that later in the meeting, the following sentiment arose: "Perhaps we expect too much of ministers[.] [T]hey're human." Seymour decided that he would not attend the February meeting of the diaconate so that congregational leadership could consider the challenges staff were facing without his looming presence.[102]

The following meetings cooled frustrations for a few months before Eastman delivered a third letter to members of the staff and fellow members of the diaconate, including many new members of the diaconate who had little context with which to situate the particulars of his grievances. In the letter, he chronicled a personal conflict that had developed between Seymour and himself. Eastman asserted that Seymour had accused him of being the "Chief Inquisitor" of an examination of the church's personnel. Eastman explained that he had "not worshipped at Binkley lately" because of this tension with Seymour, but he hoped that he might return soon.[103] At the following meeting of the diaconate, Seymour apologized to the new deacons who may have been confused by Eastman's letter, and claimed the letter was

With moveable seating, the new sanctuary could accommodate more attendees than the original sanctuary, which became the congregation's fellowship hall. Photo thanks to Megan Hollenbeck.

After conducting baptisms in another church for a few years, Binkley constructed an outdoor baptistry to perform baptisms before the addition of the new sanctuary. From the Robert Seymour Papers (04554), North Carolina Collection Photographic Archives, Louis Round Wilson Special Collections Library, University of North Carolina at Chapel Hill.

The church's new baptistry straddled the narthex and sanctuary, symbolizing an individual's rebirth as a member of the congregation upon baptism. From the Robert Seymour Papers (04554), North Carolina Collection Photographic Archives, Louis Round Wilson Special Collections Library, University of North Carolina at Chapel Hill.

A view from the baptistry into the sanctuary. Olin Binkley's portrait hangs in the background. Photo thanks to Megan Hollenbeck.

"misrepresentative" of his opinion on the matter. Eastman was not in attendance to be able to openly address the conflict.[104]

This third letter from Bill Eastman shows how the conflict over the construction of the new sanctuary never really ended but merely faded away. As families frustrated by the decision left the church or stopped attending, the conflict became less pronounced. Over the summer of 1984, as those opposed to the decision slowly removed themselves from the process, congregational leadership focused its attention more upon the transition into the new sanctuary. With "construction in full swing," members became increasingly curious about how the new sanctuary would change the life of the church.[105] Each Sunday, congregants were able to see the building's progression and imagine the finished product.

On the first Sunday in November 1984, Binkley gathered for its first worship service in the new sanctuary. The large, open, square space was based on an interpretation of Noah's Ark, with large wooden arches cresting up toward a window-filled roof. A baptismal pool resided at the entrance of the sanctuary, fixed both inside and outside the worship space. Individuals seeking to make a profession of faith and receive baptism entered the waters from outside the sanctuary and emerged from their immersion on the sanctuary side of the pool. The liminality of the baptismal pool symbolized the role of baptism in the life of a Baptist congregation. While Binkley accepted individuals who received baptism from other Christian traditions, the location of the baptismal pool in their sanctuary served as a reminder of the importance of baptism in becoming a member of the congregation.

In the following weeks that preceded worshipping in the new sanctuary, members of the diaconate discussed their reactions and thoughts. New patterns of serving communion had to be conceived and organized. Instead of permanent pews affixed to the single-leveled floor, the new sanctuary utilized movable chairs, pulpits, and communion tables. This gave Binkley the opportunity to begin experimenting with seating patterns and holding services in the round. Within two years of worshipping in the new space, the Worship Committee analyzed seating arrangements that maximized capacity. Average attendance in the first couple of years of gathering in the new sanctuary hovered at 300, but spiked on holidays like Easter, which in 1986 counted 487 individuals in attendance. While the new sanctuary had been constructed to alleviate concerns about space and the possibility of holding two worship services, the committee concluded that it seemed "most probable" that two Sunday services would still be necessary by the end of the decade.[106]

The New Sanctuary in Retrospect

In 1985, a year after the new sanctuary had been constructed, a few congregants were anonymously interviewed about the state of the church. They all highlighted the decision to construct a new sanctuary as the most "divisive decision in the church's twenty-seven-year history." One congregant explained, "The members from the early years had long held a dream to build a sanctuary but were awaiting the proper time." On the other hand, however, newer members believed that "the decision to build meant channeling resources away from missions and outreach. They did not share the dream of building the sanctuary."[107] Another congregant described the first of these groups as the "old guard," which was "typically associated with the University of North Carolina Chapel Hill." The second group, the congregant explained, had become members in the late sixties and early seventies and appreciated Binkley's "fellowship and application of Christian principles such as peace, justice, and simple living."[108]

The tragedy of the construction of a new sanctuary hinged on the tension between these two groups. There was great nostalgia at Binkley, another congregant explained, especially for the early years—"the years when the church was organizing and began meeting on the UNC campus." There was "excitement and the energy of starting a new church, of building something new and different." This story of a "small group of pioneers" creating a new type of Baptist congregation had allured the newer members to Binkley. The older, founding generation, however, was allured as well. They were allured at the prospect of becoming that large, steepled establishment both recognized and respected within the wider Chapel Hill community. While they clung to their memories of Binkley as it once was, the older members ironically pushed Binkley toward a different identity—toward establishment. Newer members who had joined Binkley because of its unique Baptist identity and approach to ministry felt blindsided. Some eventually left.

During these anonymous interviews in 1985, some congregants lamented the current state of Binkley. "Now that the sanctuary was built," one member responded, "there was no tangible goal to strive for." The member contended that "enthusiasm was down." Another congregant responded that despite the church's impressive history, "Binkley had not actually accomplished much racial inclusiveness." Yet another "felt that Binkley did not have the concern for the poor it once did."[109] These anonymous interviews paint an unpleasant picture of the new sanctuary as an odd shrine to Binkley's founding years. The sanctuary changed the congregation's identity in an attempt to preserve the legacy and reputation of its past. The rise of the college-town church that defined itself against the town's large, steepled congregations had fallen in line with them.

Framing the sanctuary conflict in such stark binary terms helps to show how significant it was in pushing the congregation in a new direction, but it also obscures the ways in which the congregation continued its community engagement over this period. Throughout this stressful season, Binkley helped to start a local chapter of Meals on Wheels to provide hot meals to "homebound older adults and persons with disabilities." The congregation provided the organization office space as well as numerous Binkley volunteers.[110] The church also began a partnership with Habitat for Humanity during this time. In 1982, the congregation sent a small team to Americus, Georgia, where the organization began. Soon after, the congregation became instrumental in helping to start a local chapter of Habitat in the Chapel Hill area. The church helped sponsor the building of numerous local houses and took trips to work with Habitat chapters in Virginia, South Carolina, and Georgia.[111] Elements of the old Binkley remained alive through these types of social outreach ministries, but the congregation's tone shifted in the process of building the new sanctuary.

Binkley's rise to prominence in Chapel Hill in many respects mirrored the national rise of the religious left throughout the 1970s. Both this local congregation and the national movement faced questions regarding to what ends they would utilize their newfound cultural power. Binkley chose to reshape its identity as a prominent religious establishment in Chapel Hill. This decision, however, meant that Binkley lost some of its more countercultural tendencies. At the same time, the decision also provided Binkley a greater platform within the local community through which it could effect change. The question going forward would be whether the congregation gave up too much of its countercultural, justice-oriented identity to effectively utilize this platform that took such a toll to build.

It is important to recognize that the platform that Binkley created through the construction of a new sanctuary was indeed political but not overtly partisan. The congregation decided that it was advantageous to have a larger, formal sanctuary that could not only meet the demands of its growing membership, but also meet the stature of its growing reputation. There were politics—questions of power—involved in the building's construction. The decision, however, was not partisan. At the same time, groups like the Moral Majority were creating platforms through which conservative evangelicals could effect change through partisan politics on a national stage. Understanding Binkley's decisions in the 1970s and 1980s through

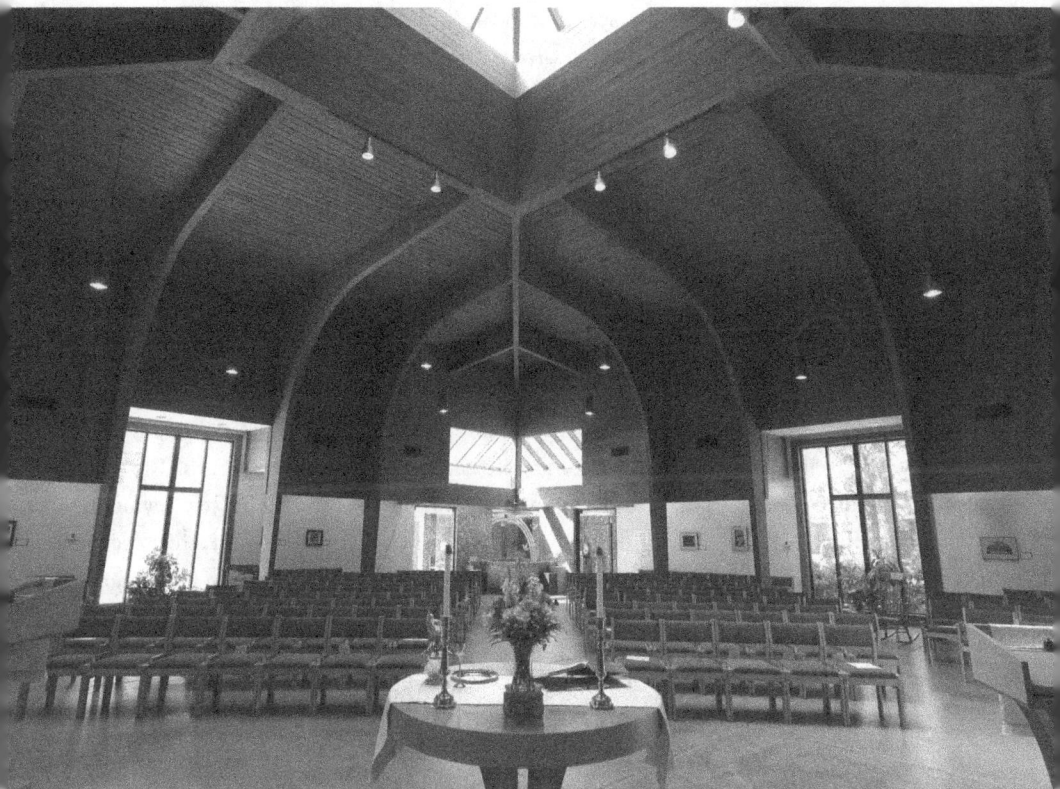

The back of Binkley's sanctuary. Photo thanks to Megan Hollenbeck.

this lens helps reveal how conservative evangelicals became so much more influential in US political life than progressive Christians. Binkley, like much of the religious left, sought to invest in and capitalize on their cultural power coming out of the 1960s much more so than their partisan political power. From Binkley's position as a local religious community, this entailed investing in their building.

Part of the reason Binkley decided to invest in its cultural power was to ensure the congregational legacy. For so much of its early history, Binkley relied upon Bob Seymour to be the congregation's voice in the public sphere. He had earned a great deal of respect in the community and was synonymous with Binkley. One congregant remarked that he possessed "such a strong voice" and as a result was quite an intimidating figure. It was "Bob's Church," and people looked to the pulpit for leadership.[112] The process of investing in Binkley's cultural capital by building a new sanctuary also served to help differentiate Binkley's voice from Seymour's. The construction of Binkley's sanctuary was in many ways the swan song of Rev. Seymour, who four years after the building project was completed retired in 1988, thirty years after Binkley's founding. His impressive twenty-nine-year history with the congregation saw the growth of Binkley from a small band of less than one hundred members and no building to a congregation of more than five hundred members and a brand-new sanctuary capable of housing them. The new sanctuary helped ensure that the congregation would be able to continue its work within the community once Seymour retired.

The end of Seymour's tenure as Binkley's pastor was greatly lamented, but for some in the congregation it was probably also a little welcomed. He had what some described to be an "assertive leadership" style, and one congregant even characterized him as "untrusting," echoing Bill Eastman's earlier characterizations. Seymour's advocacy for the church to build a new sanctuary may have been necessary for Binkley to avoid larger problems of space and building use, but his approach also left the congregation confused about the church's way forward in a post-Seymour congregation.[113] In many ways, he left the congregation still conflicted about the building. This lingering conflict made succeeding Seymour's pastorate even more difficult given his stature both within the larger Chapel Hill community and among so many of the congregation's members who joined not because of the church but because of Bob.

Through its construction of a new sanctuary, Binkley solidified its identity as a Chapel Hill establishment. It was no longer the niche college-town church it had once been. Caught somewhere between these two identities, Binkley's communal life after Seymour's retirement left the future of the congregation uncertain. On the surface, Seymour left his successor a new building and endless opportunities through which to lead the congregation into the future. At the same time, he also left his successor a congregation deeply fractured by a long and drawn-out conflict. The church held a deep admiration for his nearly thirty years of congregational leadership and community engagement, but they also now held a deep skepticism of pastoral authority more generally. Many questions loomed over the future of Binkley Memorial Baptist Church at the time of Seymour's retirement, but the congregation had the resources, the desire, and now the platform with which to chart a new course. No one expected, however, that this new course would be set in motion by a twenty-four-year-old gay divinity student.

4

Binkley in Transition

IN 1992 JOHN BLEVINS, a Duke University School of Divinity student and member of Binkley Memorial Baptist Church, received an invitation to be a guest on *The Maury Povich Show*. The *New York Times* similarly reached out to the twenty-five-year-old soliciting an interview. All the media attention had Blevins "scared to death." He was in the process of seeking a license to preach the Gospel through Binkley, which would have been rather uninteresting to major news out-lets—except that Blevins was seeking licensure as an openly gay man. As he later remembered of the process, "I was trying to figure out what my faith meant" and "what my sexuality meant." Requesting a license to preach meant that he was also asking Binkley to join him in this process of discernment. The congregation, while progressive, had many members who were uncomfortable with the idea of ordain-ing, much less licensing, an openly gay man. Many members, however, were quite ready to wrestle with questions of faith and sexuality. In April 1992, despite the plethora of competing ideas and thoughts about sexuality among its membership, Binkley licensed Blevins and became national news.[1]

While conservative evangelicals of the late twentieth and early twenty-first cen-tury garnered much attention for their opposition to homosexuality, historian Heather White has noted that the origins of this opposition emerged not from fun-damentalist preachers but from liberal Protestants. The development of the "ther-apeutic sciences of psychiatry and psychology" was appealing to liberal Protestants in the 1940s and 1950s who came to characterize homosexuality as a disorder.[2] It was the Revised Standard Version, a translation of the progressive National Council of Churches, that introduced the term "homosexual" into the biblical text for the first time. As liberal Protestant approaches to sexuality evolved throughout the twentieth century, conservative Christians came to adopt early-liberal Protestant therapeutic ideas and adapt them, for instance, to programs of conversion therapy. As White explains, "The certainties about religious orthodoxy and sexual identity defended on the Right and the Left carried forward assumptions already influenced by liberal Protestants."[3]

Binkley Memorial Baptist Church's engagement with the topic of sexuality surrounding the licensing of Blevins marked a period of transition for the congregation. On the heels of a conflict-ridden building project and the retirement of longtime pastor Bob Seymour, the congregation was indeed in transition. The licensing of Blevins reveals how the evolution of liberal Protestant thought created conflict within local congregational settings. Not every member of the congregation responded similarly to the quickly changing religious and secular discourse around the topic of homosexuality.[4] Many longtime members could remember sermons from Binkley's pulpit where Seymour had expressed hesitancy to affirm all the components of what he deemed the "sexual revolution" of the 1960s. By 1990, however, Binkley had called a new minister, Dr. Linda Jordan. She along with many members of the congregation were more open to considering the ordination of gay individuals. When the congregation faced the question of licensing Blevins, conflict ensued. Echoing the division that festered during the building of the new sanctuary, some congregants sought to license Blevins as a testament to Binkley's progressive spirit, while others remained hesitant or even openly opposed to what they deemed a product of this "sexual revolution."

This chapter addresses what became known to some members as the "licensing controversy" in Binkley's history, but it marks a larger transition in the life of the church. It shows that liberal congregations responding to issues of human sexuality had the challenge of establishing a common discourse and understanding of sexuality around which they could collectively reason and agree. As progressive as Binkley may have been, the topic of human sexuality posed a challenge precisely because the congregation struggled with how to talk about it. Binkley's willingness and ability to address racism in the 1960s Jim Crow south did not easily translate to discussions of sexuality thirty years later. Even those who favored licensing Blevins had different reasons for supporting him. Whereas scholars have often discussed how the politics of liberal Protestantism and sexuality have played out on a national level, Binkley provides a case study for how these discussions took place at the congregational level.[5] While numerous Baptist scholars and practitioners published historical and practical work on the subject of sexuality in the years following Binkley's decision, the licensing of Blevins in 1992 was a trailblazing event for a Baptist congregation anywhere and particularly in the south.[6] Such a decision shaped the congregation's identity moving forward out of the twentieth and into the twenty-first century.

Baptists and Sexuality

The denominational resources that Binkley had to support their process of thinking through issues of human sexuality in the early 1990s were almost nonexistent—or, perhaps put another way, were predominately one-sided. The Southern Baptist Convention offered its first resolution on homosexuality in 1976. The previous year, the federal government had lifted its ban on hiring gay and lesbian individuals in civil service positions, and the SBC's resolution reflected a concern that homosexuality was becoming an "open lifestyle." The convention acknowledged the "autonomy of the local church to ordain ministers" but urged "churches and agencies not to afford the practice of homosexuality any degree of approval through ordination, employment, or other designations of normal life-style."[7] The idea that gay and lesbian individuals may be working for the federal government was disturbing enough that messengers to the SBC's annual meeting sought to ensure that such individuals would not find employment within any facet of Southern Baptist life.[8]

The 1976 resolution would be the first of six resolutions the SBC would pass on this topic over the next fifteen years. Resolutions increasingly utilized harsh language as conflicts over human sexuality became more prominent in the United States. When Anita Bryant launched her campaign against gay rights in response to an anti-discrimination ordinance in Miami, Florida, the Southern Baptist Convention praised her "courageous stand against the evils inherent in homosexuality."[9] In another resolution, messengers resolved that they deplored "the proliferation of homosexual practices."[10] The convention suggested that efforts to make homosexuality more accepted within broader society were concocted by "liberal humanistic politicians."[11] In 1988, the SBC linked homosexuality with the "spread of AIDS" and resolved that "while God loves the homosexual . . . homosexuality . . . is an abomination in the eyes of God."[12] The resolutions passed from 1976 to 1991 represent the opinions of the majority of messengers from each of these respective gatherings. While the convention became increasingly conservative throughout the 1980s, objections to homosexuality remained consistent with resolutions from the previous decade.

During the same period, Binkley's other Baptist denominational partner, the American Baptist Churches USA (ABCUSA), maintained a quieter national profile regarding issues of human sexuality. In 1973, Rick Mixon, an American Baptist seminary graduate and openly gay man, approached his congregation, Lakeshore Avenue Baptist Church in Oakland, California, in pursuit of ordination. Although not unanimous, the church affirmed Mixon's call to ministry. When the congregation brought Mixon before the regional ordination council of the ABCUSA, however, they blocked his ordination. For more than two decades, Lakeshore would put Mixon forward as a candidate for ordination to no avail. During this time, Mixon founded American Baptists Concerned for those individuals within the ABCUSA who identified as "lesbian, gay, bisexual, transgender, intersex, queer, questioning, and allies." After circumventing the regional body, Mixon ultimately received ordination at Lakeshore Avenue on San Francisco Gay Pride Day in 1996, twenty-three years after first seeking ordination.[13]

As questions of sexuality created conflict at the regional level within the ABCUSA, the national organization did not attempt to make a statement on sexuality until 1987. Meeting in Pittsburgh, delegates discussed a statement of concern regarding homosexuality. The statement claimed that scripture "repeatedly depict[s] homosexuality as a social and moral evil" and concluded that "the unrepentant homosexual has no claim to full acceptance in the Christian community." After "considerable discussion," the statement failed to garner a majority of the delegates and was defeated by a vote of 408 yes, 474 no, with 71 abstentions.[14]

Such was the climate among the SBC and ABCUSA surrounding the issues of human sexuality in the 1970s and 1980s. Binkley Memorial Baptist Church affiliated with both denominational groups, but Binkley would not have agreed with the statements or attempted statements of either respective group. At the same time, however, Binkley was not as progressive a congregation as Lakeshore Avenue, which supported Mixon in the 1970s. During these two decades at Binkley, issues of sexuality percolated throughout the congregation in private, only on a few occasions manifesting themselves in the public work of the church.

Sexuality at Binkley and Seymour's Legacy

Although Bob Seymour retired in the late spring of 1988, his legacy within the congregation was far reaching. The thirty-year-old church had not known another senior minister. Seymour was well known throughout Chapel Hill, and Binkley had come to rely on him to be its progressive voice in the community. For much of its earliest history, Binkley Baptist remained focused on issues of racial justice and civil rights. Such a focus would intersect with stereotypes of the hyper-sexual Black man, the Black woman seductress, and the sexually pure white woman—but for Binkley these intersections remained a subtext. At the same time, over the course of Seymour's tenure, he spoke on a handful of occasions explicitly about questions of human sexuality. While his views evolved over the course of his pastorate, not all opinions and views within the congregation evolved the same way.

In 1966, before either the SBC or ABCUSA broached such questions, Seymour publicly took an opportunity to explicitly address Binkley on questions of human sexuality but chose to remain tentatively silent and hesitantly skeptical of same-sex relationships. In May of that year, Seymour delivered a sermon entitled "The New Morality." He began the oration clearly stating, "There is considerable anxiety today over the future of the American family—and for good reason." As Seymour understood the country's changing culture, society was in the midst of a "sex revolution the likes of which our world has never seen."[15]

Amid his statistics and general characterizations of this "sex revolution," Seymour identified a singular concrete example, the recently published study entitled *Towards a Quaker View of Sex*. Initially published in 1963, with a revised edition published in 1964, this short volume sought "to consider what Quakers could say to homosexuals and to others who found that society strongly condemned their sexual feelings and who found, too, that the expression of those feelings could lead to victimization, blackmail, and imprisonment."[16] The work made few definitive conclusions, acknowledging that this search was "a move forward into the unknown." Instead of "simple obedience to a moral code," there requires a "high standard of responsibility, thinking and awareness" not only among individuals but within community.[17] While the volume put forward no simple or clear-cut answers, it remained committed to caring for those individuals who feared for their lives because of their sexual and romantic attraction.

Seymour relied upon this volume as a principal example of "The New Morality," but he never made an explicit reference to homosexuality in his sermon. There were likely members of Binkley's congregation who were well aware of the nature of this volume, just as there were others who were unaware. Seymour toed a fine line dancing around the question of same-sex relationships. He praised this "New Morality" for holding the "principle of love" above the "bondage of law."[18] He compared the changing culture to the challenges Jesus posed to the Pharisees. Divorce served as a helpful example: while some denominational groups maintained a rigid commitment to the traditional morality forbidding divorce, other Christians recognized that questions of divorce ought to weigh "what is best for all parties involved."[19] In this sense, Seymour declared "The New Morality" a welcome change to American society.

At the same time, Seymour remained hesitant to accept everything the "New Morality" had to offer Christians. "The removal of rules in favor of the sole principle of love," he confessed, "may leave me with a greater burden to bear than I am able to manage alone." Seymour explained that he agreed with the new morality in principle, but that he was "not altogether ready to surrender the traditional morality."[20] Although his sermon never referenced homosexuality or same-sex relationships, these questions were at the forefront of Seymour's mind. Throughout much of the sermon, he focused more closely on questions of divorce and sexual relationships outside of marriage—issues that were quite divisive within Baptist congregations of the period. Seymour clearly remained uncomfortable with elements of *Towards a Quaker View of Sex,* but his views on sexuality, like those of many liberal Protestants, would evolve over the next few decades.

In the fall of 1982, Seymour published his schedule of sermon topics for the following eight months, as he normally did. In February, he scheduled a sermon in which he would openly address the congregation on his evolving views in a sermon titled "The Church and Homosexuality." It was coupled with another sermon the week prior that tackled the issue of abortion. Seymour explained that both topics were becoming more and more prevalent in society. The church, he contended, cannot "remain silent" on these issues. From the outset of his sermon in late February, Seymour held that "there is no one official position" with regard to abortion or homosexuality, and as such, "there is room for diversity of opinion."[21] As this marked the first time Seymour openly addressed the question of homosexuality from the pulpit, there certainly was a diversity of opinion within the congregation that Sunday morning.

Seymour began his sermon by addressing the oft-cited passages from the biblical text used to condemn homosexuality. He suggested that the prohibitions in Levitical laws were more concerned with "curtailing population growth" and that the story of Sodom and Gomorrah similarly focused on the sin of "inhospitality." Jesus, he reminded his congregation, "never says anything at all about homosexuality," and Paul's condemnation must be interpreted in light of a cultural context with "no understanding of the existence of what we recognize as an inversion of sexual identity."[22] Seymour wanted to instill within his congregation the recognition that the biblical text is far more complicated and nuanced than it is clear and direct.

The science of the period, Seymour continued, also remained divided between the theory that "homosexual orientation" was "learned" and the theory that it was "inherited." As part of the evolution of thought on sexuality, in the previous decade, the American Psychiatric Association removed homosexuality from its list of mental illnesses and instead referenced "sexual variations." Seymour explained that his study of the topic had helped him to recognize "the presence of both masculine and feminine characteristics in each of us." Throughout the sermon, he conflated questions of gender, sexual orientation, and sex within the confines of a single category. As a result, he

proclaimed a newfound meaning to Genesis 1:27—"God created them male and female." Seymour proposed that "God did not simply create two sexes, God made each
of us both male and female."[23] Such a provocative statement with its use of "them" as a
singular pronoun also had implications for later debates surrounding transgender and
non-binary individuals, who at the time Seymour was not even considering.

Seymour identified parallels between racial discrimination and the discrimination faced by those within the emerging LGBTQ community, equating questions
of human sexuality with his experiences fighting for racial justice in the 1960s. He
worried that sexuality would become "the most divisive issue in the church since
slavery."[24] The founding of the Universal Fellowship of Metropolitan Community
Churches (MCC) in 1968 as a denominational group "for homosexuals" concerned
Seymour. The MCC had grown steadily since its founding, boasting 111 congregations at its tenth anniversary. Historian Melissa Wilcox has argued that the growing attention to homosexuality among mainline denominations aided the steady
growth of the movement.[25] Seymour worried that this new denomination functioned as "another form of segregation within the Christian community."[26]

The sermon concluded with a call to be neighborly toward homosexual individuals,
citing the 1978 book *Is the Homosexual My Neighbor?*[27] Seymour recognized that in a
congregation the size of Binkley, meeting in the south, there would be little consensus
on questions of human sexuality. He acknowledged that there could be members of
his congregation that held "rejecting-punitive positions" toward "homosexual persons" as well as those who practiced a position of "un-conditional acceptance" and
everything in between. Despite differences of opinions, he encouraged Binkley to
practice a shared spirit of neighborliness. Seymour closed the sermon explaining that
God had brought him to the belief that "God shows no partiality, but in every sexual
orientation everyone who fears God and does what is right is acceptable."[28]

Seymour's change of opinion between 1966 and 1983 could be attributed to several societal factors. Increased attention to questions of human sexuality among
Christian denominational bodies, including statements passed by the Southern
Baptist Convention, as well as cultural moments like the Stonewall rebellion in
1969 and the growing AIDS epidemic all likely contributed to his evolution of
thought. Perhaps even more important were the number of individuals who sought
Seymour's counsel, whether they were personally wrestling with their own sexual
orientation or had a friend or family member who was.[29] He recalled years later that
following his 1983 sermon he was amazed by the "range of responses" and saw that
his "counseling increased sharply."[30]

Seymour did not take the opportunity to address the subject from the pulpit again before his retirement in 1988, but the few times he did choose to speak on the subject were significant. Many individuals in the congregation were deeply influenced by Seymour's addressing such a complex and divisive issue in a Sunday morning sermon. It was likely the first time many congregants had ever heard a sermon on the topic, and many congregants would remember Seymour's words for years to come. At the same time, he left the congregation divided on the issue. Perhaps navigating the congregation through a contentious building project had left him unable or unwilling to give more energy to such a controversial issue.

Binkley did not fully engage with questions of human sexuality as a congregational body again until John Blevins requested ordination in 1991. Blevins's request spurred a yearlong study by the diaconate and resulted in numerous individuals and families leaving the congregation. It revealed deep division within the church and echoed elements of disagreement that arose over the sanctuary building project. Binkley's ultimate decision to license Blevins resulted in the church's formal removal from the North Carolina Baptist Convention as well as the Southern Baptist Convention. This conflict, however, took place under the leadership of a new senior minister.

The Calling of Linda Jordan

Binkley took roughly two years to call its next senior minister, during which time Associate Minister Bill Hoyle carried out "day-to-day ministerial responsibilities."[31] Following the search process, Binkley made the decision to call a woman, Linda Jordan, to lead the congregation into its next chapter of life and ministry. Unlike Seymour, who avoided attending Baptist institutions of higher education, Jordan attended Furman University in South Carolina and later the Southern Baptist Theological Seminary in Louisville, Kentucky. While this had been the typical course of study for many Southern Baptist ministers born in South Carolina, Jordan was far from typical. Women in the Southern Baptist Convention had only recently begun to pursue ordination. Addie Davis became the first ordained Southern Baptist woman when she received ordination at Watts Street Baptist Church in Durham, North Carolina, in 1964.[32] Only eight years later, in 1972, Jordan graduated from Southern Seminary. That year, she accepted a call to serve as an associate pastor at First Baptist Church in Champaign, Illinois, an American Baptist church, where she was ordained in 1973.[33]

Jordan's ministerial and vocational experience made her well suited to lead Binkley. By the time she arrived in Chapel Hill, Jordan had chaplaincy experience in collegiate, military, and hospital settings. While serving as a military chaplain in the United States Air Force, Jordan accepted an invitation to fill the pulpit one Sunday for a Presbyterian congregation in Ocean Springs, Mississippi. The church had never heard a woman preach before. Jordan recalled receiving such positive feedback that the congregation's pastor and clerk of the local Presbytery referred her to Presbyterian congregations across the Gulf Coast. Gautier Presbyterian Church in Mississippi called Jordan to serve as pastor shortly thereafter. She served in this capacity for ten years, during which time she earned a doctor of ministry from Presbyterian-affiliated San Francisco Theological Seminary. She later served as the interim pastor of the historically Black Ladson Presbyterian Church in Columbia, South Carolina, shortly before coming to Binkley. Jordan was well positioned to understand the challenges facing a progressive, well-educated, ecumenical Baptist congregation in Chapel Hill.[34]

During her call process, questions of sexuality were already at the forefront of some congregants' minds. While under consideration, Jordan provided the church with a statement regarding her marital status. She explained that "she did have a wedding but not a marriage. The wedding was annulled."[35] While serving as pastor in Mississippi, she shared a house with her good friend Emilie Hall. Following the death of Hall's sister, Jordan and Hall assumed responsibility for Hall's niece. "Although I am single," Jordan explained to the congregation, "I have had the benefit of stable and loving relationships which have nurtured my self-development immensely."[36]

During a church conference on March 25, 1990, one member of the congregation pushed Jordan on her relationship with Hall. The member allegedly asked Jordan directly, "Are you gay?" Jordan answered in the negative. The congregation did not press the question further and called Jordan to serve as pastor with only a few dissenting votes. The directness with which this one congregant questioned Jordan's sexual orientation signaled a challenging and difficult pastorate to come. Not only was she following in the footsteps of the ever-present founding pastor and father of a traditional nuclear family, Robert Seymour, but she also had to endure the sexism that came with the territory of serving as the first woman senior pastor of a self-proclaimed progressive congregation.

After her first year, Binkley's Evaluation Committee solicited the congregation's thoughts on the "effectiveness" of Jordan in the areas of "administration, staff relations, and absenteeism." The evaluation was eventually made public in a congregational newsletter and reported that Jordan had received "an overall rating of 4.1 on a 1–5 scale."[37] Bob Seymour had never been so publicly subjected to such an "effectiveness" rating. Throughout Jordan's tenure as senior pastor, congregants looked to other authorities for expertise. As Jordan recalled, Seymour "continued to act as the minister" throughout her pastorate, and his associate minister, Bill Hoyle, "continued to stay" at Binkley well into Jordan's tenure.[38]

Blevins's Request for Licensure

Less than a year into Jordan's tenure at Binkley, a new church member, John Blevins, requested ordination. A self-described "cradle Baptist," Blevins had felt the call to ministry in high school. Remembering this time in his life years later, he described himself as "a man who was praying not to be gay" but who knew deep down that he was. Binkley, he remembered, helped him "to integrate" his sexuality with his faith, and as a result he sought the church's affirmation through ordination.[39] Jordan had concerns about Blevins's request, but not because of his sexuality. Baptist congregations have varied understandings of ordination and its practice in the local church. For many, including Jordan, ordination necessitated a specific call to a position in ministry. Since Blevins remained a divinity student without a congregational call to ministry, he did not require ordination. Instead, the diaconate, following Jordan's recommendation, thought it best to begin a process to consider licensing Blevins to preach rather than ordination. This slight distinction granted Blevins the authority to fill pulpits and preach, affirming his calling, but would not grant him the status of ordained clergy. While Blevins was openly gay and never sought to hide his sexual orientation, the meeting minutes made no mention of his sexuality. The diaconate appointed a committee to evaluate John Blevins along with Ann Marie Marshbanks, a longtime member of the congregation, as candidates for licensure.[40]

When the diaconate met again in June, the licensure committee recommended unanimously to license Marshbanks, but Blevins posed more of a problem. The committee voted two to one to bring a recommendation to license Blevins to the rest of the diaconate. Carol Stevens moved quickly to accept the recommendation, but a lengthy conversation ensued regarding scripture, the congregation, educational resources, and more. Rather than accept the committee's recommendation, the diaconate chose to take the process more slowly and discuss the situation in more detail at their summer retreat the following month.[41]

In preparation for this retreat, Robert Bratcher and Byron McCane prepared position papers in favor of and against licensing Blevins. Both men typified Binkley's close relationship to higher education in North Carolina's Research Triangle. Bratcher grew up the child of Southern Baptist missionaries and served himself as a missionary to Brazil before working for the American Bible Society. His accessible translation of the New Testament published in 1966 as *Good News for Modern Man* paved the way for a complete translation of the Christian Bible in 1976, known as the *Good News Bible*.[42] McCane, although not a renowned scholar, was an archeologist finishing his PhD in New Testament in the Religion Department at Duke University.[43]

Bratcher's position paper questioned whether the congregation had a right to judge Blevins based on his sexual orientation. He cited the scriptural texts often used against homosexuality, but suggested, "We are not ruled by the Jewish Torah nor are we compelled to think as Paul thought, or to act as he did." For Bratcher, Christians ought to "welcome all who wish to follow Jesus" and not differentiate a "second-class" membership that places restrictions on an individual's ability to serve Christ. He argued, "Ordination does not mean elevation to a higher rank or class of Christians: it means the church's recognition and endorsement of that person's response to God's call to a definite service, a particular ministry." Blevins easily met Bratcher's standards not only for licensure but also for ordination.[44]

Countering Bratcher, McCane's paper attempted to strike a neutral position that neither supported nor totally opposed licensing Blevins. Rather than citing various passages of scripture condemning homosexuality, he highlighted a growing consensus among "trained biblical scholars" that "homosexual behavior" is a sin. After weighing the pros and cons of ordaining or licensing a gay individual, McCane challenged the "desire for inclusiveness" as a justification for licensing Blevins. According to McCane, "Inclusiveness is not, and never has been the Gospel of Christ." Instead, it functions akin to "an idol of our culture." As he concluded his position paper, McCane answered both "yes" and "no" to whether Binkley should license Blevins. Yes, because according to McCane, Blevins "clearly has the gifts and calling for ministry." No, because licensure "affirms, celebrates, or legitimates his homosexuality." While McCane personally opposed licensing Blevins, he strove to keep his opinions vague.[45]

When discussing the positions of Bratcher and McCane in July at the diaconate retreat, the congregational leadership determined that it would be best to postpone any decision to license Blevins in order to prepare the church for the decision. The leadership then planned several educational opportunities for the congregation over the coming year to think through the issue. On July 23, 1991, Jim Wells, a psychiatrist and the chairperson of the diaconate, sent a newsletter to the congregation to inform them of upcoming programming. Wells explained that Blevins had requested to be licensed to preach and had made his sexual orientation known to the diaconate. To think through the issues, he encouraged congregants to participate in a new adult Sunday school class on "Sexuality and Spirituality." Additional Sunday-evening programming and periodic speakers provided other opportunities for congregants to inform themselves on these issues.[46]

Pastor Jordan echoed Wells's letter the following month, informing congregants that she would be preaching a four-week sermon series on sexuality and spirituality. She explained that discussions of sexuality were "forbidden in [her] own religious upbringing" and that she was "proud of the fact that Binkley has always nurtured an atmosphere of openness and a willingness to engage in controversial issues." Rather than provide the congregation with a definitive answer on questions of sexuality, Jordan desired to help frame the discussion the congregation would engage in over the coming months.[47]

On September 22, 1991, Jordan delivered the first of her four sermons on sexuality. Rather than begin with the most pressing issue of homosexuality, Jordan more thoughtfully encouraged the congregation to begin thinking about the broader relationship between sexuality and spirituality. The two "are fundamentally related in biblical faith," she explained. "Sexuality is not just a function; it is an identity." Jordan pushed the congregation to consider sexuality as part of humanity's God-created identity. Sexuality was not a mark of sinfulness; Christianity, she contended, had become too rooted in a dualistic view of the world that considered physical pleasure to be the "enemy of spiritual life."[48] Rather than see these two things as separate and opposed to one another, Jordan encouraged the congregation to consider the physical and the spiritual as constituent parts of the whole person.

She built upon this idea in her following two sermons about Christian conceptions of love. Too often, Jordan argued, Christians position the Greek idea of Eros—sensual and romantic love—against that of Agape—"self-giving and unconditional love."[49] Instead she encouraged the congregation to see both Eros and Agape as good and proper forms of love. The biblical text is full of examples of erotic love as important for human flourishing. From a theological perspective, Jordan argued that God participates in Eros as much as God participates in Philia (brotherly love) and Agape. Intimacy and physical affection, she explained, "are essential if we are ever to know love."[50] Within the biblical text, Jesus consistently touches and provides intimacy for those who need it most. Rather than view sexuality and physical intimacy as taboo within the Christian context, Jordan argues that they are natural to our human existence and should not be disregarded within the context of the church.

Jordan's fourth and final sermon in this series on human sexuality brought the congregation back to the explicit question of homosexuality. In this sermon she confessed that she genuinely wished to "avoid the subject of homosexuality," explaining that "anything I can say in these few minutes is likely to be misunderstood and at best can only be partial and inadequate." Even so, she contended that no issue currently facing Christianity is "as complex, personal, and volatile as that of homosexuality."[51] She began her sermon by sharing about her friend Bruce, whom she met while serving the Presbyterian church in Mississippi. Bruce, she explained, served as a "prominent citizen in the community" with a "winsome family," including his wife, who also served as his business partner, and their three children. After years of working with Bruce in the community, Jordan awoke one morning to hear the shocking news of Bruce's untimely death. Even more shocking, she continued, was when she and the community found out that Bruce was gay.[52]

Jordan found that both she and the larger community struggled to make sense of Bruce's sexual orientation. The community "hovered between denial and confusion." Bruce's story not only threw into question his identity, but the identity of those who knew and loved him. Drawing upon the biblical parable of the Good Samaritan, Jordan called for a shedding of prejudice and a recognition of both "homosexual and heterosexual persons as created in the image of God and therefore deserving of the greatest love, wisdom and fairness that the earthly church is capable of giving." She concluded with a public acknowledgement of gratitude for the gay persons who had met with her regularly and helped her wrestle with the issue of sexuality and the church. The sermon served to encourage Binkley's membership to continue to "listen and learn" during this season in which the congregation would be thinking through the decision to license Blevins.[53]

The Diaconate's Decision

A couple of months following Jordan's sermons on the subject, the diaconate began taking steps toward a recommendation for the congregation. As chairperson of the diaconate, Jim Wells penned a letter to the church informing its members of the challenging questions human sexuality posed to the life of the congregation. "There is mounting evidence," he wrote, "that sexual orientation is often, if not nearly always, determined before birth rather than as a learned response to a dysfunctional family system." Wells compiled a brief packet of resources that he placed in the church's library for congregants to review. The packet included articles entitled

"Are Some People Born Gay?" and "Can Homosexuals Change?" Additionally, he provided copies of Bob Seymour's 1983 sermon as well as Bratcher and McCane's position papers. The packet concluded with resources of opposition to homosexuality including an article by New Testament scholar Richard Hays and the 1976 resolution of the Southern Baptist Convention.[54] The inclusion of Seymour's sermon instead of any of Jordan's reveals the challenges Jordan faced in leading the congregation through such a polarizing decision. While many congregants had moved on from Seymour's leadership, there remained those who had yet to accept how Binkley was changing.

Before the diaconate could make a final recommendation, they sought to hear from an expert who opposed the ordination and the licensing of gay individuals. The diaconate struggled to find an individual willing to come and speak with them. Richard Hays, from Duke University, declined an invitation to come and offer his perspective. Instead, Hays recommended Steven Hoogerwerf, who had already been serving as the interim associate pastor at Binkley. Hoogerwerf received his PhD in theology and ethics from Duke University before joining Binkley's ministerial staff. He was a trained counselor and ethicist who had firsthand experience providing counseling services to gay and lesbian individuals. At their meeting, he led the diaconate through a detailed twenty-page, well-cited academic interpretation of both sides of the debate. The presentation ranged widely as he summarized the opinions of Hays and other scholars invested in questions related to sexuality and Christianity. Following Hoogerwerf's presentation, all that was left to do was meet with Blevins and make a recommendation to the Church Council for how to proceed.[55]

On January 27, the diaconate met with John Blevins for a Q & A session moderated by Jim Wells. Questions were submitted ahead of time to provide Blevins an opportunity to think about and prepare his responses. After speaking with Blevins, the diaconate met the following week and voted to recommend the congregation accept and approve him for licensure. The vote was taken by written ballot with fifteen votes in favor of the recommendation and seven against, with one abstention. With the approval of the diaconate, the decision to license Blevins to preach the Gospel became a matter for the whole congregation to weigh. Determining how to proceed with this process remained an open question and would become a serious point of contestation among members opposed to licensing a gay man.[56]

The Licensure Controversy Begins

The deacons moved quickly to release the result of their vote to the congregation in the newsletter the following day, February 4, but they were not fast enough. On February 5, many of Binkley's membership, rather than hearing the news from the church, learned of the diaconate's decision from the front page of the *Raleigh News and Observer*.[57] The article made a few inaccuracies that frustrated Jordan, who wrote to the paper's managing editor clarifying the difference between licensing and ordaining as well as the paper's wrongful assertion that Blevins would become the first openly gay Baptist minister. Jordan criticized the paper, claiming it had "violated the ethical standards of good and responsible journalism."[58] With news of the diaconate's decision breaking so quickly, the congregation needed to clarify not only the next steps in the process, but also what the congregation would be deciding.

Jim Wells encouraged congregants to meet and discuss the matter with their respective contacts on the diaconate. Within a few days, members of Binkley received a fact sheet outlining the decision-making process and providing clarifying information regarding licensure. The document clearly stated that licensing Blevins would not be "equivalent to ordination," as the local newspaper had suggested.[59] While many members of the church had been following the progress of the diaconate over the past several months, the diaconate recognized the stakes of this matter and wanted to ensure that all Binkley members felt prepared to participate in making this important decision.[60]

Not all of Binkley's membership, however, had followed the process and educational programming over the past six months. The news caught many of the congregation's more conservative members by surprise. Tony Jenkins complained in a letter to the congregation's leadership dated ten days after the local paper's story ran that he was informed of the diaconate's recommendation from the "front page of the local newspaper" before receiving the church newsletter.[61] Infuriated by the decision, Jenkins wrote to "relinquish all service positions and duties of membership . . . effective immediately." He expressed feeling "frustrated, betrayed, and deceived" by the "handling of John Blevins's licensure," and he thought the diaconate had spent the past several months attempting to force Blevins upon the congregation. Rev. Jordan's sermon series on sexuality, he complained, "seemed to abuse her position of power." The fact that the diaconate had not heard from any experts "who opposed the licensure of homosexuals" particularly frustrated Jenkins, who had come to believe that Blevins was using Binkley "to make a statement about homosexuality." The three-page, single-spaced letter concluded sorrowfully explaining that the members of Binkley could not "agree as to what the kingdom of God is, much less how to advance it." Leaving no room for reconciliation, Jenkins bid Binkley a "final farewell."[62]

Upon reading Jenkins's letter rescinding his membership, Jim Wells attempted to do some damage control. He encouraged his fellow deacons to read the letter and reach out to Jenkins.[63] Wells himself penned an apologetic eight-page letter that attempted to provide context and clarity to the process the deacons followed in making their decision to recommend Blevins to the larger congregation. Finding the news coverage "unfortunate," Wells explained to Jenkins that "every effort to avoid it was made."[64] He acknowledged that the diaconate had not been unanimous on every vote, but that they "reached apparent consensus on every decision concerning the process."[65] In addition to providing context, Wells explained some of the reasoning behind the diaconate's recommendation. Not only did he express his belief that "God calls us to support homosexual unions," but also that Blevins "has real talents, which he can fruitfully bring to our larger Community of Faith."[66] This was not a stunt or means of pressing the congregation to do something against its will; Wells believed he was following the will of God.

Jenkins's letter, however, was only the beginning. Once the news of Binkley's decision hit the local papers, the story garnered significant public attention. On the day Wells responded to Jenkins, the *Los Angeles Times* and later the *Chicago Tribune* both ran stories on the potential "ordination."[67] In the Raleigh paper, members of the public began weighing in on the decision through letters to the editor. One local pastor wrote in to say that Binkley denied "the word of God and speaks neither for Baptists nor for Jesus Christ."[68] Another woman explained that within the NRSV there are "clear indications that homosexuality is indeed against God's law."[69] Not all opinions, however, were negative. One man, titling his write-in "Cheers to Binkley," wrote, "I know many gays and lesbians who struggle with their faith due to the homophobia so prevalent in our religious institutions. We straights could learn much from their struggle."[70] The diaconate's decision quickly thrust the church into the public eye. Any congregational decision would have to fight against the polarization of the American public.

Binkley, however, was not alone in the ire and praise it drew from the media. At the same time Binkley was working through the process of licensing Blevins, Pullen Memorial Baptist Church in nearby Raleigh, North Carolina, was in the process of wedding a gay couple. Pullen, founded in 1884, shared a similar progressive theological orientation to Binkley.[71] Both congregations were affiliated with the Southern Baptist Convention and the American Baptist Churches USA, and when

William Finlator retired as Pullen's pastor in the early 1980s, he decided to begin attending Binkley. From 1986 until 1988, Pullen's pastor, Mahan Siler, preached a few sermons on sexuality, and in 1990 the congregation decided to begin a "series of discussions called the Open Forum on Homosexuality and the Church."[72] A year later, in September, a gay couple requested that Siler bless their union. After a few months of congregational discussion, Pullen was set to vote on the issue in February 1992—all while Binkley was navigating the decision to license Blevins. The media routinely covered the two congregations together in their reporting.

The North Carolina Baptist newspaper, the *Biblical Recorder,* in particular, paid close attention to the fallout from both Binkley's and Pullen's decisions. While most Baptists in the state were not in favor of either congregation's actions, a significant number of denominational leaders sought to exercise caution in responding, desiring to preserve the Baptist practice of congregational autonomy. Lamar King, a member of a North Carolina Baptist panel tasked with thinking about the state denomination's response, thought expulsion of the two congregations would create a "slippery slope." He explained, "I'm afraid that if we begin excluding groups based on what we perceive their sins to be . . . let's face it, there'll be no end to it."[73] For some, responding to Binkley was less an issue of sexual orientation and more an issue of local church autonomy. Leaders like King believed the denomination should not be policing local congregations. That was God's responsibility.[74]

Many Baptists around the state, however, disagreed. In their opinion, licensing an openly gay man to the ministry served as a breach of fellowship within the denomination. Barry Crocker's opinion published in the *Biblical Recorder* explained, "No matter how strongly we may proclaim that what one church does will not affect the others, it still will!"[75] Individuals worried that North Carolina Baptist mission programs might "be tainted by such actions."[76] Numerous churches and regional associations around the state adopted resolutions in response to Binkley's and Pullen's decisions, and many of these congregations and associations paid to have their resolutions published in the Baptist paper.[77] An open letter from Rosewood First Baptist Church implored of Binkley, "Please, please don't ordain and set apart as God's messenger one who is so breaking God's standard of living."[78]

Whatever Binkley's decision would be, the congregation would make it under intense public scrutiny. The church's moderator, Dick Helwig, scheduled a congregational meeting for March 22 to discuss the diaconate's recommendation and another meeting for April 5 to take a final vote on the recommendation. Additional small-group discussions took place as needed. The church library also housed a notebook to serve as a written forum for members of the Binkley community to submit letters containing their opinions on the matter.[79]

During the two-month period between the release of the diaconate's recommendation and the congregation's vote, a sizable opposition emerged within the congregation. This group sought to focus their opposition less upon Blevins's licensure and more upon their frustration with the diaconate's process. One opponent of licensure explained, "There has developed in our congregation a fear of being thought to fear homosexuals . . . we might call this homophobia phobia!"[80] As much as this group worried about whether they reflected an open spirit of welcome to all people, they remained equally worried that Binkley might be falling prey to the political agenda of the sexual revolution rather than adhering to the will of Christ. This group was led by many longtime members of Binkley whose thoughts on human sexuality more closely reflected Bob Seymour's 1966 sermon on the new morality rather than Linda Jordan's sermons delivered almost three decades later.

The primary leader of those opposed to the licensing or ordaining of an openly gay congregant was John Humber, the longtime Binkley member and handyman who oversaw the church building's maintenance for many years in the 1970s. Humber had completed doctoral work in history at UNC Chapel Hill but never finished the degree.[81] He believed the church's process had erred in considering Blevins's licensing before the congregation had come to a more general consensus regarding sexuality. Humber argued that Binkley needed "a policy concerning sexuality that can be uniformly applied to all persons regardless of their individual characteristics."[82] Sexuality, Humber suggested, was a private matter and "should remain as such." Because Blevins had "openly announced" his sexuality, the congregation needed to think through "an overall statement of belief and policy regarding the issue."[83] For Humber, individuals were not born gay, they chose to be gay. Knowing that Blevins was gay might associate Binkley with "promiscuity and other irresponsible conduct" that society often associated with individuals who practiced this "choice of lifestyle."[84] Humber pressed for the church to make a statement on sexuality before they considered whether they should license Blevins.

Echoing Humber, Jim Cansler—the former Baptist Student Union director and associate vice chancellor of student affairs at UNC Chapel Hill—and his wife, Dot, likewise believed the process had been biased and ill conceived.[85] In a private letter to the congregation's moderator, the couple argued that the diaconate had not created a space for "opposing views to be freely aired."[86] At the beginning of March, the Canslers penned a five-page open letter to the congregation outlining their personal convictions on the matter. They lamented and characterized Blevins's request as "regrettable" because it kept the congregation from considering the question of human sexuality "apart from its personal embodiment by him." They encouraged the congregation to view the issue of sexual orientation "as an extension of the sexual revolution of the late 1960s" and nothing more.[87]

Allen and Pat Kelley, another couple opposed to the licensing of Blevins, also composed an open letter to the congregation a few days after the Canslers' letter. The Kelleys implored the Church Council to "make an immediate decision to postpone" the vote.[88] They initially articulated a desire for a cooperative process, stating, "We must seize the opportunity John has given us; work with him and ourselves; and come forward as an informed community of faith."[89] The couple quickly changed their tune in private a few days later after considering how "unprepared" the congregation was to make a decision. If the congregation could not be more adequately informed, the Kelleys wrote to Pastor Jordan, then "the real Binkley is dead."[90]

The real Binkley, however—Olin Trivette Binkley, after whom the congregation was named—was very much alive. While he and his wife were not members of the church, they did keep up with the congregation through newsletters as well as their daughter, Pauline Binkley Cheek, who along with her family were members of the church. Jordan visited the Binkleys periodically and even discussed the licensure issue with them so that the church's decision would not take them by surprise.[91] After the diaconate recommended that the congregation license Blevins, both John Humber and the Canslers began corresponding with Olin and his wife. After hearing from the voices opposed to the whole process, Mrs. Binkley became particularly distressed by the prospect of the congregation voting to license Blevins. Various letters and newspaper articles led Mrs. Binkley to write a letter to Jim Wells, without consulting her husband. In her letter she explained that neither she nor her husband would "be able to affirm a decision to license or ordain" Blevins.[92]

Mrs. Binkley's decision to voice her and her husband's opposition marked a departure from how the two had associated with the congregation in the past. They were not members. While they attended services on special occasions when Dr. Binkley spoke, they primarily observed the congregation from afar. Even so, they were respected and beloved among the founding members of the congregation who had seen fit to name their church after Dr. Binkley. With the namesake of the church apparently behind them, the opposition to licensing Blevins coalesced around a commitment to proper procedure—a commitment that masked a deeper homophobia and fear of changing cultural attitudes around sexuality within the church. The Binkleys became a tool through which the opposition hoped to stall the process.

Those individuals who supported the licensing of Blevins, however, held wildly divergent opinions, many of which were also the product of various degrees of homophobia. As diaconate chair, Jim Wells thought critically of the procedural complaints from more conservative members of the congregation. He seemed to agree that "it would be helpful for [the congregation] to make a statement about sexuality in general" before or apart from the decision to license Blevins.[93] He began soliciting opinions from members of the diaconate regarding what such a statement might look like and whether consensus could be drawn around such a statement. The responses Wells received from his fellow deacons were quite mixed and showed little if any consensus. One member of the diaconate recorded eight divergent opinions she observed from deacons throughout the recommendation process. These ranged from beliefs that "same-gender sexual orientation is not a part of God's intended plan for creation" to "human sexual intimacy, and the circumstances of its practice, should not be an inherent barrier to church membership or licensure."[94] Another member of the diaconate felt that amidst all the diversity of opinion, "a consensus statement would force a compromise which," she argued, "would not be representative of the complexity of the issue."[95] One deacon echoed the sentiment of complexity, suggesting that the diaconate had not "fully discussed all of the issues/implications" of their recommendation.[96]

Many members of the diaconate were concerned that Wells was pushing the congregation to make a statement on sexuality when they were only personally comfortable with licensing Blevins. One deacon, who supported Blevins, felt that "promiscuity and AIDS are two very good examples of reasons that Binkley Church should not issue a blanket approval of homosexuality."[97] Others simply wanted to recommend Blevins and put their "period at that point."[98] These members of the diaconate were comfortable with accepting Blevins's call to ministry and saw "no reason why his request should be expanded to a full scale endorsement of homosexuality."[99] If a general statement were to be included, another deacon believed the congregation should emphasize the importance of monogamy in a sexual relationship.[100]

Still other members of the diaconate were quite comfortable with supporting Blevins and even a statement, should it be necessary. Eva Clontz jokingly recorded her opinion, stating, "In the community of faith we welcome all (regardless of age, sex, race, color, national origin, handicap, veteran status, sexual orientation or basketball loyalty)."[101] One deacon reasoned that Blevins should be licensed because of the congregation's commitment to seeing every member as a minister—licensing or ordination was a mere formality.[102] Many deacons alluded to the story of Jesus telling the crowd to let those who had not sinned cast the first stone against a woman charged with adultery. "Who am I, a sinner, to say 'no' to" Blevins, reasoned Lanie Freeman.[103]

In the two weeks leading up to the congregational vote on April 5, Binkley held four open meetings for discussion. The first of these meetings gathered more than 150 members, while subsequent gatherings were much smaller. One of the Thursday discussions included only ten members. Following these preliminary discussion meetings, the congregation braced for a final vote. On the evening of the fifth, 266 members of Binkley arrived at the church conference prepared to vote their conscience. John Humber, titling his remarks "Binkley Church At A Crossroads, A Majority Moving Out On Its Own Or a Community of Faith Moving Together," rose to propose that the congregation defer a vote on licensure. He suggested the congregation compose a "policy statement" for licensing and ordaining "anyone to the ministry" as well as an additional statement of belief regarding the "role and place of homosexuality within the church." As he returned to his seat and discussion ensued, Humber recalled noticing that longstanding friendships began to rupture.[104]

After Humber returned to his seat, Jim Wells offered an amendment to the diaconate's proposed recommendation to approve licensing Blevins. Wells took the criticism that the congregation needed a general statement on sexuality before licensing Blevins and, after compiling the opinions of the diaconate, offered one. The proposed amendment, or "Preface" as it was called, was not meant to imply unanimity but to provide context for the decision. The amendment praised God "for the gift of sexuality." One of the amendment's paragraphs read: "We therefore commit ourselves as a community of Christians to ask God's guidance in helping us find a means of allowing homosexual men and women to pledge their faithful and life long relationship. Such a permanent, selfless and monogamous covenant can truly promote the good of both partners and deserves the support and encouragement of God's people."[105] Introduced the night of the vote, there was much initial discussion regarding whether such a statement was proper. Members like Jim Wilde supported the Preface because they did not want the decision to only be about John. Wilde did not want to allow the congregation's decision to be "revised in retrospect."[106] Following Robert's Rule of Order, however, the question was called, and the congregation approved the amendment 142 in favor, 87 against, with 36 abstentions.

As the nearly four-hour evening wore on, members opposed to licensing Blevins pushed again to postpone the vote on the newly amended motion.[107] Many in the congregation, tired by the process, wanted to move on and affirm Blevins with a vote. By the time the final vote was taken, fourteen members had already left the gathering. The final vote tally was 145 to 107 in favor of licensure.[108] John Humber recalled leaving the church that night overhearing a member, John Stokes, saying in exasperation, "We lost the vote." Jim Cansler quickly retorted, "No, John. We lost a Church."[109]

The Consequences of Licensure

Two days after the congregation's decision to license Blevins, the *News and Observer* ran articles announcing the congregation's decision. The recently licensed divinity student explained to the paper that he did not think "Binkley's actions will make a quick society change" but that he "hoped that people will be able to see beyond my being a gay minister and see me simply as a minister."[110] Blevins was correct that the congregation's decision did not bring swift societal change, but the result did lead to far-reaching consequences not only for Binkley but also for wider Baptist denominational life.

Few, if any, congregational votes this contentious end after the final tabulation. This vote at Binkley was no different. The following month "a support group of those members who" opposed the vote gathered to determine their next steps. This group of roughly forty members remained deeply troubled by the process of amending the final vote. They desired to bring Binkley "back to the point of departure on the night of" the vote.[111] Michael Berkut, professor emeritus of biochemistry at UNC, believed that the amended "Preface" to the resolution was unconstitutional according to the church bylaws. "It is disgusting and an abhorring inference," he claimed, "that penile penetrations of the anal orifices between sexually active gay men is equated to God's gift of sexuality between that of a husband and wife."[112] The group led by Humber believed that their best course of action was to craft a constitutional amendment requiring that "policy motions" be approved by a three-fourths majority of all resident members through mail-in ballots.[113] They reasoned that less than half of the church had been in attendance for the final vote. Perhaps if they could get those who were absent to weigh in on the decision, they could change the outcome.

Following an additional month of conversations, Binkley agreed to rescind Wells's amendment "on the basis of procedural concerns and a sense of fairness" to those who opposed the recommendation.[114] Blevins's licensure, however, still stood. For some members, this was not enough. As many as thirty families left to find other churches in and around Chapel Hill. John Humber followed this path and began attending another congregation. Even so, however, he took the time to write and self-publish an eighty-two-page pamphlet outlining his thoughts and experiences of the conflict entitled *The Tragedy and Ordeal of Binkley Baptist Church.* While he strove to remain unbiased in his account, his personal investment in the project often skewed his interpretations of the letters and documents that he had compiled over the preceding months. He accurately noted, however, how difficult the process was for the congregation internally. These internal challenges were only compounded by the vast amount of media attention the congregation received throughout the entire process.

Not only did the decision have consequences for Binkley's membership, but the congregation's actions also created conflict at the state and national levels within the Southern Baptist Convention. The General Board of the North Carolina Baptist State Convention met at the Caraway Conference Center on May 20 to decide how Binkley's decision would affect the church's standing in the state denominational body. The initial response of the state had been one of restraint, but mounting opposition to Binkley as well as to Pullen Memorial Baptist Church's decision began to turn the tide. While local autonomy certainly remained something Baptists around the state valued, it was not enough to bear the weight of sexual orientation. The group resolved to expel both Binkley and Pullen from the state convention.[115]

When the Southern Baptist Convention met in Indianapolis in June 1992, shortly after the North Carolina Baptist Convention had made their decision, the writing was on the wall for both Binkley and Pullen. After months of public media scrutiny and debate within local denominational associations, the Southern Baptist Convention was poised to adopt a recommendation to expel the two churches. The gathering of Southern Baptists from around the country concluded that Binkley's and Pullen's actions "in regard to homosexuality are contrary to the teachings of the Bible" and are "offensive to Southern Baptists." The messengers voted to declare that both congregations were "not in friendly cooperation with the Convention nor sympathetic with its purposes and work and, therefore, the Southern Baptist Convention withdraws fellowship from these churches."[116] Binkley and Pullen were no longer Southern Baptist congregations.

Disfellowshipping from Binkley and Pullen was not enough, however, for the Southern Baptist messengers in Indianapolis. Following this recommendation, the gathered body determined to amend the Southern Baptist Convention's constitution. Amid the "appearance of elation regarding withdrawing fellowship from the churches," a messenger from Louisiana moved to adopt a recommendation on church membership to the SBC. The current constitution required churches to be "in friendly cooperation with this Convention and sympathetic with its purposes and work" in addition to being a "bona fide contributor to the Convention's work." The amended constitution added to these requirements that "among churches not in cooperation with the Convention are churches which act to affirm, approve, or endorse homosexual behavior."[117] Binkley's actions led to the re-writing of the Southern Baptist Convention's constitution. Opposition to homosexuality became a benchmark for participation within SBC life.[118] The *New York Times* reported, "Southern Baptists have banished two congregations for accepting homosexuals and set in motion a precedent-setting change in bylaws to exclude other churches that ever do the same."[119]

In the years following Binkley's decision, the congregation embarked on a long process of recovery from the conflict. Many of the wounds from building the new sanctuary had been reopened over the course of licensing Blevins. Jordan recalled hearing one congregant in a business meeting compare the process of approving the sanctuary to the process of licensing Blevins.[120] Congregational giving decreased as numerous families left the church. Two years later, in February 1994, Linda Jordan resigned as pastor of the congregation. Jordan explained in her resignation letter that she believed many members were "dissatisfied with both the quality of my ministry and my style of leadership."[121]

Reflecting on her time at Binkley years later, Jordan described her decision to support Blevins as one of "the few times in life where you truly know the right thing to do." While the public media attention and the congregational conflict were certainly stressful, she remembered choosing to leave Binkley for other reasons. The congregation never really seemed to value her authority as pastor, and Bob Seymour never let go of his former position. Instead of joining another local congregation upon retirement as many ministers do, Seymour chose to remain active at Binkley. Jordan remembered descending from the pulpit on Sunday mornings to greet congregants in the narthex of the church, only to find Seymour doing the same thing as if he were still pastor.[122]

Founding members never seemed to let go of Seymour, either. Jordan found the congregation's relationship with its former pastor to be unhealthy. In many ways the church had seemingly valued Seymour's opinions on sexuality more than they had Jordan's: Seymour's 1983 sermon on the issue had been held up as important reading material, whereas Jordan's sermon series was rarely cited by membership either in favor of or against licensure. Seymour remained a gregarious and outgoing individual with a penchant for what some saw as autocratic leadership during the building of the sanctuary. These qualities undercut Jordan's authority, making it difficult for her to minister.[123]

Jordan remembered Bob Seymour stopping by her office one day to offer her some advice. She recalled saying, "Bob, you have given a lot to this church. I hope you can let go of being the pastor." He retorted, "I'll always be the pastor of this church." Jordan responded, "I believe you." After this exchange, Jordan made the decision to resign.[124]

Lurking underneath Binkley's conflict over homosexuality was a conflict about the role of women in church leadership. Seymour led the congregation as the head of a typical nuclear family. His wife played the organ, and he had two children. Jordan's identity as a congregational leader was different. She was a woman, and she was not married. With Seymour unwilling to leave the church that he helped nurture and build, the congregation had to choose whom to look toward for leadership. Much of the historical record of this conflict comes from the perspective of men, and even Mrs. Binkley's decision to speak up against licensing Blevins was framed as important because of her husband. As much as this story is one of homophobia, it is a story of sexism as well. Many in the congregation likely did not recognize how their attention may have been pulled to one, both, or neither of these issues.

After obtaining his licensure and graduating from Duke, Blevins moved to Chicago to begin ministering to children and adults diagnosed with HIV and AIDS. He left the church to continue its study of faith and sexuality. The congregation repealed the amended "Preface" in June 1992 and subsequently began the process of crafting a more formal policy statement on sexuality. That same year both Jordan and Pullen Memorial pastor Mahan Siler received the Citizen Award from the *Independent Weekly,* a local area magazine, for their courageous support of LGBTQ individuals.[125] In 1994, Binkley voted to "establish a committee on inclusive services" and later joined the Association of Welcoming and Affirming Baptists (AWAB).[126] Binkley's process of becoming a welcoming and affirming congregation would also encourage the newly formed Alliance of Baptists (formerly the Southern Baptist Alliance) to study the issue of human sexuality. Both Binkley and Pullen Memorial Baptist Church were member congregations of the Alliance, and when the young organization met for their annual convocation in Charlotte, North Carolina, in April 1992, the organization appointed its Task Force on Human Sexuality. Following the lead of partner congregations like Pullen and Binkley, over the next two years the Alliance's task force composed a statement for the larger denominational body. Binkley, along with Pullen's focus on human sexuality, pushed the Alliance of Baptists to pass a statement affirming a diversity of opinions within this small progressive Baptist group as well as to adopt a non-discrimination hiring policy with regard to sexual orientation.[127]

The process of licensing Blevins became a foundational story for understanding Binkley in the following years. This process was not clean. While the church may have voted to affirm Blevins, the reasoning among congregants varied widely. Some believed that sexual orientation should have no bearing on one's Christian convictions, and others personally affirmed Blevins while at the same time holding many homophobic ideas and beliefs. The process of licensing Blevins shows how changing discourses around religion and sexuality created challenges for individual congregational bodies. Members of Binkley found themselves at varied places within this changing discourse around sexuality. Some members continued to speak about issues of sexuality in the language of the "sexual revolution" as Bob Seymour once did in the 1960s. Other members saw their language evolve to discuss sexuality as a type of innate orientation with which individuals are born. Still others saw their opinions fall between these two poles. Amid this diversity of thought, the congregation coalesced a majority that favored licensing Blevins and later became welcoming and affirming of all LGBTQ persons.

After leaving Binkley and moving to Chicago, John Blevins was not formally invited to return to Binkley until September 29, 2019. In the years between leaving Chapel Hill and this return, he recalled informally slipping into the back of Binkley's sanctuary on a handful of Sunday mornings when he was in town. The Sunday morning of September 29 served as a "way of coming full circle." Blevins expressed his "deep and profound gratitude" to the congregation for their support twenty-seven years before. He wanted the congregation to know that the "connection" forged through his licensing was greater and "more powerful than the rupture" the church experienced because of the conflict. Providing a short narrative of his life after leaving Binkley, Blevins shared that he had received his doctor of theology in pastoral care and counseling and had begun teaching in Emory University's School of Public Health as an expert in the intersection of religion and public health. With tears in his eyes, he told the congregation, "You gave me a gift. And I just want to say thank you."[128]

While not everyone involved in this period of Binkley's history remembered the conflict in this way, licensing Blevins served as a significant point of transition within the history of the congregation. It marked a new beginning and revealed a diversity of opinions within this progressive congregation. Not everyone thought alike. As certain members left, lamenting the congregation's decision, Binkley solidified its support and affirmation among LGBTQ individuals. This did not mean that the congregation as a whole came to a consensus around a common discourse around sexuality and Christianity, but they established more of a consensus than existed previously. In doing so, they opened the door to a new period in the life of the church.

Every Member a Minister

WHEN JEAN AND DON WESTBROOK moved to Chapel Hill in the early 2000s, they began their search for a church community. As they explored the surrounding area, they consistently asked residents a variety of questions from "What is the most open church?" to "What is the most socially conscious church?" The more they asked, the more they discovered that "no matter how [they] worded the question, the answer was always Binkley Baptist." As a result of the nearly unanimous answer, the Westbrooks became members in 2007.[1] As the couple quickly learned, by the early twenty-first century Binkley had a distinct reputation in the surrounding community. For some new and old residents, this progressive reputation was an attractive quality. As the congregation welcomed new members into the life of the church, these individuals brought with them energy and enthusiasm for engaging the local community. Robert Seymour no longer provided the congregation's leadership and vision, and Linda Jordan's tenure as pastor revealed that the congregation was not interested in returning to a model where the pastor held all the authority. Instead, by the middle of the 1990s, Binkley was primed to fully live into its longtime slogan, "every member a minister."

While Binkley was an ecumenical congregation, it still had Baptist roots. The proclamation that every member of Binkley was a minister echoed nineteenth-century German Baptist Johann Oncken, who adopted the phrase *"Jeder Baptist ein Missionar"* (every Baptist a missionary).[2] Pinpointing the origins of the congregation's use of the phrase would be difficult, but the sentiment behind the phrase had been instructive in Binkley's ministry from its earliest days. Robert Seymour had long encouraged congregants to utilize their professional vocations as opportunities for ministry. His leadership during the congregation's early years, however, provided clear direction for the church as he enlisted certain congregants to serve the church by serving in the community. By the middle of the 1990s, many of Binkley's congregants were more hesitant of this type of top-down pastoral leadership and instead sought to lead themselves. As a result, pastoral authority within the congregation took on a new form, and individual members began more fully directing Binkley's engagement with the wider community. This new dynamic created challenges for the congregation as members possessed strongly held convictions and priorities that did not always align with one another.

Living into the slogan "every member a minister" presented a unique array of opportunities and challenges for Binkley. The licensure of John Blevins solidified Binkley's progressive theological identity, and members took this as an opportunity to expand upon this identity and push the congregation in new directions. Pastoral leadership in turn became more focused on leading, guiding, and balancing the energy within the congregation. Not everyone always agreed on what issues and ministries to prioritize, and sometimes the congregation's commitments and convictions came into conflict with one another. As each member brought with them deeply held convictions regarding sexuality, race, gender, poverty, immigration, the environment, and more, the congregation as a whole faced the daunting task of seeking to craft an intersectional ethic grounded in shared theological commitments.[3] In many ways, Binkley was still haunted by the conflicts surrounding the building of the sanctuary and the licensure of John Blevins, which both resulted in numerous families leaving the church. The fear and threat of another similar conflict loomed, and the collective trauma of those events stubbornly persisted.

Like many progressive Christian congregations, Binkley struggled to make sense of its identity in light of the emergence of the religious right in American politics. While the church had been aligned with the progressive principles of the Democratic Party of the 1960s, the election of Richard Nixon in 1968 ushered in a more conservative spirit in US politics.[4] By the 1980s, organizations like the Moral Majority had closely wedded conservative, evangelical Christians to the Republican Party. These movements represented an organized and concerted effort to change American politics. Binkley was far less organized. While numerous members participated in Democratic Party politics, the congregation as a whole had priorities beyond partisan politics. Whereas conservative, evangelical ministers could wield their authority to steer churches toward the Republic Party, Binkley's ministerial leadership did not hold the same sway over the congregation. While Binkley certainly differentiated itself from the religious right, creating a collective identity amid the diversity of its progressive commitments was a challenge.

This chapter examines the ways Binkley forged ahead as one of Chapel Hill's most progressive religious institutions at the dawn of the twenty-first century. Drawing upon the energy of new members and a new vision of pastoral leadership, Binkley expanded its ministry focus to include concerted efforts into health ministries, refugee resettlement, climate justice and more. The congregation would also reaffirm and build upon preexisting commitments to racial justice and LGBTQ inclusion. The chapter concludes with an analysis of the contentious ordination process of Ray Speller, a Black ministerial intern at Binkley from 2011 to 2013. Speller's views on sexuality did not completely overlap with Binkley's, and his ordination process presented a challenging dilemma regarding how the church should think about the intersection of their congregational commitments. The painful and difficult process ultimately led to Speller's withdrawal from ordination at Binkley. The episode showcases the limitations of liberal Protestantism and the need for progressive congregations to think beyond traditional "liberal" categories.

Changing Pastoral Leadership

The transition from the congregation's founding pastor, Bob Seymour, to Linda Jordan's four-year tenure, as the previous chapter demonstrates, was far from smooth. Seymour's continued presence at Binkley following his retirement created an environment in which Jordan struggled to receive the congregation's respect as the new pastor. He continued to wield immense informal power in the congregation and remained an outspoken and active leader within the local Chapel Hill community. In addition to challenges surrounding pastoral authority, the congregation had been expelled from the SBC over the licensing of John Blevins. While the church and the denomination no longer represented one another ideologically, the formal expulsion was jarring. Binkley needed to figure out its identity apart from the SBC, yet it continued to experience the lingering and nagging reverberations from the decision to build the sanctuary. Binkley did not need a pastor to come in and lead the church into a new era; the church needed a pastor who could help its membership process how they got to this point. While both Jordan and Seymour had roots in Southern Baptist life, the two senior pastors that followed, Jim Pike and Peter Carman, had roots in American Baptist life. Their experience in the ABCUSA shaped their leadership styles in distinct ways.

The immediate task of helping Binkley move on from the licensure conflict fell upon Jim Pike, an American Baptist pastor who at the time served as the senior pastor of the Community Church of Wilmette, Illinois, a congregation in the suburbs of Chicago. Called to Binkley in 1996, Pike had a unique history with the church that allowed him to better navigate some of Binkley's congregational politics. This was not the first time he had considered serving in a pastoral role at Binkley. When the congregation called Tom Clifton to serve as associate pastor in 1973, Pike had also been under consideration. At the time, he was an associate pastor at First Baptist Church of Madison, Wisconsin. Binkley flew him down to Chapel Hill, and years later he remembered "sitting in a car in the church parking lot with Bob Seymour talking about ministry."[5] As much as Pike came to admire the congregation from his visit, it also affirmed that he no longer felt called to serve as an associate pastor, and he turned down the position. After Seymour's retirement in 1989, Walter Parrish, executive minister of the American Baptist Churches of the South (ABCOTS), approached Pike about applying to succeed Seymour. Family health complications, however, kept Pike from considering the position. Finally in 1996, Binkley and Pike's timing and calling aligned. After the congregational meeting in which the membership voted to accept Pike's call to serve as senior pastor, Bob Seymour exclaimed, "It took us 22 years to get you to say Yes!" The former pastor's excitement over Pike's leadership stood in stark contrast to his relationship with Linda Jordan. Seymour's approval greatly aided Pike's ability to navigate congregational politics as well as unify and lead the congregation into the new century.[6]

Pike was not a product of the south. He grew up immersed in American Baptist life, attending youth conferences in Green Lake, Wisconsin, at the annual American Baptist Assembly. While he was a student at Indiana State University, he spent one summer as a soloist for evangelistic rallies in the surrounding rural community. Over the course of this summer, Pike became disillusioned with this type of evangelism and began to question the revivalist enterprise. At one event, a host pastor handed him a bottle of Johnson's baby oil and asked him to anoint a woman and pray for healing. He refused. The event served as a formative moment for Pike, and he came to see his refusal as a "back door call to ministry." As he saw it, God needed ministers who could speak to people who found revivals and anointing oil off-putting, just as he had.

Following college, Pike decided to attend seminary and even entertained the possibility of attending the Southern Baptist Theological Seminary in Louisville, Kentucky, the flagship school of the SBC. He later remembered opening the school's acceptance letter and reading the salutation, "Dear Brother Jim," which was enough to dissuade him from attendance. Instead, Pike matriculated at Colgate Rochester Divinity School in Rochester, New York. Here, he was exposed to a more ecumenical and liberal approach to Christianity within the American Baptist tradition. Walter Rauschenbusch, known for his advocacy of the Social Gospel, taught at the school at the turn of the century and helped solidify the school's more liberal identity. In his coursework, Pike took classes from Bill Hamilton, a theologian who

Jim Pike preaching at the church's fiftieth anniversary celebration.

participated in the Death of God movement, which questioned traditional forms of theism within an increasingly secular society. He also completed his field education with a local Presbyterian church. When Pike arrived in Rochester, he described himself as politically conservative, but by his graduation he later explained that he had "been politicized for justice causes."[7]

Pike remained at Binkley for eleven years, and following his retirement in 2011, the church began another search-and-call process that resulted in the calling of Peter Carman, another senior minister with roots in American Baptist life. Carman was born to American parents in India, and they taught at a local seminary and researched world religions before his father joined the faculty at Harvard Divinity School in the late 1960s. Carman grew up in a household where interfaith conversations were a regular occurrence and "Hindu, Christian, Muslim and Jewish scholars often dropped in to chat."[8] Baptized at the age of twelve at the Harvard University Memorial Chapel, Carman had a rich ecumenical background. While an undergraduate at Haverford College in Pennsylvania, he attended local Quaker meetings. Upon graduation, he matriculated at Yale Divinity School.[9]

Carman's time at Yale was far different and far removed from the Yale that Binkley's founding pastor Robert Seymour had attended. Whereas Seymour attended Yale at the conclusion of World War II, Carman's education coincided with the final decade of the Cold War. Committed to local peace and justice movements, he served as a social action coordinator for student groups around New Haven. He continued advocacy work on nuclear disarmament that he began as an undergraduate at Haverford, which also included nonviolence training. After he graduated from Yale, Carman received ordination at the First Baptist Church of Wallingford, Connecticut, and accepted a calling to serve as the associate minister of First Baptist Church Pittsfield, Massachusetts. In this position, Carman helped lead Christian educational programming, plan youth events and activities, and encouraged the congregation to engage with pressing issues of social concern.[10]

Carman accepted a call to come to Binkley after seventeen years as the senior pastor of Lake Avenue Baptist Church (LABC), one of the oldest American Baptist congregations in Rochester, New York, which had a rich and progressive history. Shortly after Carman arrived at Binkley, he helped guide the congregation through a process of becoming welcoming and affirming of LGBTQ+ individuals. During his pastorate, the church also began welcoming several student refugees from Burma, and by the end of his pastorate, these few individuals had blossomed into a large and vibrant community.[11] The call to serve Binkley intrigued Carman, who had both turned down and been turned down from other pastorates in the years leading up to his arrival in Chapel Hill. Conversations with the search committee at Binkley were "key in moving from interest to a sense of call." Carman felt that there were areas of his ministry at Lake Avenue that "might translate well at Binkley."[12]

Although both are "Baptist," the cultural differences between the SBC and the ABCUSA are striking, and both Pike and Carman reflected these differences in their approach to leadership at Binkley. The Triennial Convention, which traces its legacy to the ABCUSA, had a rich tradition organized around separate but related and cooperative societies. Power within ABCUSA denominational circles because of this history was more diffused across a variety of societies and agencies, whereas within Southern Baptist life, power was centralized within the denominational convention. Historians rightly note that the Southern Baptist Convention was founded when Baptists in the South sought to nominate and appoint two enslavers to serve as missionaries, and the larger Baptist denominational infrastructure denied their appointment. In addition to its pro-slavery founding, however, the SBC was also an attempt to centralize power into a single institution. These organizational and bureaucratic differences would shape and influence how congregations and pastors organized and understood religious authority.

While Binkley had long been a member of both the SBC and the ABCUSA dating back to the 1960s, Pike and Carman sought to nurture more of an American Baptist spirit within the congregation. When Pike arrived at Binkley in 1996, he recalled, "I did a lot of listening." There was so much grief and loss as well as a feeling of being 'disowned' from the SBC that he considered himself more of a "healing pastor."[13] Rather than lead or push the congregation in any particular direction, Pike understood his responsibility to be one of nurturing new members and inviting their involvement. Amid Binkley's great diversity of interests and agendas, Pike believed that the "pastor's role was to help keep a balance."[14] Following Pike, Carman likewise recognized that within the Southern Baptist tradition of pastoral leadership, "Bob [Seymour] was always going to be 'Herr Pastor'" at Binkley. He instead sought to craft his role and identity as more of an "organizing pastor." Carman described Binkley not as a congregation with a single, unified reality; instead, he recognized that like many larger congregations, Binkley had multiple realities, and, echoing Pike, that a pastor's job was to balance those realities.[15]

As Carman transitioned from serving LABC, he faced the challenge of navigating the bureaucratic SBC denominationalism that remained engrained at Binkley. While the congregation had not been Southern Baptist for more than sixteen years upon his arrival, vestiges of the culture remained, which could partly be seen in its vast network of committees and councils. This more centralized and highly organizational structure meant the pastoral staff had no shortage of meetings to attend. Gatherings of the Church Council as well as meetings of the diaconate were one thing, but when Pike arrived, the congregation had "32 standing committees." He described the congregation's bureaucratic infrastructure simply: "It was a lot."[16] Carman remembered that the church often had "trouble recruiting" for such an expansive organizational infrastructure. At the same time, creating such an expansive infrastructure in the first place required what he described as the "active leadership of church members."[17]

Making congregational decisions within this vast committee network proved challenging. Pike came to jokingly say, "Binkley doesn't process things, we puree them."[18] The legacy of the conflicts surrounding the construction of the sanctuary and the licensing of John Blevins gave the congregation pause around big decisions. Pike worked to incorporate models of consensus decision-making processes around significant and potentially contentious issues to ensure that everyone's voice was adequately heard. This sometimes meant that decisions took longer to reach. For example, during Pike's pastorate, he helped oversee a renovation of the congregation's facilities that lasted almost the entire duration of his ministry at Binkley. He described the renovation process as very time consuming. "Everyone in the congregation was involved," he remembered. "I thought it important that every voice that wanted to be heard would be heard." There were "dozens of meetings. Maybe hundreds." Such an approach to leading the congregation through the renovation was decidedly different from Seymour's approach to building the sanctuary.[19]

In addition to the leadership of a senior pastor, since the 1970s Binkley enjoyed the leadership of two associate ministerial positions. This continued during Pike's and Carman's time as senior pastor. The men and women who served as associate ministers provided leadership in areas of Christian education, youth, and more. Dale Osborne, in particular, provided continuity on the ministerial staff by serving as an associate minister from the early 1990s into the twenty-first century. Shortly after the licensure of John Blevins, Linda Jordan had informed Osborne about the position, and he quickly applied due to the congregation's commitment to "outreach ministries locally, nationally, and internationally." His work with the congregation's youth and families continued to be "the most demanding and rewarding part of his ministry" fifteen years after first starting.[20] Additional associate ministers Gretchen Jordan, Robin Brooks, Beth Honeycutt, and Stephanie Ford provided additional leadership in the areas of Christian formation. These members of the congregation's professional ministerial team similarly strove to facilitate the leadership of congregational members, guiding committee work and organizing events and programming.

Throughout Binkley's history, the congregation encouraged members to take leadership roles in both the church and the community. The use of the phrase "every member a minister" captures the ways in which the church called upon members to consider the ways in which their personal and professional lives might intersect and provide opportunities to serve the local community. At the same time, like many Southern Baptist churches, for much of this history the congregation had leaned upon the vision and leadership of their pastor. Seymour's charismatic presence provided the congregation a centralized figure of authority, and his retirement raised the question as to whether this model of top-down leadership best suited the congregation going forward into the twenty-first century. While this style of leadership may have worked for a young congregation with few resources, Linda Jordan's short tenure as pastor following Seymour revealed that the congregation was certainly not ready for a woman to lead in this way and perhaps had moved beyond this style of leadership entirely. During Jordan's tenure, Binkley had to wrestle with what

Members from Binkley's ministerial staff over the years. *Top left:* Raimundo César Barreto, Jr., Bill Currin, Jim Pike, Bob Seymour, Tom Clifton, Bill Hoyle, Julie Strope, and Bob Keever. Bottom Left: Ed Huggins, Dale Osborn, Denise Cumbee Long, Gretchen Jordan, Bishop Gene Hatley.

it meant for a woman to serve as pastor and what it meant for a gay member of the church to seek the label of "minister." The phrase "every member a minister" presented a challenging reality to live into. As a bastion of progressive religion in Chapel Hill, Binkley also attracted many retired clergy and chaplains who were quite literally ministers. At the same time, many members simply held strong convictions and agreed with the church's progressive orientation. Its ministerial staff had to adjust to this reality.

Binkley's Theological Diversity

In the 1980s, scholars noticed the decline of denominational affiliation within American Christianity.[21] Denominations no longer had the same type of cultural power they once did within American society. In the early twentieth century, evangelical groups sought to bridge the theological particularities of niche denominational groups in favor a more generic, "fundamental" Christian faith.[22] By the end of the century, divisions in American Christianity were increasingly framed around politics and divisive cultural issues like abortion and same-sex marriage. At the congregational level Binkley's theological outlook both affirms the declining influence of denominational bodies on the American religious landscape and reflects how denominationalism continued to shape congregational decisions. Despite its Baptist name, Binkley long attracted congregants from outside Baptist life due to its commitment to ecumenism. Even in the 1970s the church appealed to couples who came from different denominational backgrounds, like Melinda and Jim Wilde, who were Southern Baptist and Episcopalian, respectively.[23] As time progressed, Binkley found that more and more of its membership had backgrounds in other denominational bodies.

By the late 1990s, retired pastor Bob Seymour delivered a local lecture on ecumenism in which he recalled a recent Sunday when Binkley welcomed nine people for membership—"Two came from a Lutheran congregation, two from Methodist congregations, one from a Presbyterian congregation, and only four from other Baptist churches."[24] Denominational background increasingly became less of an issue when accepting new members. Theological questions relating to baptism and membership had been settled in the congregation's founding era when the church decided to recognize baptisms from outside Baptist congregations. By the late twentieth and early twenty-first centuries, however, Binkley began expanding its ecclesial practices to accommodate this denominational diversity. During Jim Pike's pastorate, Binkley offered opportunities for members of the youth group who had been baptized as infants to "choose to go through a ritual of confirmation." This became a way Binkley practiced their ecumenism: by engaging and sometimes adopting and adapting practices found within the wider Christian church.[25]

At the same time, the decline of denominationalism that fostered such ecumenism at Binkley did not mean that the influence of denominational distinctions was unimportant or nonexistent. By the time Peter Carman became pastor in 2008, he reflected on the fact that many of Binkley's membership had not grown up Baptist. Instead, "they were Catholic, Presbyterian, Methodist, UCC, Disciples, AME, [and] Pentecostal." Fostering a collective congregational vision out of such diverse denominational backgrounds proved difficult. As previously noted, even the cultures within Southern Baptist circles and American Baptist circles were different enough to shape organizational and bureaucratic processes. Such a breadth of denominational backgrounds marked a significant breadth of theological diversity as well. Not only this, but denominational identity also intersects with geographic, cultural, and aesthetic differences. Carman found it challenging to preach to such a diverse congregation who may have found his preaching either "not artistic enough" on the one hand or "too political" on the other. Balancing and drawing these many denominational identities together took patience and care.[26]

Amid the congregation's variety of denominational backgrounds, Binkley maintained a distinctively liberal Protestant approach to theological practice and spirituality. Over the course of Carman's pastorate, he came to characterize Binkley's theological orientation as neither "evangelical" nor even "really Christocentric."[27] Instead, the church placed significant energy and focus on spiritual practices and prayer, emphasizing silence and meditation. Jim Pike found this denominational and theological diversity to be a "rich gift" that led the congregation to try "blending many different spiritual practices." Under Pike's leadership, Binkley began intentionally incorporating artwork into worship services and even started renting a giant canvas labyrinth for use in the sanctuary. The church also began regular Taizé services.[28] Inspired by an international, ecumenical community in Taizé, France, these short services focused on contemplative practices that drew upon a "creative mix of literature, music, and visual artistic expression."[29]

By the late twentieth and early twenty-first centuries, Binkley had drifted, both in intentional and unintentional ways, from its founding as an ecumenical, evangelical congregation in the southern college town of Chapel Hill. While the congregation's ecumenism remained, as more of its membership came from backgrounds outside of the Baptist tradition, Binkley shed much of the evangelical identity that contributed to characterizing its founding. Instead, the church resembled more of

During Pike's tenure as pastor, Binkley began setting up a labyrinth in the sanctuary during Holy Week. Photo thanks to Megan Hollenbeck.

a predominately white, mainline Christian congregation. Through this denominational diversity, however, the church was pushed and pulled in multiple directions as congregants prioritized different theological and social agendas. The struggle to create an intersectional ethic that sought to address interlocking injustices in tandem with one another was a constant battle for Binkley—one that Binkley both won and lost. Limited resources made prioritizing certain commitments necessary, but individual congregants worked to ensure that their personal commitments were represented within the collective.

Expanding Ministry Opportunities

From its founding, Binkley strove to be involved in the community by initiating and contributing to a variety of local causes and ministries. From the local Interfaith Council for Social Services to Habitat for Humanity to Meals on Wheels, there was never a shortage of ministry opportunities at Binkley. By the middle of the 1990s, however, the congregation began to expand its ministry footprint in different ways and different directions. Rather than having specific ministries, the congregation began to address larger areas of focus that had either gone unnoticed by the congregation or were new areas opened up by its progressive identity. Through the church's vast network of committees in conjunction with its emphasis on every member's responsibility as a minister, Binkley began to build out its ministry emphases. Some of these areas required more financial commitment and dedication, whereas others were less time consuming and costly. Some required Binkley to reorient the ways in which the congregation thought about both itself and its larger theology. This expansion of Binkley's areas of ministerial focus provided new ways for the congregation to engage the world around them.

One of the new areas of ministerial focus for Binkley during this period revolved around health and well-being. The congregation counted a significant number of medical professionals, including both nurses and doctors, among its membership. These individuals came together to help form a Health Ministries Committee. The group planned blood drives and organized health fairs that resembled a Social Gospel approach to public health. The group even planned healing services, creating new congregational practices that stretched the theological boundary for many congregants. Liberal Protestants for much of the twentieth century decried the idea of healing services, which were often found within more charismatic and Pentecostal traditions, but as historian Pamela Klassen has shown, some liberal

Protestant groups "cultivated their own version of supernaturalism, as they cut across Protestant denominations, embracing ecumenism, socialist critique, and sometimes even the scientifically mystical allure of parapsychology." Biomedical science did not function antagonistically toward Christianity through this lens; rather, Binkley's health and wellness services became an extension of Christianity's central message of healing.[30] Binkley's ecumenism and willingness to engage other denominational and religious groups opened the congregation to envision what these practices and ministries could look like.

Under this larger umbrella of health ministries, Binkley also engaged in more targeted and specific programming. Spurred on by Binkley members who had family members struggling with mental health disorders, a new group called the Binkley Brainstormers facilitated gatherings where individuals could share resources and advocate for greater attention on mental illness.[31] In 1999, the Health Ministries Committee helped establish what became known as Margaret's Supply Closet. Named after deceased relatives of Binkley members, Margaret's Closet became a room in the church that collected and organized medical equipment from crutches and wheelchairs to more technical and specific items. The Health Ministries Committee maintained the equipment for "people in the church and beyond who were having health problems." When the closet became overstocked, the congregation donated excess items to other agencies in need.[32] Through these efforts, Binkley's membership encouraged the congregation to think about the intersection between health, faith, and ministry.

In addition to health ministries, Binkley also expanded its commitment to consider the needs of the larger global community from their context in Chapel Hill. In an increasingly globalized world, humanitarian and larger geo-political events that once seemed distant to Chapel Hill were now easier and more accessible to engage. One congregant, Mary Lou Smith, encouraged Binkley to become more active in advocating for the rights of Palestinians. She founded a local organization, the Coalition for Peace with Justice, that sought the Israeli withdrawal from occupied lands gained after the Six-Day War.[33] Through Smith, the Israeli-Palestinian conflict became a more important and discussed matter within the congregation. Other members of Binkley helped form a partnership with the Pinheiro Church of Maceio, Brazil. Facilitated through the Alliance of Baptists' relationship with the *Alianca Baptista do Brasil,* Binkley and the Pinheiro Church sought to model a new type of ministry partnership that avoided the challenges and legacies of colonialism and imperialism typified through the traditional missionary enterprise. Travel between North Carolina and Brazil was not centered around service projects but relationship building between the two faith communities.[34]

The congregation also began to think globally within their local community as Chapel Hill welcomed an increasingly cosmopolitan and global population. As a large college town, Chapel Hill welcomed residents from all around the globe, which transformed some of the ways Binkley engaged the local community. As geo-political events destabilized regions around the world, Binkley worked to help resettle refugee families in the local community. Beginning in 1975, Binkley participated in the resettlement of a small number of Vietnamese families, and in 1993 the congregation partnered with two other local congregations to settle four-teen Burmese refugees. By 2005, Binkley had formally established a Resettlement Committee to maintain an active and consistent role in helping resettle refugees in the larger Research Triangle of North Carolina. As part of this work, the congregation formally sponsored families and helped them adjust to life in a new place. Peter Carman had experience with this work, having come from Lake Avenue Baptist Church in Rochester where he pastored a congregation with a large population of Burmese refugees, many of whom were Baptist because of nineteenth-century American Baptist missionary efforts in the country. After a few years into Carman's pastorate at Binkley, the congregation began to welcome a few new Chin members and opened their facilities to a Karen congregation that utilized the church's build-ing—both are ethnic groups native to Burma.[35]

Throughout its history, Binkley encouraged congregants to think about political engagement and advocacy as a form of social ministry. This included not only vot-ing, but also running for public office. Howard Lee's successful mayoral campaign in 1969 and his subsequent career in politics provides a good example. In addition to Lee, Binkley welcomed numerous individuals into its membership who were committed to public service and political engagement. Anne Barnes, who helped run two of Howard Lee's campaigns, and Verla Insko both served multiple terms in the North Carolina House of Representatives, and Edith Wiggins became the sec-ond Black woman to serve on the Chapel Hill Town Council in 1996.[36] Beginning in 1987, Binkley member David Price was elected to represent North Carolina's fourth congressional district in the United States House of Representatives. Price, a Democrat, served in this capacity well into the twenty-first century, only losing once in the 1994 midterm elections known as the "Republican Revolution." For these Binkley members, engaging in the political and democratic process became a form of lived ministry.

In the 1990s, many of Binkley's longtime members focused their political energies on combatting the death penalty in North Carolina. Prior to the Supreme Court's decision to reinstate the death penalty in 1977, the state ranked fifth in state executions.[37] In cooperation with the North Carolina Council of Churches, Binkley members helped to found and support People of Faith Against the Death Penalty (PFADP), a local nonprofit established in 1994. That year, the state was set to execute Kermit Smith Jr. for crimes he committed in 1980. For the newly appointed executive director of PFADP, Leigh Eason, the case presented an opportunity to pressure the state and its predominately Christian citizenry to ask in blunt terms whether "the death penalty is Christian or not Christian. Is the death penalty right or wrong?"[38] In the years following its founding, PFADP and its Binkley supporters petitioned the governor on numerous occasions to grant clemency to individuals on death row.

The state's governor at the time, Jim Hunt, a Democrat, was uniquely positioned to hear Binkley's protests. When Hunt was a law student at the University of North Carolina in the 1960s, he attended Binkley. While serving as governor from 1977 to 1985 before serving again from 1993 until 2001, Hunt explained to the *North Carolina Independent* that Binkley "embodies what I believe Christianity is all about." Despite growing up a Presbyterian, Hunt remembered that Binkley appealed to his belief that God calls God's followers to "be involved in our communities in order to make life better for our fellow men and women."[39] Through his connection to Binkley, Hunt shared the congregation's commitment to faithfully engage the needs of the local community. Unlike many members of Binkley's congregation, however, Hunt saw no problem with enforcing the state's death penalty. If God called God's followers to make life better for our neighbors, Hunt believed the death penalty did just that.

In 1998, the state was scheduled to execute John Noland, a convicted murderer. In response, Seymour and PFADP recruited another well-known Binkley member, Dean Smith, to petition Hunt to stay the execution. Smith, at this time retired from his illustrious thirty-six-year career as head coach of UNC Chapel Hill's men's basketball team, actually knew Noland. As a head coach, he regularly scheduled visits to hospitals, schools, and prisons with student athletes as a type of public ministry. Noland was a big fan of the Tar Heels, and Smith had spoken with him on multiple occasions while visiting Raleigh Central Prison with student athletes. When Smith and the PFADP coalition went to petition Hunt in a now-famous meeting, he raised his finger to the governor and firmly declared, "You're a murderer." He turned his finger and continued around the room, "and you're a murderer, and you're a murderer, and I'm a murderer." Smith reasoned that the legal execution of a state citizen was a communal act that was neither morally justified nor effective in deterring criminal acts. Hunt respectfully listened but refused to grant the request.[40] Binkley may have been an institution that championed a progressive form of Christianity, but its congregants were far from unified on theological or social issues. Both Hunt and Smith had been shaped and formed by their time at Binkley to greater or lesser degrees, but the two were not of one mind.

John Noland died by lethal injection on November 20, 1998. In a written statement composed hours before his execution, Noland expressed gratitude for the outpouring of love and support from those who had fought to stay his execution. "Love surrounds me, comforts me, makes me very happy in my last hours." He continued, "Love from our God, my family, members of Sisk Memorial Baptist Church, Binkley Baptist Church, [and] People of Faith Against the Death Penalty."[41]

Hunt denied clemency for inmates on death row seven times between 1998 and 1999, and it was not until December 1999, after serving as governor of North Carolina for a combined fourteen years, that he commuted an inmate's sentence. The former Binkley member had not reached some sudden epiphany about the death penalty; rather, the merits of the individual case led him to this particular decision.[42] The time between Hunt joining a small, progressive Baptist congregation as a graduate student and becoming one of the longest-serving governors in United States history reveals a lot about Binkley. In the span of just over forty years, the congregation had managed to cultivate personal relationships with two of the most recognizable figures in North Carolina—Jim Hunt and Dean Smith. Both believed in an active Christian faith that engaged the public square—a belief that Binkley had nurtured—but the issues and positions that shaped and formed this engagement differed.

Hunt had long since been a member of Binkley, but his connection to the congregation highlights the challenges a progressive church like Binkley faced in holding the boundaries of its fellowship together. As the church embraced its progressive identity in the wake of Blevins's licensure, the expansion of ministry opportunities and areas of ministerial focus opened the doors to internal disagreements and conflicts. Smith and Hunt were members at Binkley at the same time in the 1960s when civil rights were a congregational priority that held the community together. Over thirty years later, the death penalty proved to be an issue that went too far for Hunt (or at least too far for his political career). As Binkley evolved and adopted more progressive ministries, not all congregants came to the same understanding and agreement. While the congregation never sought to impose doctrinal or social beliefs on its membership, the gravity of the majority's opinion put pressure on members to conform. This social pressure, however, was only so strong as members prioritized and nuanced their beliefs differently.

The congregation's inability to convince Hunt reveals the limits of the church's political involvement. Binkley's attempts to rely on moral suasion within the political arena could not compare to the raw political power wielded by conservative evangelicals within Republican circles.[43] Progressive Christianity did not have the same organized voting power with which to hold politicians accountable for their voting records and actions. Binkley had developed an impressive network within North Carolina political life as evidenced by its ability to arrange a meeting with the governor. That soft influence cannot be discounted. Offering up a moral voice within a system that values votes, money, and power, however, does not always yield concrete results. For Binkley, the costs of giving up that moral voice in favor of pursuing more tangible outcomes was too high. Although the congregation had cultivated an impressive network of connections to local politics through its membership, as a community, the church understood its political engagement as grounded in its moral authority and distinct from partisan politics.

The "Green(e)ing" of Binkley Baptist Church

Spurred on by new congregants, the environment and climate justice became another area of ministry expansion at Binkley around the turn of the century. Scientists and activists during the latter half of the twentieth century issued numerous national and global calls to examine the damage humans were causing to the planet. Rachel Carson's 1962 work documenting the adverse effects of pesticides, *Silent Spring,* marked one of the earliest works in the environmental movement. Carson's work raised environmental alarm only four years after Binkley's founding, but despite her call and others, the church paid relatively little attention to the environment for much of its history. The congregation's turn to address environmental issues within both the life of the community and its theological outlook around the turn of the century was not marked by a growing consensus or significant congregational attention; rather, this turn became the project of a new member, Herman Greene.

Joining Binkley in 1996, Greene had no memories or experiences from the congregational conflicts surrounding the construction of the sanctuary or licensure of John Blevins. He joined the congregation as it transitioned under the pastoral leadership of Jim Pike. Raised in a moderate Southern Baptist congregation in

Gainesville, Florida, Greene, like many of Binkley's members, cultivated his faith within the context of a college town. It was not until Greene left Gainesville to pursue a master's degree at Stanford University, however, that he truly began to see the relationship between his faith and community activism. While in California, Green learned how to link justice issues related to civil rights and poverty to the Baptist faith of his upbringing.[44]

A perpetual student, it was not until 1981, after Greene had received a master of theology from the University of Chicago as well as a juris doctor from UNC, that he began to think about the relationship between the environment and his faith. While attending Park Slope Methodist Church in Brooklyn, New York, he became acquainted with Thomas Berry, a Roman Catholic priest and self-described "geologian."[45] Berry was a cultural historian of religions, and by the 1970s, he became consumed by the ecological crisis facing the earth. Through his study of the changing environment, Berry saw the impending need to transition his theological perspective of "human history to cosmological history."[46] Hearing Berry speak on the "Spirituality of the Earth" in 1981 forever changed Greene's theological perspective, and he continued to return to and find Berry's life and writings influential.

Three years after joining Binkley, in 1999, Greene helped initiate the formation of an Earth Ministry Committee within the congregation. As he described it, the committee's primary intention served to expand "awareness of the members of the committee, first, and the congregation, second." Meetings included time for the roughly ten-person group to discuss the times and places in which they had touched and been touched by nature. The group also studied ecologically informed theological and spiritual works. Within the broader life of the congregation, Greene and the Earth Ministry Committee helped to plan Thanksgiving and Earth Day Sunday services by providing liturgies and preparing special altar-table arrangements.[47]

Greene found that despite Binkley's "outstanding record in dealing with social issues," accepting "that creation should be a focus of the ministry, witness, and theology of the church was difficult" for Binkley.[48] He surmised that the congregation's theological outlook remained too "anthropocentric." Focusing too much on human salvation, either physical or spiritual, allowed members of Binkley to view humanity as outside or above the natural world. The congregation's classically liberal roots allowed it to see the inherent worth of everyone, but as Greene saw it, Binkley needed a "new understanding and vision" that allowed congregants to see the connectivity of the individual not just to the rest of human society, but to the rest of creation.[49]

Greene sought to use his work with the Earth Ministry Committee as a springboard for testing the implementation of a "Creation Season" into the liturgical life of Binkley. Greene first envisioned this project while pursuing his doctor of ministry through United Theological Seminary in Dayton, Ohio. He hoped this Creation Season would help integrate an "ecological consciousness" into the life of Binkley and perhaps encourage and inspire other congregations to follow suit. Although not a member of the congregation's staff, Greene worked closely with Binkley's ministerial staff including Senior Pastor Jim Pike, Associate Pastors Dale Osborne and Robin Brooks, and Minister of Music Leandra AnafShalom. From January to June 2003, Greene helped to plan Binkley's first Creation Season for the fall of that year.[50]

Each Sunday during Creation Season, congregants sang hymns and heard special choir anthems that centered around the earth and creation. Artwork and banners displayed throughout the church and sanctuary sought to accentuate similar themes. While the Earth Ministry Committee had designed and created altar tables in the past for specific occasions, throughout Creation Season, their curated designs appeared each Sunday. Special events including a blessing of the animals and a vegetarian potluck for the Feast Day of St. Francis were added to the church calendar. Educational programming on ecology and the environment took place throughout the fall on Wednesday evenings and Sunday mornings. Associate Pastor Dale Osborn organized, and the church sponsored, a youth whitewater rafting trip as well as a family bird-watching excursion.[51] Greene's project sought to incorporate the environment into every facet of congregational life.

At the start of Creation Season in early October 2003, Greene delivered an inaugural sermon entitled "What Now?" Through this oration, he sought to help the congregation situate humanity within a far larger picture of creation, highlighting the relatively short history of humanity's ten-thousand-year existence in comparison to earth's five-billion-year history. Greene explained that Christians are taught to read the Bible to imagine God's kingdom in ways that are much too limiting. "When you read the Bible with ecological eyes," Greene explained, "all creatures great and small, human and non-human alike, become parts of God's great reign of love." He wanted Binkley to begin recognizing the wideness of creation.[52]

Greene celebrated Binkley as a congregational heir to a "wonderful liberal tradition" but warned that this tradition "will not carry us into the future." He critiqued modernity's vision of an "ever-growing economy, democracy and world peace" as failing to account for the limitations of the natural world. Greene argued that Binkley had an "unusual opportunity" to shape a "constructively post-modern . . . progressive wing of Christianity."[53] For some of Binkley's membership, the prospect of shaping a uniquely post-modern, progressive wing of Christianity proved intriguing. Decentering humanity and, in the process, the individual offered the opportunity to engage in a holistic vision for congregational ministry. Some of Binkley's members, however, were not as convinced that climate justice should be the theological lynchpin in reorienting the congregation's priorities. As a progressive congregation, Binkley created a space for marginalized persons, and for members committed to racial justice and LGBTQ inclusion, two groups long decentered within Christian communities, these issues were also pressing.

Binkley and Barbee Chapel

From Binkley's founding, addressing racial injustice and segregation had been a core tenet of how the congregation described itself and understood its identity. At the same time, it remained a predominately white church throughout its history. In 1996, the congregation worked to reinvigorate its commitment to racial justice and equality by beginning a formal partnership with the local Barbee Chapel Missionary Baptist Church, later renamed Barbee's Chapel Harvest Word Church and Ministries. This historically Black congregation in Chapel Hill traced its history to the late nineteenth century when former slaves of Willis Barbee, whose grandfather had helped finance the construction of Chapel Hill Baptist Church, broke away to establish their own congregation.[54] The precursors of this congregational partnership began during Linda Jordan's tenure at Binkley. While much of her pastorate remained overshadowed by the licensure of John Blevins, Jordan also cultivated a friendship with Bishop Hatley through the Coalition of Chapel Hill-Carrboro Clergy, which the two co-chaired. Hatley and Jordan helped unite Black and white local religious leaders, and they also sought to work together on the congregational level. The two ministers began monthly conversations between members of the two churches, which laid the groundwork for a formal partnership.[55]

Initially this partnership revolved around monthly meetings during which members from both congregations spent an hour or two "catching up on each other's news, from the arrival of grand babies, health challenges, new jobs and retirements." Nancie McDermott explained that at these gatherings members from both churches also talked about "social justice issues . . . from incidents in the schools, the achievement gap, workers' rights and the fight for a living wage."[56] While gatherings often had agendas, they were more about conversation and cultivating relationships. One summer, some Binkley members proposed that the two churches take a break from these monthly meetings for the summer since the group was not working on any specific projects at the time. A member from Barbee Chapel, Lorena Mills, responded to the suggestion contending that she didn't think the "reason for meeting was to plan and execute events, but to be in relationship with each other, to talk and reach out across all the pervasive and powerful forces of racism and injustice." Recognizing the "wisdom and truth in her response," the monthly meetings continued as a staple of the two congregations' commitments to one another.[57]

As the relationship continued to evolve, Binkley and Barbee Chapel arranged to swap pastors a couple of Sundays each year and even hold joint worship services. Through these joint services, both congregations experienced different styles and approaches to worship often involving special musical and choral arrangements. During Jim Pike's pastorate, he and Bishop Hatley sometimes sang at these joint services.[58] The congregations also partnered on building homes together with Habitat for Humanity. The largest project the two churches worked on together, however, was their biennial yard sale, designed to raise money for various ministries. These joint yard sales served as an extension of Binkley's practice of holding yard sales and Christmas bazaars beginning in the 1970s. Under the partnership with Barbee Chapel, these events would take on a life of their own. Peter Carman recalled that they might more aptly be described as an "extravaganza" rather than a yard sale.[59]

In preparation for the biennial event, both congregations received all kinds of donations from their members that organizers categorized and priced. One year, Kimberley Eastman remembered that Dean Smith "donated a bunch of his neckties to the 'Men's Haberdashery' department." Her father purchased one for each of his male relatives for Christmas.[60] The 2008 yard sale took roughly 250 Binkley and Barbee members three weeks of "intensive volunteer hours of sorting, setting up, and pricing." When the date of the event finally arrived, it only took five hours to generate $36,000. That year the two congregations divided the profits equally. Binkley's share of the profits went to support the resettlement of three refugee families in Chapel Hill as well as disaster relief funds organized by both the Baptist Peace Fellowship of North America and the American Baptist International Ministries. Barbee Chapel, in turn, allocated its profits to a local education initiative targeting the educational achievement gap in the local school system.[61] In future years, the two congregations agreed to donate all proceeds to shared local ministry priorities.[62] Whereas monthly meetings provided a time of personal and intimate gathering between the two congregations, joint worship services, these large yard sales, and other ministry projects shaped a larger, more public-facing dynamic between the two churches.

As successful as their partnership was, the relationship between Barbee Chapel and Binkley was not always smooth and easy. Pike remembered that some Binkley members questioned whether the proceeds of the biennial yard sale should be evenly split between the two congregations. Binkley, as a larger and financially better-endowed congregation, often provided more staffing for the event, causing some members to question this division. Having all proceeds directed toward shared goals helped remedy some of these complaints. Similarly, in the early years of the partnership, Pike remembered that Bishop Hatley preached a sermon at Binkley where he "spoke of 'white privilege' before it was a familiar concept in a way that offended folks who heard it for the first time." Such an indictment rubbed a few Binkley members the wrong way, and as a result, these few individuals decided not to participate in future joint worship services.[63] The partnership forced Binkley to think about equity. While it may have made some congregants uncomfortable, it did not stop the partnership from continuing to evolve and mature.

Binkley was proud of its history and support of the civil rights movement, and for many congregants, partnering with Barbee Chapel served as an extension of this legacy. At the same time, coming to terms with the realities facing Black Americans thirty years later was an eye-opening experience for some members. As much as Binkley wanted to help address the challenges facing Black Americans in the late twentieth and early twenty-first centuries, its remembered history sometimes got in the way. Former pastor Bob Seymour, as well as some members of the congregations, struggled with some of Bishop Hatley's characterizations of the realities facing Black residents in Chapel Hill.

In June 1994, Bishop Hatley published an article entitled "Racism is Alive and Well in Chapel Hill" in the *Chapel Hill News*. That year the town was struggling with how to proceed when it was revealed that LaVonda Burnette, a twenty-three-year-old Black woman, had lied about her educational background in her successful campaign to serve on the local school board. Local officials began the process of establishing the rules for holding a recall election.[64] Against this backdrop, Hatley penned an op-ed after hearing a prominent unnamed clergyman declare that things were so much better for Blacks then they were in the 1950s. Hatley contended that the forms of discrimination had simply changed. They were no longer "obviously overt, but covert ranging from denial of employment promotions, lack of adequate persons in management . . . to blatant systematic institutionalizations of grievance procedures designed to prevent complaints."[65] Seymour assumed that the prominent clergy member Hatley had referred to was him and took an opportunity to voice his opinion.

Seymour responded in an open letter criticizing and offering corrections to the Black minister's characterizations of race relations in Chapel Hill. He tried to explain to Hatley that Chapel Hill had "seen major changes" since the period of Jim Crow and that those changes "should not be belittled." He argued that society was moving in a direction in which race would "become increasingly irrelevant." The number of Black publicly elected officials, for instance, signified this improvement. Seymour insinuated that Burnette was elected due to "reverse racism" and that Chapel Hill voters had sought to elect her "BECAUSE she is [B]lack!" He defended the University of North Carolina for not employing enough Black faculty due to the small "percentage of [B]lack PhDs available in America." While there was work that needed to be done in educating more Black individuals with advanced degrees, Seymour did not believe UNC should be criticized for this larger systemic problem.[66]

Toward the end of his letter, Seymour admitted that he was troubled by Hatley's "endorsement of the opinion that white America still thinks every [B]lack as a 'n——.'" Hatley had not used such a pointed phrase; rather, he implied that regardless of educational status or profession, race was still the first thing the country saw—"you are still called a n——."[67] This struck a nerve with Seymour, who pushed back, calling this the "worst kind of racial stereotype against white people," and concluded, "I don't think you really believe this." For Seymour, Bishop Hatley had offered up some "disturbing indictments" of his "white sisters and brothers."[68]

Seymour's attempts to correct and reframe Bishop Hatley's perceptions of racism in Chapel Hill missed the realities of the present by celebrating the victories of the past. It demonstrated the ways in which white supremacy and racism can co-exist within the most vocal and outspoken white supporters of racial justice. Burnette was ultimately pushed to resign, and local officials awarded her position to the white woman who had lost to her by 113 votes.[69] Binkley's relationship with Barbee Chapel helped the congregation, Seymour included, to recognize some of ways in which white supremacy operated. The partnership helped reveal the challenges that continued to press upon racial minorities in the late twentieth and early twenty-first centuries. Seymour's comments at the beginning of the congregations' partnership marked a starting point from which the predominately white congregation could grow and evolve over the course of the churches' relationship. After more than a decade of partnership between the two congregations, Binkley began engaging on a small scale the difficult questions related to the difference between the "theoretical affirmation and personal inclusion of persons of color" and the reality of building a "multicultural congregation that is rooted both in Mainline Baptist and Black Church practices." During Peter Carman's tenure, he found the congregation had energy around "collectively addressing white supremacy."[70] That energy, however, was also met by energy to tackle many other systemic injustices in the local community and wider world.

The Consequences of LGBTQ Inclusion

The decision to license John Blevins in 1992 marked the beginning of Binkley's transition toward a new progressive identity, but the process through which the congregation came to affirm Blevins's right to preach was fraught to say the least. While this moment in the congregation's history caused many families to leave, Binkley continued to experience reverberations of their newfound identity in the years following. It took the congregation a few years to process their decision and come to a common understanding of their identity as a church that welcomed LGBTQ individuals. It was not until Jim Pike's first Church Council meeting as pastor in 1996 that the board of outreach voted to join the Association of Welcoming and Affirming Baptists (AWAB), an organization with roots in the American Baptist Churches USA and committed to LGBTQ inclusion within Baptist congregational life. It took the congregation another year to formally apply for and receive official membership status within the para-denominational group. Binkley's membership gave the congregation better language with which to articulate their inclusion of all persons. As the issue of human sexuality became more of a wedge issue within American politics, Binkley responded with conviction and sometimes received resistance and even condemnation.

In 1999, two members of United Church of Chapel Hill, Larry Ellis and Jim Raymer, sought to hold a ceremony marking their commitment and love for one another, but the church's sanctuary was in the process of renovation. There were few congregations in the area that would affirm the couple's relationship. As a result, Binkley volunteered to host what local papers reported as a "gay union."[71] Sixteen years before the Supreme Court ruled in *Obergefell v. Hodges* (2015) that same-sex couples had the right to marry, Binkley welcomed Ellis and Raymer to use their facilities for the ceremony. Thanks to the process of becoming an AWAB congregation, Binkley had already a developed a "Holy Union policy" to guide the church in hosting the couple's ceremony.[72] The congregation had no problem opening its doors for the couple to celebrate their love for one another.

One month later, however, Binkley received a letter from Westboro Baptist Church condemning the congregation's decision to host the ceremony. Pastored by Fred Phelps, Westboro Baptist Church was a small congregation in Topeka, Kansas, comprised largely of Phelps's family. They gained a national reputation in 1998 for picketing the funeral of Matthew Shepard, a gay University of Wyoming student who was brutally tortured and left to die outside the town of Laramie. For Westboro, this marked the beginning of a strategy of picketing funerals, church services, and other public gatherings across the country with brightly colored and evocative signs.[73] Binkley caught their ire. Phelps addressed his letter to "Brother Pike" and accused Pike of using Binkley to "spit in the Face of Christ." According to Pike, the letter concluded, "Apostate churches (like yours) cater to sodomites and a sinful lifestyle that will destroy the life, damn the soul and doom the nation . . . Yours In Christ." Phelps sent letters to the local papers and the Chapel Hill police explaining their intention to picket a Sunday morning service at Binkley.[74] They wanted to create a spectacle.

In preparation for Westboro Baptist Church's arrival, Binkley planned for an opportunity to "witness to the inclusive love of God for all of God's children." On May 16, 1999, Fred Phelps and Westboro arrived in front of Binkley Memorial Baptist Church with signs proclaiming, "God Hates Fags" and "Your Pastor is Lying." Inside the church, over four hundred members of Binkley sat to participate in what had already been planned as Youth Sunday. According to Pike, Binkley's youth group had been given the opportunity to back out of the service under the circumstances. They "steadfastly refused."[75] That morning, Westboro Baptist was restricted to protesting across the street from the church property with "police in squad cars" stationed "out of view." The sanctuary, Bill Eastman recalled, "kept filling to capacity" with Binkley members and caring friends from other congregations in the community, as well as a few scattered police officers.[76] According to the *Raleigh News and Observer*, the service was characterized by "messages of compassion and inclusive love" delivered by teenage members of the Binkley community.[77]

The Westboro protests were a significant moment in the life of the congregation and served as a real and tangible consequence of Binkley's convictions. While several families left Binkley after the licensure of John Blevins, the Westboro protests marked a different kind of consequence. Both Westboro and Binkley claimed to be Baptist churches; however, both held wildly divergent theological perspectives. Both congregations characterized the very edges of Baptist life in the United States. For Binkley, the protests only strengthened their resolve that the congregation's stance was a prophetic witness to God's inclusive love of all people.

Most Americans, however, did not hold similar views on human sexuality, and two years later, one of Binkley's longest-standing community partnerships was

upended due to the congregation's stance on human sexuality and LGBTQ individuals. Since the early 1960s Binkley had sponsored Boy Scout Troop and Cub
Scout Pack 820, providing a facility for the group's nearly two hundred members.
Harry Jensen Jr. began attending Binkley in 1959 and helped to start the troop. He
served as Scoutmaster for more than fifteen years, leading numerous camping trips
to all parts of North Carolina with many other Binkley members who were also
involved in the troop.[78] In 2001, the congregation's charter with the Boy Scouts of
America (BSA) was up for renewal, and members of the church were divided as to
how to proceed. Throughout the 1990s, the Boy Scouts had prohibited gay membership, and in 2000 the Supreme Court upheld the BSA's right to do so.[79] For
some members of the congregation, the answer was clear: "the Troop must go."[80]
Despite years of hosting the organization, these members were easily willing to end
their relationship with the BSA.

Not everyone felt the same way. Some of Binkley's members had been deeply
involved in Scout life for years.[81] Pastor Jim Pike, having been a Boy Scout growing
up, sought to find a way to retain the ministry of hosting the Boy Scouts while at
the same time honoring Binkley's commitment to the inclusion of LGBTQ individuals. The church, as a hosting institution, proposed a "conditional charter" to the
national organization that would recognize the congregation's anti-discrimination
policy. The amended charter, however, was rejected. Given that the congregation's
amendment was at odds with the national policy of the BSA, the local Occoneechee
Council rejected Binkley's proposal and severed ties with the congregation. The
local papers explained that there were "no hard feelings between the scouts and
the church."[82] The decision was one of conviction for Binkley, but also for the Boy
Scouts of America. That conviction cost something for both institutions. For some
in the congregation, the real tragedy was that "the children are the ones who are
suffering from this."[83]

The inclusion of LGBTQ individuals continued to be a driving commitment and
motivation for Binkley into the twenty-first century. That commitment came with
its challenges. The protests of Westboro and decisions of the BSA marked clear and
distinct consequences of this commitment, but they did not cause Binkley to waver
in their resolve. Instead, the congregation garnered a clearer and more distinct identity within the community that attracted Christians who were tired of conservative
theologies that offered unfulfilling answers to some of society's most pressing and
sensitive issues.

The Challenges of Liberal Protestantism

As every new member brought their own unique theological beliefs and practices into the congregation, the church and its leadership had to balance how to respond and act in the wider community. Budgetary limitations meant that the congregation could not fund and support everything. From long-standing ministries including the local Interfaith Council, Meals on Wheels, and Habitat for Humanity to newer commitments of refugee resettlement, health ministries, and environmental justice, Binkley had a lot to balance and negotiate. Amid all of their congregational commitments, some of Binkley's members in the late twenty-first century felt that the congregation sometimes tried to do too much. Rather than "focus on the most important issues," Binkley merely kept a "toe-hold" in a variety of areas.[84] One congregant contended that when it came to balancing their commitments, the church had a "hard time focusing" on which issues to prioritize.[85] The challenge became how to choose which issues and commitments merited more attention than others. Many members had sought out Binkley because, as a unique progressive Baptist congregation, it would be more receptive to their deeply held personal convictions than a more conservative congregation. Picking and choosing which issues and ministries to prioritize could often feel a lot like picking and choosing which congregants would be prioritized. As Binkley negotiated its priorities, sometimes conflicts and tensions flared.

In the fall of 2010, Binkley welcomed Raymonda "Ray" Speller to serve as a ministerial intern. He was a Black, second-year divinity student at Duke Divinity School in nearby Durham and had been placed at Binkley for his second year of field education. Just as the congregation had welcomed James Forbes in the early 1960s, Binkley now welcomed Speller. A native of Suffolk, Virginia, Speller was raised in a charismatic, nondenominational Black Christian tradition and was theologically formed within this tradition.[86] Serving in a predominately white, mainline congregation like Binkley was a new experience. After the first three or four weeks he "wasn't sure [he] could stick it out," but he slowly began to find a place teaching Sunday school and serving in a variety of other capacities. Speller found his time as intern so meaningful and fruitful that he joined the congregation after his one-year field education and continued attending during this third year of divinity school.[87]

Peter Carman, who served as pastor at the time, described Speller as a "wonderful preacher" who captivated Binkley's membership. Carman remembered one Wednesday evening when Speller artfully explained the concept of "speaking in tongues" to a liberal, mainline congregation in ways that resonated and made sense.[88] For Speller, the practice functioned as a "way of reforming God's community" and "breaking down barriers." Speaking in tongues was an invitation "into the body of Christ." This description aligned with Binkley's commitment to inclusion even if the practice of speaking in tongues was quite foreign to many members. Outside the walls of the congregation, Speller helped coordinate Binkley's volunteers for a Habitat for Humanity build in conjunction with Barbee Chapel Church.[89] He enjoyed getting to know congregants on this level and "seeing folks outside the church."[90]

As Speller reached the conclusion of his seminary training, he asked Binkley to accompany him through the process of licensure and ordination—to have the congregation affirm his calling to ministry. The initial process of licensure was an "affirming process" that made Speller feel more "a part of the congregation." Through the ordination process, Speller looked inward as he sought to convey to his committee details about his faith journey and theology. Given Speller's background in a more conservative, charismatic tradition, one member of his ordination council was interested to know more about how this tradition had shaped him. "They assumed I was more conservative than I was," Speller recalled of the process, adding that they wanted to "sniff that out." As the conversation continued, this member of the ordination committee pressed Speller on his beliefs surrounding human sexuality. The young minister, however, was still "working through" where he came down on the issue of "sexual relationships outside heterosexual marriage." When asked whether he viewed same-sex relationships as sin, Speller responded that he was still thinking and working through his beliefs on the matter.[91]

Barring one abstention, the ordination council was unanimous in endorsing Speller's candidacy for ministry. The transition from this smaller ordination council's endorsement to the decision of the congregation at large, however, never happened. Speller's self-acknowledged lack of clarity on issues of sexuality concerned some church members, and as a result, he faced the difficult choice of whether to press forward in the ordination process despite the likelihood of opposition or withdrawal. Speller had conversations with some members who thought his withdrawal would help "preserve the church": some congregants worried that if put to a congregational vote, Speller's ordination would "cause some type of splitting." Rather than discussing the issues openly, Speller felt there was a "conspiracy of silence."[92] The young minister faced a daunting decision. According to Carman, Speller "got caught in the crossfire" of larger congregational dynamics.[93]

The process was incredibly painful for the church, which continued to be haunted by the conflicts surrounding the sanctuary and the licensing of John Blevins. It was not lost on Binkley's membership that Speller would be the first Black person to be ordained by the congregation, and they wanted to hold his individual conscience sacred. At the same time, North Carolina was embroiled in a conflict over the legal definition of marriage. The state was weighing whether to adopt an amendment to its constitution that defined marriage between "one man and one woman," and Binkley was active in fighting against the amendment.[94] Many congregants were concerned as to how to balance thinking through Speller's call to ministry, his personal convictions, and how those convictions might reflect back upon the congregation. Rather than reject Speller, the church put the ordination process on hold, and he withdrew his request and later sought ordination elsewhere.[95]

The process of Speller's ordination revealed the challenges and tensions Binkley sought to negotiate in a congregation with many deeply held convictions that did not always neatly overlap. On the one hand, framing Speller's ordination at Binkley crudely as a conflict between the congregation's commitment to racial justice and the congregation's commitment to LGBTQ inclusion assumes individuals and their convictions can be easily and neatly categorized. On the other hand, assuming the process was not racialized and merely reflected a question about human sexuality and nothing else fails to recognize how issues of oppression and injustice intersect with one another. As a predominately white, liberal Protestant body that came to newfound understandings of race, gender, and sexuality at different moments in its history, Binkley has the unique challenge of identifying these intersections.

That challenge was costly for the congregation. In many ways, Speller was precisely the candidate for ministry that Binkley longed to support. Speller went on to be ordained at St. Paul Community Baptist Church in Brooklyn, New York, and in 2015 he began serving as the pastor of Community Congregational United Church of Christ (UCC) in Montgomery, Alabama. Speller acknowledged that Binkley helped open his denominational point of view to consider a calling in the UCC. He also later reflected upon the unique space Binkley affords to LGBTQ persons to "feel uniquely themselves." Speller explained that in retrospect he would have "withdrawn immediately" from the ordination process to preserve that space had he understood how he might have jeopardized it.[96] Speller was precisely the candidate and minister Binkley would have longed to be associated with, but the congregation's inability to work at these intersections of race, gender, and sexuality obscured the church's ability to see this in Speller.

One of the sad ironies of Ray Speller's ordination process was that through it, Binkley failed to live up to its motto—"every member a minister." At this particular moment in the congregation's history, the boundaries of Binkley's inclusion were not wide enough for Speller's ministry. All congregations have these boundaries, but as collective bodies their boundaries are always shifting. People experience, observe, and/or overlook the intersections of racial justice, gender equality, LGBTQ inclusion, climate justice, and more in different ways. This makes it challenging for congregations to allocate limited time, attention, and resources to so many societal needs and issues at the same time. For Binkley, and for like-minded progressive congregations, negotiating these intersections defines their journey into the heart of the twenty-first century.

Binkley's commitment to "every member a minister" was always aspirational, and while the church often failed to live up to this lofty vision, it did inspire many congregants to action. Church members brought their passions and interests to bear on the life of the faith community, and Binkley's pastoral staff sought to guide and direct members into leadership positions where they might flourish. When Jean and Don Westbrook were told that Binkley was the most socially conscious church in the area, it did not mean that Binkley was perfect. As Peter Carman explained in a reflection on his pastorate, Binkley "is a living breathing worshiping household of faith." Sometimes that can be messy. That mess can be unsavory when conflicts and misunderstandings lead to certain congregational prioritizations over others, but sometimes that mess can be beautiful as a community of faith and all its members seek to live out their faith in a variety of ways.

Conclusion

AT THE FIFTIETH ANNIVERSARY of Binkley's founding in 2008, the congregation compiled a volume of memories written by founding, former, and current congregants entitled *Binkley Memories: The First 50 Years, 1958–2008.* Some of these memories were heartfelt and thoughtful descriptions of a particularly poignant moment in the life of Binkley, whereas others shared a small moment of joy or humor. Many members recounted a few of the congregation's theatrical and musical productions, including *Godspell* and *Joseph and the Amazing Technicolored Dreamcoat.* Charles Carver included a couple of recipes, including his mother's recipe for Brunswick stew, which he recalled cooking in a fifty-gallon pot for large Binkley events and gatherings. In addition to these shared memories from congregants, many of Binkley's former and current pastors wrote letters to the congregation reminiscing on their time in ministry at Binkley. Toward the end of his letter, Jim Pike, who had retired as senior minister the year before, explained, "Ministry by nature has ups and downs. No church is perfect. No pastor is perfect either. But with mutual respect and affection we served together in ministry."[1]

Throughout the history of Olin T. Binkley Memorial Baptist Church, the congregation indeed had its ups and downs. Looking back in retrospect through the lens of a congregational history provides an opportunity to think critically about important decisions that Binkley made or did not make and how these decisions influenced the church's identity. Amid the more than 330,000 estimated religious congregations in the United States, Binkley is both remarkably unique and incredibly ordinary in this respect. The congregation has taken bold and what many would call prophetic stances throughout its history, from establishing itself as an interracial and ecumenical congregation at its founding to its early work around LGBTQ inclusion to its commitment to the well-being of the local Chapel Hill community. At the same time, the ways in which Binkley processed and made difficult decisions as a collective body resemble that of many religious congregations across the United States that balance passionate members with strong opinions.

Indeed, no church is perfect. Few congregations, however, record or discuss the challenging and unsavory moments in the life of their church in significant detail. Bird's-eye views of the American religious landscape cannot account for the granular ways in which churches struggle to arrive at certain decisions or negotiate certain congregational priorities. For a uniquely progressive congregation like Binkley oriented within a Southern Baptist tradition, understanding how the church negotiated controversial decisions is pivotal in understanding its identity and place within the American religious landscape generally and Baptist life in the United States specifically. Such a congregational analysis provides another perspective for thinking about religion. Larger questions of theological doctrine become secondary to questions of balancing budgets, building maintenance, and committee work. Theoretical questions about polity become secondary to practical questions about process. Congregational life looks different on the ground.

For Binkley, congregational life was grounded in Chapel Hill, North Carolina. From its conception, the congregation's founders envisioned the church having a close relationship with the University of North Carolina. Binkley was a college-town church. Baptists cherish their belief in the autonomy of the local church, which contends that congregational beliefs and practices are not dictated by hierarchical denominational structures located in other parts of the country or world. While traditionally Baptists understand this belief as a type of freedom from larger institutions, it also opens the possibility for congregations to be free to better resemble the local context around them. Binkley took this opportunity to ground itself in the unique brand of southern liberalism that characterized UNC. Ideas of academic freedom easily translated into ideas of freedom of conscience that Baptists have long held sacred. Binkley celebrated learning and a rigorous faith that appealed to faculty, administrators, and students. The congregation sought to be a faithful voice that contributed to this brand of southern liberalism.

Over the course of its history, however, Binkley became less invested in campus life, as this study shows. When the church moved from Gerrard Hall to its permanent location in the middle of the 1960s, its relationship with the campus changed. The church slowly began to lose its connection to campus life. It started to appeal more to graduate students as well as professional and retired community members than it did to undergraduates. Binkley's maturation from a small, niche, college-town congregation to an established fixture of Chapel Hill's religious landscape in some ways resembles the changes that have taken place in Chapel Hill itself. By the end of the twentieth century, collegiate life in the United States looked far different than it had fifty years earlier, and Chapel Hill was no longer a small, quiet town. The massive growth of college campuses across the country changed how colleges like UNC operated in relationship to the surrounding community. Whereas UNC's chancellor once made Gerrard Hall available to nurture religious congregations like Binkley that could serve the growing student population, by the end of the twentieth century the school had a massive budget devoted to student life and community.[2]

What it meant to be a college-town congregation changed, and the growth of cities like nearby Raleigh and Durham—which along with Chapel Hill composed North Carolina's Research Triangle—helped shape the congregation as well. Binkley's established reputation surpassed the boundaries of Chapel Hill and appealed to people in the broader community. As a result, the church widened its conception of what constituted "local." It remained committed to the brand of southern liberalism popularized by UNC, and many members of the congregation continued to have connections to the school but not to the same extent that the church once did. Chapel Hill was now more than simply UNC, and Binkley changed along with its context.

In the same way that Binkley adjusted to its changing local context, this study also shows how a Southern Baptist congregation became an institution of progressive religion in Chapel Hill. By drawing upon the liberalism of its namesake, Olin T. Binkley Memorial Baptist Church welcomed theological contradiction. Caught between the optimism of the Social Gospel, the realism of Neo-Orthodoxy, and the energy of evangelicalism, Binkley brought together a unique amalgamation of theological beliefs and practices, something further nurtured by the congregation's founding pastor, Robert Seymour. In so doing, Binkley offered a novel theological perspective to which Baptists in the South were quite unaccustomed. It gave the church a radical edge when compared to other Southern Baptist congregations in the area.

As time wore on, Binkley continued to sharpen this radical edge. As with many liberal Protestant congregations in the twentieth century, Binkley changed and evolved theologically through expansion. The church expanded its vision of God's beloved community by adding to its theological understanding. As theological problems arose, the congregation addressed them. When women at Binkley began advocating for the congregation to use more inclusive language, the church expanded its theological understanding to think inclusively with regard to gender identity. Similarly, with the licensure of John Blevins, Binkley began to expand its understanding of the relationship between human sexuality and faith. The environment, likewise, provided another opportunity for Binkley to expand its theological perspectives and priorities. While at each of these junctures the congregation did significant theological work to incorporate these commitments into its larger collective theological perspective, it did not entail an entire collective reworking of the congregation's theological discourse.

In this way, Binkley followed the evolution of the liberal consensus of the twentieth century that centered white, male, heteronormative perspectives and experiences and slowly began seeking to add and incorporate the experiences of persons who fall outside these categories.[3] At times they struggled to see where their diverse identities and convictions intersected theologically. Ministries and priorities of the congregation tended to become siloed, vying for the congregation's attention and financial resources and occasionally creating tensions and conflicts over which ministries and commitments to prioritize. By the twenty-first century, Binkley, like many predominately white, progressive congregations, struggled to think through the ways in which their numerous justice commitments related to one another. While all congregations face the challenge of negotiating the passions and priorities of its membership, Binkley's history demonstrates how these challenges emerged within the context of a uniquely progressive church.

The congregation's evolving identity and changing theological perspectives did not emerge out of nothingness. These changes took place within an institutional context, and they played out through congregational, regional, and even national politics. Binkley's history shows that much of religious history in the United States is bureaucratic. While certainly the experiences of worship, fellowship, and Bible studies provide one image of congregational life, decisions are made through committee work and business meetings. The decisions to build a new sanctuary or license a gay divinity student, which had far-reaching consequences for Binkley, took place in congregational meetings. Conflicts over process became the battlegrounds for shaping questions of theological identity. Binkley navigated questions regarding the broader theological purpose of financial resources and building space through the process of building a sanctuary. Likewise, the church examined the relationship between sexuality and the divine through the licensure of John Blevins. Binkley's history shows that bureaucratic meeting minutes revealed these changes often in greater detail than sermons or newsletters.

Denominational structures too helped to shape Binkley's identity as a progressive Baptist congregation operating in a college town. As Binkley changed, so did the denominational bodies and organizations with which it affiliated. The church provides another lens for thinking about Southern Baptist life in the latter half of the twentieth century. Over much of this period, the gravity of the SBC eclipsed groups like the ABCUSA, the historically Black National Baptist Convention, and other Baptist denominational groups. While the "Baptist Battles" that took place in Southern Baptist life in the 1980s revealed the nuance and texture of the nation's largest Protestant body, they also kept the religious landscape focused on the SBC. The contestation between conservatives and moderates within Southern Baptist life became an all-consuming struggle that witnessed convention gatherings topping 35,000 messengers. Southern Baptist seminaries and agencies became the sites of intense struggles between denominational and institutional employees and increasingly conservative boards of directors. For Southern Baptist life in the United States, the events of the 1980s have become one of the most defining events in the latter half of the twentieth century.[4]

While Binkley may have been expelled from the convention in 1992 in large part due to the changes that took place in the SBC throughout the 1980s, the church had long stopped centering the SBC as its primary denominational body. This is not to say that the expulsion was not a significant event or that the church completely ignored the developments of the 1980s, but rather that the slow and methodical rise of conservatives within key leadership positions in Southern Baptist life did not occupy Binkley's focus. Since the 1970s, the congregation had been cultivating relationships outside of Southern Baptist life within American Baptist circles. At the congregational level in the 1980s, Binkley was far more concerned about building its new sanctuary and what this meant for its identity in the local community. As a progressive, ecumenical, college-town congregation, Binkley had never been exceedingly invested in Southern Baptist life.[5]

While denominational affiliation for many people in the United States became less and less important within American religious life beginning in the latter half of the twentieth century, Binkley continued to nurture relationships with denominational and para-denominational bodies. While the church may not have found community within the SBC, Binkley cultivated partnerships within regional, national, and international groups like the American Baptist Churches of the South (ABCOTS), the Alliance of Baptists (AOB), the Association of Welcoming and Affirming Baptists (AWAB), the Baptist Peace Fellowship of North America (BPFNA), and the North Carolina Council of Churches (NCCC). In leaving the highly centralized and hierarchical SBC, Binkley and other like-minded congregations came to affiliate with a wider array of organizations, resembling early-nineteenth-century Baptists who organized around various societies. As historian

Bill Leonard writes, these nineteenth-century Baptists worried that too much denominational connection "would undermine the autonomy of local congregations and contribute to the growth of a dreaded Baptist hierarchy."[6] For Binkley, this nineteenth-century Baptist concern was justified as the hierarchy and growing conservatism of the SBC proved limiting for the progressive congregation. Instead, this network of progressive Baptist and ecumenical organizations helped provide Binkley religious identity and denominational support during its expulsion from the SBC at a time when denominationalism was on the decline, demonstrating how denominational groups, despite their declining influence, continue to wield some power and influence at the congregational level.[7]

As conservative evangelicals across the denominational spectrum, including many Southern Baptists, sought out political power within the confines of the Republican Party, the history of Binkley reveals a different relationship between progressive Christianity and the Democratic Party in the latter half of the twentieth century and early twenty-first century. While throughout its history Binkley counted numerous politicians and activists among its members, as a religious community, its influence in political life was limited. That is not to suggest that its political influence was nonexistent. The congregation was well respected for its inclusiveness as well as its commitments to the local community, and Binkley knew how to utilize the levels of local government to push for change on a variety of issues. Most often the church's priorities aligned best with the Democratic Party, but the congregation remained focused on issues rather than partisanship. Even Democrats, like Governor Jim Hunt, were not always in alignment with the majority of Binkley's membership on issues like the death penalty. Instead of seeking political power within the sphere of Democratic political life as conservative evangelicals had within the Republican Party, the church remained an institution on the periphery of Democratic life committed more to its outsider moral authority than its insider political influence.

As much as this is a story about a singular institution, enmeshed within this narrative about a particular community of faith is also a story about its pastoral leadership, and particularly the leadership of its founding pastor, Bob Seymour, who passed away on October 11, 2020. Many members of the congregation and much of the local Chapel Hill community remember Seymour as a maverick local Baptist pastor who challenged the status quo of the Jim Crow South. For many within Binkley's membership, he was the reason they joined. He offered a progressive vision that resonated with Binkley members and pushed the congregation to live into its commitments to justice and equality in Chapel Hill.

At the same time, Seymour is more than a caricatured progressive pastor. His life was more complicated. As he wrote in his memoir, "Indoctrination in racial differences began for me from the day of my birth . . . White supremacy reigned supreme. As you learned the protocol, the system seemed to run smoothly and for the benefit of all. You become a victim of cultural osmosis from which there is no escape and no visible exception."[8] Throughout his life, Seymour strove to unlearn and resist the temptation to fall back on what his childhood had taught him about the world and his place in it as a white, heterosexual man. While he highlighted his "indoctrination in racial differences," his childhood taught him much about differences around gender, class, sexuality, and religion as well. At times in his life, he successfully pushed beyond the boundaries of his upbringing to understand human relationships and the wider world in new ways. There were other times, however, when he was unsuccessful in this pursuit.

Seymour provided Binkley with vision and energy at a time when the congregation was not even a year old. He animated the church's progressive spirit and pushed its membership to fight for a more equitable and just Chapel Hill community. As Binkley grew and matured, however, the congregation that Seymour helped bring into being began to outpace its first pastor. His understanding and approach to pastoral leadership became a point of contestation within the congregation as some members came to see him as too untrusting and autocratic. Seymour's decision to remain a member of Binkley following his retirement also created challenges for subsequent ministers. He embodied so much of Binkley's past that both he and the congregation had to work to ensure that he did not distract from the congregation's future.

Binkley grew beyond Seymour. This is not to suggest that his influence became obsolete, but rather that the congregation developed an identity apart from its first pastor. This adjustment and transition within the congregation was not always smooth. At times Seymour struggled to let go of the power and authority he once held in the congregation. One could craft a narrative in which Seymour was a one-dimensional, heroic figure who helped establish Binkley's progressive reputation in Chapel Hill; one could also craft a narrative of Seymour as a retired minister clinging to his former pulpit. Neither provides a satisfying or complex picture of the most influential figure in the history of Binkley Memorial Baptist Church. Seymour was deeply relational and committed to the people he pastored. His unyielding devotion and passion for Binkley was in turn reflected in the congregation's devotion and passion for its work and ministry.

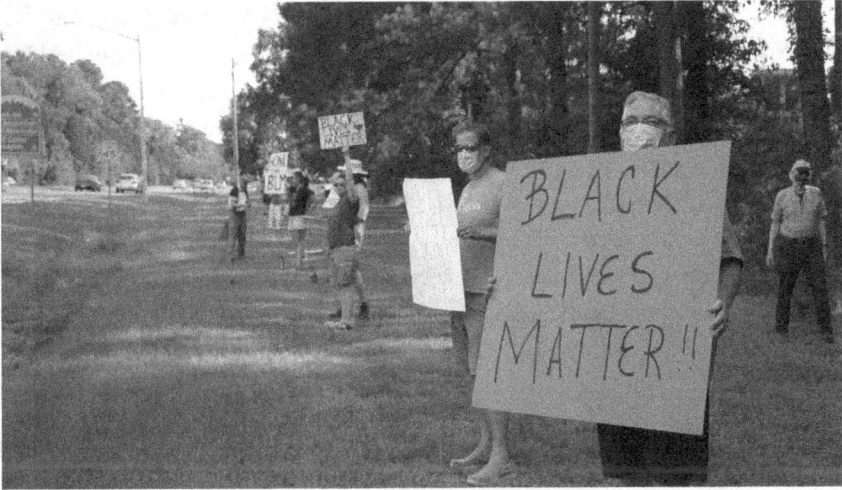

Binkley Pastor Marcus McFaul holds a Black Lives Matter sign at one of the church's Black Lives Matter vigils in 2020.

Binkley's work and ministry continues beyond the history and analysis of this study. Rather than write up and into the present moment, this project keeps a measure of historical distance between its analysis of the congregation and the present day. In 2018, the congregation celebrated its sixtieth anniversary, and in that year, Binkley called its fifth senior pastor, Marcus McFaul. Future historians both inside and outside the congregation will find in this period a church deeply committed to issues of climate change, immigration, the rights of LGBTQ persons, economic inequality, and racial justice. The challenges of the coronavirus pandemic drastically changed congregational life in the United States generally but also at Binkley. The pandemic coupled with the murder of George Floyd, an unarmed Black man in Minneapolis, and the ensuing racial unrest in the summer of 2020 led the congregation to begin hosting a series of Black Lives Matter vigils. These weekly and later monthly events sought to keep the issue of racial justice in focus at the church and in the local community. While this study highlights the congregation's challenges in forging an intersectional approach to its life and ministry, many congregants today push the church to think in these terms.

Binkley reveals much about the diversity and complexity of religious life generally and Baptist life specifically in the United States. The church resists the religious categorizations of "evangelical" and "mainline" while complicating simplistic understandings of what constitutes a "Baptist" church. It operates as a case study for understanding the unique challenges that face progressive congregations seeking to live into a theological perspective that welcomes all people regardless of their background and identity. Such acute and specific challenges provide ways for thinking about congregational life more broadly and how church bodies navigate differences of thought among membership and grow beyond their founding era. While Olin T. Binkley Memorial Baptist Church may not be the typical Baptist congregation, its history, ministry, and voice within Chapel Hill, North Carolina, make a unique and important contribution to the landscape of America's Baptists.

Notes

Introduction

1. William Meade Prince, *The Southern Part of Heaven* (New York: Rinehart & Company, Inc., 1950); Cecil Johnson, review of *The Southern Part of Heaven,* William Meade Johnson, *Journal of Southern History* 16, no. 3 (August 1950): 382–83.

2. John K. Chapman, "Black Freedom and the University of North Carolina at Chapel Hill, 1793–1960," (PhD diss., Univ. of North Carolina at Chapel Hill, 2006), 7.

3. Prince, *The Southern Part of Heaven,* quoted in Mike Ogle, "The Southern Part of Heaven: A Confederate Monument Still Standing," *Stone Walls,* October 1, 2020, https://stonewalls.substack.com/p/the-southern-part-of-heaven.

4. Ogle, "The Southern Part of Heaven."

5. See Charles Howard Hopkins, *The Rise of the Social Gospel in American Protestantism, 1865–1915* (New Haven, CT: Yale Univ. Press, 1940); Paul Carter, *The Decline and Revival of the Social Gospel* (Ithaca, NY: Cornell Univ. Press, 1956); Donald Meyer, *The Protestant Search for Political Realism, 1919–1941,* 2nd ed. (Middletown, CT: Wesleyan Univ. Press, 1988); Richard M. Gamble, *The War for Righteousness: Progressive Christianity, the Great War, and the Rise of the Messianic Nation* (Wilmington, DE: Intercollegiate Studies Institute, 2014); Heath Carter, *Union Made: Working People and the Rise of Social Christianity in Chicago* (New York: Oxford Univ. Press, 2015); Christopher H. Evans, *The Social Gospel in American Religion: A History* (New York: New York Univ. Press, 2017); Cara Burnidge, *A Peaceful Conquest: Woodrow Wilson, Religion, and the New World Order* (Chicago: Univ. of Chicago Press, 2016).

6. "Liberal Protestantism" is a complex, broad, and not altogether easily defined category. I follow in the tradition of William Hutchison and understand this group to be intent upon the "adaptation of religious ideas to modern culture," holding closely to the beliefs that "God is immanent in human culture" and "human society is moving toward realization . . . of the Kingdom of God." See William Hutchison, *The Modernist Impulse in American Protestantism* (Durham, NC: Duke Univ. Press, 1976). Other informative works on liberal Protestantism include David Hollinger, *After Cloven Tongues of Fire: Protestant Liberalism in Modern American History* (Princeton, NJ: Princeton Univ. Press, 2013);

Leigh E. Schmidt and Sally M. Promey, *American Religious Liberalism* (Bloomington: Univ. of Indiana Press, 2012); Leigh E. Schmidt, *Restless Souls: The Making of American Spirituality* (Berkeley: Univ. of California Press, 2012); Matthew Hedstrom, *The Rise of Liberal Religion: Book Culture and American Spirituality in the Twentieth Century* (New York: Oxford Univ. Press, 2013); Carter, *Union Made*; and Mark Wild, *Renewal: Liberal Protestants and the American City After World War II* (Chicago: Univ. of Chicago Press, 2019).

7. Peter Carman interview with the author, March 3, 2021.

8. For more on the Southern liberal Christian tradition see Jarod Roll, *Spirit of Rebellion: Labor and Religion in the New Cotton South* (Urbana: Univ. of Illinois Press, 2010); Elna C. Green, "*The Master-Word*: Lily Hardy Hammond and the Social Gospel in the South," *Journal of Southern Religion* 15 (2013): http://jsreligion.org/issues/vol15/green .html; Andrew McNeill Canady, *Willis Duke Weatherford: Race, Religion, and Reform in the American South* (Lexington: Univ. Press of Kentucky, 2016); for scholarship on the Black liberal Christianity that shaped the civil rights movement see Andrew Manis, *A Fire You Can't Put Out: The Civil Rights Life of Birmingham's Reverend Fred Shuttlesworth* (Tuscaloosa: Univ. of Alabama Press, 2001); David Chappell, *A Stone of Hope: Prophetic Religion and the Death of Jim Crow* (Chapel Hill: Univ. of North Carolina Press, 2005); for more on the role of white southern liberals during the civil rights movement, see Mark Newman, *Getting Right with God: Southern Baptists and Desegregation, 1945–1995* (Tuscaloosa: Univ. of Alabama Press, 2001); Douglas E. Thompson, *Richmond's Priests and Prophets: Race, Religion, and Social Change in the Civil Rights Era* (Tuscaloosa: Univ. of Alabama Press, 2017); David P. Cline, *From Reconciliation to Revolution: The Student Interracial Ministry, Liberal Christianity, and the Civil Rights Movement* (Chapel Hill: Univ. of North Carolina Press, 2016); David Chappell, *Inside Agitators: White Southerners in the Civil Rights Movement* (Baltimore, MD: Johns Hopkins Univ. Press, 1994); for work on progressive evangelical traditions see David Swartz, *Moral Minority: The Evangelical Left in an Age of Conservatism* (Philadelphia: Univ. of Pennsylvania Press, 2012); Brantley Gasaway, *Progressive Evangelicals and the Pursuit of Social Justice* (Chapel Hill: Univ. of North Carolina Press, 2014).

9. Peter Carman email message to author, February 10, 2021; Carman served as pastor from 2009 to 2014 and recalled some congregants being frustrated that he was not evangelical enough.

10. David King argues similarly in his study of the evangelical humanitarian organization World Vision in his work *God's Internationalists: World Vision and the Age of Evangelical Humanitarianism* (Philadelphia: Univ. of Pennsylvania Press, 2019).

11. For an example of a larger volume see Douglas Weaver, *Second to None: A History of the Second-Ponce de Leon Baptist Church* (Nashville, TN: Baptist History and Heritage Society, 2004).

12. Alverta Wright, *Not Here by Chance: The Story of Oakhurst Baptist Church Decatur, Georgia*, vol. I, *1913–1988* (Decatur, GA: Oakhurst Baptist Church, 1988); Alverta Wright, *Not Here by Chance: The Story of Oakhurst Baptist Church Decatur, Georgia*, vol. II, *1988–1993* (Decatur, GA: Oakhurst Baptist Church, 1993).

13. Margaret Hickerson Emery, *The First Hundred Years: A History of the Tabernacle Baptist Church of Richmond, Virginia* (Richmond, VA: Tabernacle Baptist Church, 1991), vii; Emery, another congregational member, published the work first started by Eudora Thomas, who died before completing her research and writing.

14. Marion Arthur Ellis, *By a Dream Possessed: Myers Park Baptist Church* (Charlotte, NC: Myers Park Baptist Church, 1997).

15. Mercer University Press, in particular, has published numerous works in Baptist congregational studies, including Douglas Weaver and Aaron Weaver, *Different and Distinctive But Nevertheless Baptist. A History of Northminster Baptist Church, Jackson, MS* (Macon, GA: Mercer Univ. Press, 2018); Glenn Jonas, *A Cloud of Witnesses from the Heart of the City: First Presbyterian Church, Raleigh, 1816–2016* (Macon, GA: Mercer Univ. Press, 2016); Glenn Jonas, *Nurturing the Vision: First Baptist Church, Raleigh, 1812–2012* (Macon, GA: Mercer Univ. Press, 2012); Bruce Gourley, *A Journey of Faith and Community: The Story of the First Baptist Church of Augusta, Georgia* (Macon, GA: Mercer Univ. Press, 2017).

16. Genna Rae McNeil et al., *Witness: Two Hundred Years of African-American Faith and Practice at the Abyssinian Baptist Church of Harlem, New York* (Grand Rapids, MI: Eerdmans Press, 2013); Peter Paris et al., *The History of Riverside Church in the City of New York* (New York: New York Univ. Press, 2004).

17. Weaver, *Second to None*, 12.

18. Ibid.

19. See Gourley, *A Journey of Faith and Community,* and Jonas, *A Cloud of Witnesses*, which respectively detail the origins of Baptist and Presbyterian life and theology.

20. David B. Marshall, "The Return of Denominational History," *Acadiensis* 39, no. 2 (2010): 121; Amy Koehlinger and Jeannine Hill Fletcher, "Pursuing a Field of Critical Catholic Studies," *American Catholic Studies* 125, no. 3 (Fall 2014): 6.

21. Carol Kammen, "How to Write a Congregational History," *Journal of Presbyterian History* 91, no. 2 (2013): 56–67.

22. Kammen, "How to Write a Congregational History," 56–67.

23. Institutional histories generally have the capacity to more thoroughly integrate the wider social and historical context into their narratives. See T. Laine Scales and Melody Maxwell, *Doing the Word: Southern Baptists' Carver School of Church Social Work and Its Predecessors, 1907–1997* (Knoxville: Univ. of Tennessee Press, 2019).

24. James Wellman, "Turning Word into Flesh: Congregational History as American Religious History," *Journal of Presbyterian History* 91, no. 2 (2013): 75–76.

25. See works including David Hall, *World of Wonder Days of Judgment: Popular Religious Belief in Early New England* (Cambridge, MA: Harvard Univ. Press, 1989). Leigh Schmidt, *Holy Fairs: Scotland and the Making of American Revivalism* (Grand Rapids, MI: Eerdmans, 2001); David Hall, ed., *Lived Religion in America: Toward a History of Practice* (Princeton, NJ: Princeton Univ. Press, 1997).

26. Robert Orsi, *The Madonna of 115th Street: Faith and Community in Italian Harlem*, 3rd ed. (New Haven, CT: Yale Univ. Press, 1988), xxxvii. See also Orsi, *Thank You, St. Jude: Women's Devotion to the Patron Saint of Hopeless Causes* (New Haven, CT: Yale Univ. Press, 1996). This work also provides a helpful framework for thinking about the relationship between lived religion and congregational histories. While focused on the popular Roman Catholic practices of devotion to St. Jude, the work emerges out of the history of Our Lady of Guadalupe Church in Chicago.

27. Nancy Ammerman, *Studying Lived Religion: Contexts and Practices* (New York: New York Univ. Press, 2021), 7.

28. See Mark Chaves, *Congregations in America* (Cambridge, MA: Harvard Univ. Press, 2004); Nancy Ammerman et al., *Studying Congregations: A New Handbook* (Nashville, TN: Abingdon Press, 1998).

29. See Amanda Porterfield, *Corporate Spirit: Religion and the Rise of the Modern Corporation* (New York: Oxford Univ. Press, 2018).

30. Robert Orsi, *Between Heaven and Earth: The Religious Worlds People Make and the Scholars who Study Them* (Princeton, NJ: Princeton Univ. Press, 2004), 5–6.

31. Orsi, *The Madonna of 115th Street*, xi.

32. Kate Wagoner Maynard, "At Binkley Church I learned . . . ," in *Binkley Memories: The First 50 Years 1958–2008*. This collection of essays and reflections was compiled at the fiftieth anniversary and produced by the church. Maynard wrote that at Binkley she learned, "Potlucks are my favorite meal, and no one makes deviled eggs quite like southerners."

33. Russell T. McCutcheon, *Critics Not Caretakers: Redescribing the Public Study of Religion* (New York: SUNY Press, 2001); Michael Slater, "Can One Be a Critical Caretaker?," *Method and Theory in the Study of Religion* 19 (2007): 332–42; Atalia Omer, "Can a Critic Be a Caretaker too? Religion, Conflict, and Conflict Transformation," *Journal of the American Academy of Religion* 79, no. 2 (2011): 459–96; Russell T. McCutcheon, "A Direct Question Deserves a Direct Answer: A Response to Atalia Omer's 'Can a Critic Be a Caretaker too?,'" *Journal of the American Academic of Religion* 80, no. 4 (2012): 1077–82; K. Merinda Simmons, "Regulating Identities: The Silences of Critical Caretaking," *Method and Theory in the Study of Religion* 25, Issues 4–5 (2013): 362–81.

34. "Richard O. Whitaker, Binkley Member 1958–1980," in *Binkley Memories: The First 50 Years 1958–2008*.

35. Robert Seymour, "Our Story, History," box 31, Robert E. Seymour Papers #4554, Southern Historical Collection, Wilson Library, Univ. of North Carolina at Chapel Hill.

36. "Don Freeman, Binkley Charter Member," in *Binkley Memories: The First 50 Years 1958–2008.*

37. Alison Greene, "Reckoning with Southern Baptist Histories," *Southern Cultures* 25, no. 3 (2019): 46–67.

38. Seth Dowland, *Family Values and the Rise of the Christian Right* (Philadelphia: Univ. of Pennsylvania Press, 2015); Marie Griffith, *Moral Combat: How Sex Divided American Christians and Fractured American Politics* (New York: Basic Books, 2017).

39. See Daniel K. Williams, *God's Own Party: The Making of the Christian Right* (New York: Oxford Univ. Press, 2010); Darren Dochuck, *From Bible Belt to Sunbelt: Plain-Folk Religion, Grassroots Politics, and the Rise of Evangelical Conservatism* (New York: W. W. Norton, 2012); Angie Maxwell and Todd Shields, *The Long Southern Strategy: How Chasing White Voters in the South Changed American Politics* (New York: Oxford Univ. Press, 2019). These and additional works can obscure how the Democratic Party and its candidates also invoke religion in a myriad of ways. See David Weiss, ed., *What Democrats Talk About When They Talk about God: Religious Communication in Democratic Party Politics* (Lanham, MD: Lexington Books, 2010); Ruth Braunstein, ed., *Religion and Progressive Activism: New Stories about Faith and Politics* (New York: New York Univ. Press, 2017).

1. Founding a College-Town Church

1. "Getting to Know Binkley: Frequently Asked Questions," Binkley Memorial Baptist Church, accessed February 11, 2020, http://www.binkleychurch.org/about/index/faq.

2. Thomas Kidd, *Who Is An Evangelical? The History of a Movement in Crisis* (New Haven, CT: Yale Univ. Press, 2019), 9.

3. This four-part definition is known as the Bebbington Quadrilateral. See David Bebbington's *Evangelicalism in Modern Britain: A History from the 1730s to the 1980s* (London: Routledge, 1989).

4. For the addition of the Holy Spirit into the Bebbington Quadrilateral, see Thomas Kidd, *The Great Awakening: The Roots of Evangelical Christianity in Colonial America* (New Haven, CT: Yale Univ. Press, 2007); Timothy E. W. Gloege, *Guaranteed Pure: The Moody Bible Institute, Business, and the Making of Modern Evangelicalism* (Chapel Hill: Univ. of North Carolina Press, 2015), 12–13. Gloege suggests that conservative evangelicals might be better defined through a type of aesthetics emerging out of mass-marketing strategies.

5. Kidd, *Who Is An Evangelical?*, 2.

6. See Brantley Gasaway, *Progressive Evangelicals and the Pursuit of Social Justice* (Chapel Hill: Univ. of North Carolina Press, 2014); David Schwartz, *Moral Minority: The Evangelical Left in the Age of Conservatism* (Philadelphia: Univ. of Pennsylvania Press, 2012). Both Gasaway and Schwartz address the rise of a more progressive or left-leaning evangelical. Binkley's founding precedes the movement both scholars discuss, and while the congregation holds similar progressive agendas, the label is not particularly accurate.

7. Walter Shurden, "The Southern Baptist Synthesis: Is it Cracking?," in *Not An Easy Journey: Some Transitions in Baptist Life* (Macon, GA: Mercer Univ. Press, 2005), 200–215. Shurden identifies the Charleston Tradition, the Sandy Creek Tradition, the Georgia Tradition, and the Tennessee Tradition.

8. Andrew Smith highlights this tension well in his work *Fundamentalism, Fundraising, and the Transformation of the Southern Baptist Convention, 1919–1925* (Knoxville: Univ. of Tennessee Press, 2016).

9. See Malkhaz Songulashvili, *Evangelical Christian Baptists in Georgia: The History and Transformation of a Free Church Tradition* (Waco, TX: Baylor Univ. Press, 2015).

10. A location can shape a congregation in numerous ways. Sometimes a congregation may even resist the elements of their local context, choosing to see themselves at odds with the world around them. Such resistance emphasizes how important location and context are in shaping congregations.

11. Blake Gumprecht, *The American College Town* (Boston: Univ. of Massachusetts Press, 2008), 20.

12. See Andrew Hibel and Kelly A. Cherwin, "Hidden Opportunities and Challenges in the College Town Job Market," in *The New American College Town: Designing Effective Campus and Community Partnerships,* ed. James Martin and James E. Samels & Associates (Baltimore, MD: Johns Hopkins Univ. Press, 2019), 188; See also John Thelin, *A History of American Higher Education*, 2nd ed. (Baltimore, MD: Johns Hopkins Univ. Press, 2011).

13. Gumprecht, *The American College Town*, 1; some scholars have suggested that college towns range in the degree to which the college or university influences their local context, and some schools can even be rather disconnected from the local town. James Martin and James E. Samels, "The New American College Town," in *The New American College Town*.

14. Gumprecht, *The American College Town*, 13.

15. Ibid., 4.

16. Martin and Samels, "The New American College Town," 6.

17. Ibid., 7.

18. See Charles J. Holden, *The New Southern University: Academic Freedom and Liberalism at UNC* (Louisville: Univ. Press of Kentucky, 2012), 1–24.

19. Holden, *The New Southern University*.

20. William Snider, *Light on the Hill: A History of the University of North Carolina at Chapel Hill* (Chapel Hill: Univ. of North Carolina Press, 1992), 211.

21. James Atwater, interviewed by Jennifer Nardone, February 28, 2001, K-0201, Southern Oral History Program Collection (#4007), Southern Historical Collection, Louis Round Wilson Special Collections Library, UNC-Chapel Hill.

22. See John K. Chapman, "Black Freedom and the University of North Carolina at Chapel Hill, 1793–1960," (PhD diss., Univ. of North Carolina at Chapel Hill, 2006).

23. Snider, *Light on the Hill*, 202–37.

24. "Junius Scales, Communist Sent to U.S. Prison, Dies at 82," *New York Times,* August 7, 2002.

25. See Mark A. Sheft, "The End of the Smith Act Era: A Legal and Historical Analysis of Scales v. United States," *American Journal of Legal History* 36, no. 2 (1992): 164–202; "Junius Scales, Communist Sent to U.S. Prison, Dies at 82," *New York Times,* August 7, 2002.

26. Daphne Athas, *Chapel Hill in Plain Sight: Notes from the Other Side of the Tracks* (Hillsborough, NC: Eno Publishers, 2010), 144.

27. Sheft, "The End of the Smith Act Era," 177; Junius Irving Scales and Richard Nickson, *Cause at Heart: A Former Communist Remembers* (Athens: Univ. of Georgia Press, 1987).

28. "University of North Carolina Welcomes New Student Secretary," *Biblical Recorder,* February 13, 1946; "New Notes," *Biblical Recorder,* June 11, 1947; "Baptist State Convention," *Biblical Recorder,* December 1, 1948.

29. J. C. Herrin, "A piece of Baptist History," *Biblical Recorder,* April 26, 1952.

30. Scales and Nickson, *Cause at Heart.*

31. Federal Bureau of Investigation, "Julius Irving Scales," CE 100–607, Charlotte, NC, December 12, 1953.

32. See Michael McVicar, "Apostles of Deceit: Ecumenism, Fundamentalism, Surveillance, and the Contested Loyalties of Protest Clergy during the Cold War," in *The FBI and Religion: Faith and Nation Security before and after 9/11,* ed. Sylvester Johnson and Steven Weitzman (Oakland: Univ. of California Press, 2017), 85–107.

33. A. C. Howell, *A History of the Chapel Hill Baptist Church, 1854–1924* (Chapel Hill, NC: n.p., 1945); in the Old South following the Civil War, many Black members left integrated congregations to establish their own congregations. See Charles Irons, "North Carolina's Black Baptists and the Predicament of Emancipation," in *Between Fetters and Freedom: African American Baptists Since Emancipation,* ed. Edward Crowther and Keith Harper (Macon, GA: Mercer Univ. Press, 2015), 28–56.

34. Curtis Freeman, "Let the Doors of the Church Be Open: Martin Luther King, Jr. and the Baptists in Chapel Hill, North Carolina," box 33, Robert E. Seymour Papers #4554, Southern Historical Collection, Wilson Library, Univ. of North Carolina at Chapel Hill. Hereafter abbreviated RSP.

35. Carolyn DuPont, *Mississippi Praying: Southern White Evangelicals and the Civil Rights Movement, 1945–1975* (New York: New York Univ. Press, 2013).

36. "The Reverend J. C. Herrin . . . ," Julius Caesar Herrin, MS615, Z. Smith Reynolds Library Special Collections & Archives.

37. "Parallels Obvious in BSU and Presbyterian 'Probes,'" *Durham Morning Herald,* March 21, 1954.

38. "The Reverend J. C. Herrin . . . ," Julius Caesar Herrin, MS615, Z. Smith Reynolds Library Special Collections & Archives.

39. "Recommendations of Committee Concerning BSU Secretaries," *Biblical Recorder,* April 10, 1954.

40. Blake Gumprecht, *The American College Town,* 13–15.

41. The Yates Baptist Association, North Carolina, Eighth Annual Session (1956), 54, Internet Archive, https://archive.org/details/minutesofsession4956yate/page/n473 /mode/2up.

42. The Yates Baptist Association, North Carolina, Ninth Annual Session (1957), 64, Internet Archive, https://archive.org/details/minutesofsession5760yate.

43. "Bill Moffitt, Binkley founding member," in *Binkley Memories: The First 50 Years 1958–2008.*

44. Courtland Smith, "An Interpretive History of the First Ten Years," in *Essays on the First Fifty Years of the Olin T. Binkley Memorial Baptist Church,* The Olin T. Binkley Papers, box 106, folder 4, Z. Smith Reynolds Library Special Collections & Archives. Hereafter abbreviated OTBP.

45. Anthony W. Allen, "Dr. Olin Trivette Binkley (1908–1999): Pastor, Educator, President of Southeastern Baptist Theological Seminary" (master's thesis, Southeastern Baptist Theological Seminary, 2001), Proquest Dissertation Publishing, 1403711.

46. Allen, "Dr. Olin Trivette Binkley."

47. Henlee Barnette, "Dr. Olin T. Binkley: Saint and Scholar," May 2001, box 20, folder 10, OTBP.

48. This is typified in Reinhold Niebuhr's *Moral Man and Immoral Society* (New York: Charles Scribner's Sons, 1932).

49. Allen, "Dr. Olin Trivette Binkley," 20; Olin Trivette Binkley, "The Antievolution Movement in Relation to Public Education in the United States" (PhD diss., Yale Univ., 1933), Proquest Dissertation Publishing, 9781084831551.

50. Olin T. Binkley, *From Victory Unto Victory* (Nashville, TN: Broadman Press, 1945), 30.

51. Binkley, *From Victory Unto Victory,* 38.

52. Olin T. Binkley, *The Churches and the Social Conscience* (Indianapolis, IN: National Foundation Press, 1948).

53. David Stricklin, *A Genealogy of Dissent: Southern Baptist Protest in the Twentieth Century* (Lexington: Univ. Press of Kentucky, 1999), 24.

54. Binkley, *The Churches and the Social Conscience,* 32–33.

55. Ibid., 34.

56. "June 30, 1958," box 107, folder 5, OTBP.

57. Ibid.

58. Ibid.

59. Olin T. Binkley to Fred Ellis, July 10, 1958, box 107, folder 5, OTBP.

60. "August 4," Olin T. Binkley Journal, box 123, folder 5, OTBP.

61. Dr. Binkley to John T. Wayland, August 8, 1958, box 52, folder 2, OTBP.

62. "The Resolution of Purpose," The Olin T. Binkley Memorial Baptist Church Service of Organization Program, box 106, folder 13, OTBP.

63. Ibid.

64. "The Challenge," September 21, 1958, box 129, folder 12, OTBP.

65. Courtland Smith, "An Interpretive History of the First Ten Years," in *Essays on the First Fifty Years of The Olin T. Binkley Memorial Baptist Church,* box 106, folder 4, OTBP.

66. Snider, *Light on the Hill,* 246–49.

67. Chapman, "Black Freedom and the University of North Carolina," 170–71.

68. "The Affirmation of Faith," The Olin T. Binkley Memorial Baptist Church Service of Organization Program, box 106, folder 13, OTBP.

69. "The Church Covenant," The Olin T. Binkley Memorial Baptist Church Service of Organization Program, box 106, folder 13, OTBP.

70. Annual of the Southern Baptist Convention (1958), 391, Southern Baptist Historical Library and Archives, https://sbhla.org/digital-resources/sbc-annuals/.

71. Robert Seymour, *"Whites Only": A Pastor's Retrospective on Signs of the New South* (Valley Forge, PA: Judson Press, 1991), 77; Art Chansky, *Game Changers: Dean Smith, Charlie Scott, and the Era That Transformed a Southern College Town* (Chapel Hill: Univ. of North Carolina Press, 2016), 33.

72. Courtland Smith, "An Interpretive History of the First Ten Years," in *Essays on the First Fifty Years of The Olin T. Binkley Memorial Baptist Church,* box 106, folder 4, OTBP.

73. "Church History," Mars Hill Baptist, accessed January 19, 2020, https://marshillbc.org/church-history/.

74. "Counties with higher lynching rates have low voter turnout today, SC research finds," *Palmetto Politics,* July 12, 2019, https://www.postandcourier.com/politics/counties-with-higher-lynching-rates-have-low-voter-turnout-today/article_627132ba-9375-11e9-b335-3f61123ae128.html.

75. Seymour, *"Whites Only,"* 12.

76. Ibid., 9.

77. Ibid., 21; Robert Seymour, interviewed by Bruce Kalk, May 21, 1985, C-0020, Southern Oral History Program Collection (#4007), Southern Historical Collection, Louis Round Wilson Special Collections Library, UNC-Chapel Hill.

78. Seymour, *"Whites Only,"* 10–14.

79. Ibid., 16.

80. Ibid., 18; Seymour, interviewed by Kalk, May 21, 1985.

81. Seymour, *"Whites Only,"* 29–34.

82. See Will D. Campbell, *Brother to a Dragonfly* (New York: Continuum International Publishing Group, 1977).

83. Seymour, *"Whites Only,"* 34.

84. Ibid., 35.

85. Ibid., 40.

86. Robert Seymour, "John Gill: Baptist Theologian (1697–1771)" (PhD diss., Univ. of Edinburgh, 1954), 1–2; 313–14.

87. See Marion Arthur Ellis, *By a Dream Possessed: Myers Park Baptist Church* (Charlotte, NC: Myers Park Baptist Church, 1997).

88. Seymour, *"Whites Only,"* 46–47; Ellis, *By a Dream Possessed,* 33–34.

89. Seymour, *"Whites Only,"* 48–56.

90. Robert Seymour, "Introduction . . . ," box 33, RSP.

91. Seymour, *"Whites Only,"* 51, 53, 56.

92. Ibid., 61–66.

93. Ibid., 62–63; Seymour, interviewed by Kalk, May 21, 1985.

94. Robert Seymour, "The Church in a University Community," box 30, RSP.

95. Robert Seymour to Mr. J. W. Moffitt, January 13, 1959, box 33, RSP.

96. Olin T. Binkley to Robert Seymour, October 24, 1958, box 33, RSP; John T. Wayland to Robert Seymour, October 20, 1958, box 33, RSP.

97. Robert Dorr to Robert Seymour, January 20, 1959, box 33, RSP.

98. Charles M Jones to Robert Seymour, January 24, 1959, box 33, RSP.

99. "The Olin T. Binkley Memorial Baptist Church Service of Organization," September 21, 1958, box 106, folder 13, OTBP.

100. "Constitution," September 21, 1958, box 129, folder 12, OTBP.

101. Fred Ellis to Olin Binkley, July 31, 1958, box 107, folder 5, OTBP.

102. The Yates Baptist Association, North Carolina, Tenth Annual Session (1958), 26, Internet Archive, https://archive.org/details/minutesofsession5760yate.

103. The Yates Baptist Association, North Carolina, Eleventh Annual Session (1959), 26, Internet Archive, https://archive.org/details/minutesofsession5760yate.

104. Robert Seymour to Olin T. Binkley, September 2, 1959, box 107, folder 5, OTBP.

105. Olin T. Binkley to Robert Seymour, September 5, 1959, box 107, folder 5, OTBP.

106. "Memorandum Concerning Church Constitution," box 129, folder 12, OTBP.

107. The Yates Baptist Association, North Carolina, Twelfth Annual Session (1960), 28, Internet Archive, https://archive.org/details/minutesofsession5760yate. Warren Carr, pastor of the more progressive Watts Street Baptist Church in Durham, North Carolina, opposed the committee's recommendation.

108. Untitled memo, October 31, 1960, box 107, folder 6, OTBP; the brief document has a handwritten note underneath the text stating, "Olin T. Binkley Sent to Nashville by Ben Fisher on October 31, 1860."

109. Robert Seymour to Olin Binkley, November 4, 1960, box 107, folder 5, OTBP.

110. Olin Binkley to Robert Seymour, November 30, 1960, box 5, folder 107, OTBP; in this letter he sent a check for $150; Olin Binkley to Robert Seymour, September 5, 1959, box 107, folder 5, OTBP.

111. Courtland Smith, "An Interpretive History of the First Ten Years," in *Essays on the first Fifty Years of the Olin T. Binkley Memorial Baptist Church,* box 106, folder 4, OTBP.

2. Town and Gown

1. "Yearbook 1961–1962," reel 2, Binkley Memorial Baptist Church (Chapel Hill, NC) records, CRMF992, Z. Smith Reynolds Library Special Collections & Archives, Wake Forest Univ., Winston-Salem, NC, USA. Hereafter abbreviated BMBCA.

2. Though still predominately white, the congregation sought to find a retreat center that would welcome Black members and any Black guests who might attend. "Report to the Church Council from the Christian Education Committee," January 27, 1962, reel 1, BMBCA.

3. See David Chappell, *A Stone of Hope: Prophetic Religion and the Death of Jim Crow* (Chapel Hill: Univ. of North Carolina Press, 2004); Andrew Manis, *A Fire You Can't Put Out: The Civil Rights Life of Birmingham's Reverend Fred Shuttlesworth* (Birmingham: Univ. of Alabama Press, 2001); Paul Harvey, *Through the Strom, Through the Night: A History of African American Christianity* (Lanham, MD: Roman & Littlefield, 2011); much of this work centers on how Black men utilized religion during the civil rights movement. For more on the way women navigated the role of religion in civil rights, see Courtney Pace, *Freedom Faith: The Womanist Vision of Prathia Hall* (Athens: Univ. of Georgia Press, 2019).

4. See Martin Luther King Jr., *Stride Toward Freedom* (Boston, MA: Beacon Press, 1958).

5. Emblematic of this type of interpretation is John Lee Eighmy, *Churches in Cultural Captivity: A History of the Social Attitudes of Southern Baptists* (Knoxville: Univ. of Tennessee Press, 1972); other scholars, like Sam Hill, a member of Binkley, contended that southern whites were "indifferent" to segregation. See Sam Hill, *Southern Churches in Crisis* (New York: Holt, Reinhart and Winston, 1966).

6. See Kelly J Baker, *The Gospel According to the Klan: The KKK's Appeal to Protestant America, 1915–1930* (Lawrence: Univ. of Kansas Press, 2011); Carolyn DuPont, *Mississippi Praying: Southern White Evangelicals and the Civil Rights Movement* (New York: New York Univ. Press, 2013).

7. Mark Newman, *Getting Right with God: Southern Baptists and Desegregation, 1945–1995* (Tuscaloosa: Univ. of Alabama Press, 2012).

8. For more on the changing political landscape of the 1960s, see Angie Maxwell and Todd Shields, *The Long Southern Strategy: How Chasing White Voters in the South Changed American Politics* (New York: Oxford Univ. Press, 2019); Allen Matusow, *The Unraveling of America: A History of Liberalism in the 1960s*, 2nd ed. (Athens: Univ. of Georgia Press, 2009).

9. Robert Seymour, "The Church in a University Community," box 30, Robert E. Seymour Papers #4554, Southern Historical Collection, Wilson Library, Univ. of North Carolina at Chapel Hill. Hereafter abbreviated RSP.

10. "Don Freeman, Binkley charter member," in *Binkley Memories: The First 50 Years 1958–2008*.

11. "Michael Berkut, founding member," in *Binkley Memories: The First 50 Years 1958–2008*.

12. "Cover the Campus," *Daily Tar Heel,* November 15, 1958.

13. "Lecture Series," *Daily Tar Heel,* February 3, 1960.

14. "Baptists to hear Dr. Ray Dawson," *The Daily Tar Heel,* October 9, 1960.

15. "Yearbook 1960–1961," reel 6, BMBCA.

16. "Yearbook 1961–1962," reel 6, BMBCA; "The Olin T. Binkley Memorial Baptist Church Yearbook 1968," reel 6, BMBCA.

17. "The Olin T. Binkley Memorial Baptist Church Yearbook 1968," reel 6, BMBCA.

18. Larry Enley, "Home Church, Campus Tied By Baptist Student Union," *Daily Tar Heel,* December 7, 1958.

19. "Constitution," reel 6, BMBCA.

20. "Missions Committee Report for Council Meeting," January 19, 1964, reel 2, BMBCA.

21. "Report to Church Council from the Christian Ed. Comm.," October 28, 1964, reel 2, BMBCA.

22. Rebekah J. Kowal, "Staging the Greensboro Sit-Ins," *The Drama Review* 48, no. 4 (2004): 135–54.

23. Howard Lee, *The Courage to Lead: One Man's Journey in Public Service* (Chapel Hill, NC: Cotton Patch Press, 2008), 15.

24. "Dr. Martin Luther King To Speak Here On Monday," *Daily Tar Heel,* May 5, 1960; "Overflow Crowd Attends Speech," *Daily Tar Heel,* May 10, 1960.

25. Robert Seymour, *"Whites Only": A Pastor's Retrospective on Signs of the New South* (Valley Forge, PA: Judson Press, 1991), 81.

26. Seymour, *"Whites Only,"* 81.

27. Curtis Freeman, "Let the Doors of the Church Be Open: Martin Luther King, Jr. and the Baptists in Chapel Hill, North Carolina," box 33, RSP.

28. "NSA Leader Backs Theatre Picket; Chapel Hill Clergy Votes To Boycott," *Daily Tar Heel,* January 8, 1961.

29. Seymour, *"Whites Only,"* 83.

30. "Church Council," October 20, 1963, reel 2, BMBCA.

31. "Report to Binkley Church Council," November 17, 1963, reel 2, BMBCA; "BSU Convention Adopts Korean Work Team Project and Drafts Letter on Race Relations," *Biblical Recorder,* November 9, 1963.

32. Seymour, *"Whites Only,"* 84.

33. "Dear Finance Committee," February 25, 1963, reel 2, BMBCA.

34. For more on the Student Interracial Ministry program, see David Cline, *From Reconciliation to Revolution: The Student Interracial Ministry, Liberal Christianity, and the Civil Rights Movement* (Chapel Hill: The Univ. of North Carolina Press, 2016).

35. Seymour, *"Whites Only,"* 91.

36. "Report to the Church Council from the Christian Education Committee," June 8, 1962, reel 1, BMBCA.

37. "Report to the Church Council from the Christian Education Committee," January 27, 1962, reel 1, BMBCA.

38. Seymour, *"Whites Only,"* 92.

39. "Report to the Church Council from the Christian Education Committee," July 1, 1962, reel 1, BMBCA.

40. James Forbes, "Interracial Ministry Report," box 33, RSP.

41. Seymour, *"Whites Only,"* 91–93.; Cline, *From Reconciliation to Revolution*, 48.

42. "Bert and Diane Adams to Binkley Church," in *Binkley Memories: The First 50 Years 1958–2008.*

43. "Report to the Church Council from the Christian Education Committee," April 7, 1964, reel 2, BMBCA.

44. James Forbes quoted in Cline, *From Reconciliation to Revolution*, 50.

45. Samuel Hill and Robert Torbet, *Baptists North and South: What Keeps Baptists Apart?* (Valley Forge, PA: Judson Press, 1963).

46. Hill and Torbet, *Baptists North and South*, 8.

47. "The Reverend J. C. Herrin . . . ," Julius Caesar Herrin, MS615, Z. Smith Reynolds Library Special Collections & Archives.

48. "A Memorial Service in Celebration of and Thanksgiving for the life of the Reverend J. C. Herrin," July 30, 2009, box 36, RSP; Robert Seymour, "A Personal Reflection Upon the Life and Friendship of J. C. Herrin," box 34, RSP.

49. See "Report of the Diaconate," July 5, 1963, reel 2, BMBCA; "Report of the diaconate," November 17, 1963, reel 2, BMBCA.

50. "Report of the Diaconate," January 5, 1964, reel 2, BMBCA; Watts Street Baptist Church was also an atypical Baptist congregation in the south. Later in 1964, the

congregation would ordain the first woman minister in the Southern Baptist Convention, Addie Davis.

51. "Binkley Bulletin Board," July 15, 1964, reel 3, BMBCA.

52. "Agenda for the Council Meeting," September 22, 1963, reel 2, BMBCA; "Minutes of the October 1, 1968, meeting of the Church Council," October 1, 1968, reel 2, BMBCA.

53. "Memorandum to Jack Whitaker, Fred Ellis, Robert Seymour, Yvonne Williams, and Lee Wagoner," reel 2, BMBCA.

54. "Moderator's Report," November 17, 1963, reel 2, BMBCA; "Church Council," November 17, 1963, reel 2, BMBCA.

55. "The Dedication of The Olin T. Binkley Memorial Baptist Church," September 27, 1964, reel 4, BMBCA.

56. Ibid.

57. Curtis Freeman, "All the Sons of Earth: Carlyle Marney and the Fight Against Prejudice," *Baptist History and Heritage* 44, no. 2 (Spring 2009): 71–84.

58. "Student Affairs Committee Report," October 20, 1963, reel 2, BMBCA.

59. See "Transportation to the Binkley . . . ," *Daily Tar Heel,* September 27, 1964.

60. "Minutes of the Church Council," October 14, 1964, reel 2, BMBCA.

61. "Report of Day Nursery Committee to Olin T. Binkley Baptist Church Council," reel 2, BMBCA; See "Binkley Preschool," Binkley Preschool, accessed July 28, 2020, binkleypreschool.org/about/.

62. Seymour, *"Whites Only,"* 89.

63. Howard Lee interview with author, March 29, 2021.

64. "Local Accommodations Law Proposed," *Daily Tar Heel,* June 13, 1963.

65. "Unpuzzling The Press' Many Whys," *Daily Tar Heel,* February 5, 1964.

66. "200 Protest Core," *Daily Tar Heel,* February 6, 1964.

67. "Shifting the Onus of 'Gradualism,'" *Daily Tar Heel,* February 4, 1964.

68. "Church Council," January 19, 1964, reel 2, BMBCA.

69. "Moderators Report," April 18, 1964, reel 2, BMBCA.

70. In 1964, both Pearl and Bob Seymour's names appeared on a paid advertisement in the *Daily Tar Heel* stating that they supported boycotting businesses refusing service to people based on "race, creed, or national origin." See "A Proclamation," *Daily Tar Heel,* February 28, 1964.

71. Howard Lee interview with author, March 29, 2021.

72. Art Chansky, *Game Changers: Dean Smith, Charlie Scott, And the Era That Transformed a Southern College Town* (Chapel Hill: Univ. of North Carolina Press, 2016), 80–81; Robert Seymour, *"Whites Only,"* 86–87; see also Dwana Leah Waugh, "From Forgotten to Remembered: The Long Process of School Desegregation in Chapel Hill, North Carolina, and Prince Edward County, Virginia" (PhD diss., Univ. of North Carolina, 2012).

73. Robert Seymour, interviewed by Jim Douglas, March 18, 2011, transcript R0507, Southern Oral History Program Collection, Univ. of North Carolina at Chapel Hill; Seymour, *"Whites Only,"* 87.

74. "New City Officers to be Sworn in Monday Night," *Daily Tar Heel,* May 5, 1961.

75. "Negro Students May Attend Theatre: Desegregation moves along in town," *Daily Tar Heel,* September 19, 1961.

76. Waugh, "From Forgotten to Remembered," 155.

77. Dean Smith, *A Coach's Life: My 40 Years in College Basketball* (New York: Random House, 1999), 95.

78. Smith, *A Coach's Life,* 1–7.

79. Ibid., 93.

80. Ibid., 93–94.

81. "Yearbook 1960–1961," reel 6, BMBCA.

82. Smith, *A Coach's Life,* 95–96; Seymour, *"Whites Only,"* 103; Chansky, *Game Changers,* 34–35.

83. "Long Ago, He Won the Big One," *Sports Illustrated,* November 29, 1982, 118.

84. Smith, *A Coach's Life,* 95–96; Seymour, *"Whites Only,"* 103; Chansky, *Game Changers,* 34–35.

85. Smith, *A Coach's Life,* 97.

86. Chansky, *Game Changers,* 53–54.

87. Ibid., 71–74.

88. Ibid., 74–75.

89. Smith, *A Coach's Life,* 102; Chansky, *Game Changers,* 74–75.

90. Lee, *The Courage to Lead,* 103.

91. See Jeffrey Scholes, "Religion, Race, and Sports," in *The Oxford Handbook of Religion and Race in American History,* ed. Paul Harvey and Kathryn Gin Lum (New York: Oxford Univ. Press, 2018), 304–17. Andrew Gardner, "Religion, Sport, and Congregation: Dean Smith as Basketball Coach and Baptist Churchman," *Baptist History and Heritage* 56, no. 3 (2021): 65–80.

92. Chansky, *Game Changers,* 166.

93. Lee, *The Courage to Lead,* xvi–xvii.

94. Ibid., 102.

95. Ibid., 102–3.

96. Howard Lee interview with the author, March 29, 2021.

97. Chansky, *Game Changers,* 150; Seymour, *"Whites Only,"* 124; Lee, *The Courage to Lead,* 12–13.

98. Lee interview with the author, March 29, 2021.

99. Lee, *The Courage to Lead,* 15–16.

100. "Binkley Bulletin Board," March 17, 1965, reel 3, BMBCA.

101. Lee, *The Courage to Lead,* 17–19; Billy E. Barnes interviewed by Elizabeth Gritter, November 6, 2003, transcript O-0038, Southern Oral History Program Collection, Univ. of North Carolina at Chapel Hill.

102. Anne Barnes interviewed by Kathryn Nasstrom, January 30, 1989, transcript C-0049, Southern Oral History Program Collection, Univ. of North Carolina at Chapel Hill.

103. "Chapel Hill Negro to Run for Mayor," *Raleigh News and Observer,* April 1, 1969; "Lee Outlines Campaign Proposals," *Daily Tar Heel,* April 2, 1969.

104. Lee, *The Courage to Lead,* 20–25.

105. Lee interview with the author, March 29, 2021.

106. "We Endorse," *Daily Tar Heel,* May 6, 1969.

107. Chansky, *Game Changers,* 153–55.

108. Waugh, "From Forgotten to Remembered," 1–8.

109. "Binkley Newsletter," March 18, 1964, reel 3, BMBCA; "Binkley Bulletin Board," July 15, 1964, reel 3, BMBCA.

110. Joe and Eva Clontz interview with the author, March 22, 2021.

111. Lee interview with the author, March 29, 2021.

112. Joe and Eva Clontz interview with the author, March 22, 2021.

113. See Elizabeth Flowers and Karen Seat, eds., *A Marginal Majority: Women, Gender, and a Reimagining of Southern Baptists* (Knoxville: Univ. of Tennessee Press, 2020); Melody Maxwell and Laine Scales, *Doing the Word: Southern Baptists' Carver School of Church Social Work and Its Predecessors, 1907–1997* (Knoxville: Univ. of Tennessee Press, 2019); Melody Maxwell, *The Woman I Am: Southern Baptist Women's Writings, 1906–2006* (Tuscaloosa: Univ. of Alabama Press, 2014).

114. Eva Clontz email message to author, March 22, 2021.

115. This dynamic of women's work as collective rather than individual has been observed in other historical works, like Ellen Blue, *St. Mark's and the Social Gospel: Methodist Women and Civil Rights in New Orleans, 1895–1965* (Knoxville: Univ. of Tennessee Press, 2011).

116. "The Inter-Church Council for Social Service," in *1971–1972 Director and Yearbook Olin T. Binkley Memorial Baptist Church,* reel 6, BMBCA; "Historical Timeline," Interfaith Council, accessed May 11, 2021, https://www.ifcweb.org/about/history; the organization's website recounts the work of seven unnamed local woman who founded the organization, demonstrating the ways in which women's religious work operated and functioned differently during the 1960s than the religious work of men.

117. "Yearbook 1961–1962," reel 6, BMBCA.

118. "Binkley Baptist Women Will Meet," *Daily Tar Heel,* December 11, 1965.

119. "Pauline Binkley Cheek, Binkley member 1959–64," in *Binkley Memories: The First 50 Years 1958–2008.*

120. Seymour, *"Whites Only,"* 116.

121. "Minutes of the June 4, 1958, meeting of the Church Council," June 4, 1968, reel 2, BMBCA; "Church Council Meeting," June 3, 1969, reel 2, BMBCA; "Church Council Meeting," October 7, 1969, reel 2, BMBCA; "The Church Council was called to order," July 7, 1970, reel 2, BMBCA; "Help Needed," *The Daily Tar Heel,* July 24, 1969.

122. Seymour, *"Whites Only,"* 135.

123. "Kate Maynard Wagoner," in *Binkley Memories: The First 50 Years 1958–2008*; "Lee Wagoner," in *Binkley Memories: The First 50 Years 1958–2008*.

124. "The first meeting of the new church council . . . ," May 18, 1970, reel 2, BMBCA.

3. The Rise and Fall of a College-Town Church

1. "The Diaconate of the Olin T. Binkley Memorial Baptist Church," November 30, 1970, reel 2, Binkley Memorial Baptist Church (Chapel Hill, NC) records, CRMF992, Z. Smith Reynolds Library Special Collections & Archives, Wake Forest Univ., Winston-Salem, NC, USA. Hereafter abbreviated BMBCA.

2. Robert Seymour, "Commencement Address to the Graduating Class of Chapel Hill High School," 1971, box 31, Robert E. Seymour Papers #4554, Southern Historical Collection, Wilson Library, Univ. of North Carolina at Chapel Hill. Hereafter abbreviated RSP.

3. See Robert Wuthnow, *The Restructuring of American Religion* (Princeton, NJ: Princeton Univ. Press, 1988).

4. See works like Daniel K. Williams, *God's Own Party: The Making of the Christian Right* (New York: Oxford Univ. Press, 2012); Randall Balmer, *Thy Kingdom Come: How the Religious Right Distorts Faith and Threatens America* (New York: Basic Books, 2007); for a documentary history of the rise of the religious right, see Matthew Avery Sutton, *Jerry Falwell and the Rise of the Religious Right: A Brief History with Documents* (Boston, MA: Bedford/St. Martins, 2012).

5. L. Benjamin Rolsky, *The Rise and Fall of the Religious Left: Politics, Television, and Popular Culture in the 1970s and Beyond* (New York: Columbia Univ. Press, 2019), 6.

6. Robert Seymour, "All in the Family," May 7, 2000, box 30, RSP.

7. See Rolsky, *The Rise and Fall of the Religious Left.*

8. For more on the idea of the evangelical left, see David Swartz, *Moral Minority: The Evangelical Left in an Age of Conservatism* (Philadelphia: Univ. of Pennsylvania Press, 2012); Brantley W. Gasaway, *Progressive Evangelicals and the Pursuit of Social Justice* (Chapel Hill: Univ. of North Carolina Press, 2014).

9. "The first meeting of the new church council was called to order . . . ," May 18, 1970, reel 2, BMBCA.

10. "The Church Council," January 8, 1974, reel 2, BMBCA.

11. "Church Conference," April 1, 1973, reel 2, BMBCA.

12. See Robert Wuthnow, *The Restructuring of American Religion.*

13. "Minutes of the October Meeting of the Diaconate," October 1973, reel 2, BMBCA.

14. For more on Graham's legacy and ability to adapt his messaging toward the wider culture see Grant Wacker, *America's Pastor: Billy Graham and the Shaping of a Nation* (Cambridge, MA: Harvard Univ. Press, 2014), 28.

15. "Meeting of the Diaconate," December 3, 1973, reel 2, BMBCA.

16. "Meeting of Diaconate," April 12, 1973, reel 2, BMBCA.

17. "Minutes of Diaconate Meeting," April 4, 1977, reel 2, BMBCA; Robert Seymour to Jim, June 2, 1976, reel 2, BMBCA.

18. Nancy Ammerman, *Baptist Battles: Social Change and Religious Conflict in the Southern Baptist Convention* (New Brunswick, NJ: Rutgers Univ. Press, 1990); Bill Leonard, *God's Last and Only Hope: The Fragmentation of the Southern Baptist Convention* (Grand Rapids, MI: William B. Eerdmans Publishing Company, 1990); David T. Morgan, *The New Crusades, the New Holy Land: Conflict in the Southern Baptist Convention 1969–1991* (Tuscaloosa: Univ. of Alabama Press, 1996); James C. Hefley, *The Truth in Crisis: The Controversy in the Southern Baptist Convention* 5 (Richmond, VA: Hannibal Books, 1990).

19. "Church Council Minutes," December 8, 1980, reel 2, BMBCA. Binkley adopted a statement asking for SBC president Bailey Smith to resign after Smith contended that God did not hear the prayers of Jewish practitioners. The statement Binkley passed was borrowed from Watts Street Baptist Church with one difference. Where Watts Street called Smith to resign with both "regret and sadness," Binkley took out those emotions, simply asking Smith to resign immediately.

20. Andrew Gardner, *Reimagining Zion: A History of the Alliance of Baptists* (Macon, GA: Nurturing Faith, 2015).

21. "Diaconate Minutes," September 14, 1987, reel 2, BMBCA.

22. "Ordinations to the Christian Ministry," *Binkley Memories, The First 50 Years 1958–2008*, 14.

23. "The Church Council," September 4, 1973, reel 2, BMBCA; "Sunday," October 22, 1972, reel 2, BMBCA; "The Church Council," August 29, 1972, reel 2, BMBCA.

24. Robert Seymour to Kathi Wagoner, April 12, 1978, reel 2, BMBCA; "Binkley's History The First Forty Years," BMBCA; Kate Wagoner Maynard, "At Binkley Church I learned . . . ," in *Binkley Memories: The First 50 Years 1958–2008.*

25. "Church Council Meets Monday," November 10, 1980, reel 2, BMBCA.

26. Robert Seymour to Matthew Moffitt, February 8, 1978, reel 3, BMBCA.

27. Robert Seymour to Bill and Hilda Moffitt, February 8, 1978, reel 3, BMBCA.

28. Annual of the Southern Baptist Convention (1971), 72, Southern Baptist Historical Library and Archives, https://sbhla.org/digital-resources/sbc-annuals/.

29. Ralph Elliot, *The Message of Genesis* (Nashville, TN: Broadman Press, 1961); Ralph Elliot, *The Genesis Controversy: A Eulogy for a Great Tradition* (Macon, GA: Mercer Univ. Press, 1992).

30. Lillian Calles Barger, *The World Come of Age: An Intellectual History of Liberation Theology* (New York: Oxford Univ. Press, 2018), 9; See Gustavo Gutierrez, *A Theology of Liberation* (Maryknoll, NY: Orbis Books, 1973); James Cone, *A Black Theology of Liberation* (Maryknoll, NY: Orbis Books, 1970); Mary Daly, *Beyond God the Father: Toward a Philosophy of Women's Liberation* (Boston, MA: Beacon Press, 1973).

31. "Diaconate Minutes," April 16, 1974, reel 2, BMBCA.

32. Robert Seymour, "Is the Guaranteed Annual Income Moral?," sermon, September 8, 1968, Binkley Memorial Baptist Church, Chapel Hill, NC.

33. Seymour, interviewed by Kalk, May 21, 1985, C-0020, Southern Oral History Program Collection (#4007), Southern Historical Collection, Louis Round Wilson Special Collections Library, UNC-Chapel Hill.

34. "Binkley's History he First 40 Years," BMBCA.

35. "Louise Baker, Binkley member since 1976, and Eva Clontz, Binkley member 1966–67 and returned to Binkley in 1971," in *Binkley Memories: The First 50 Years 1958–2008*.

36. "Minutes of Diaconate Meeting," October 4, 1976, reel 2, BMBCA.

37. "Diaconate Meeting," February 7, 1983, reel 2, BMBCA; "Proposal for the Use of Inclusive Language in Worship," June 6, 1983, reel 2, BMBCA.

38. "Proposal for the Use of Inclusive Language in Worship," June 6, 1983, reel 2, BMBCA.

39. "Binkley's History The First 40 Years," BMBCA.

40. See Elizabeth Flowers and Karen Seat, eds., *A Marginal Majority: Women, Gender, and a Reimagining of Southern Baptists* (Knoxville: Univ. of Tennessee Press, 2020).

41. Newsletter, "Southern Baptists for the Family and Equal Rights," vol. 1, no. 2 (October 1981), folder "Southern Baptists for the Family and Equal Rights, 1981–1985," box 7, Resource Center for Women and Ministry in the South records, David M. Rubinstein Rare Book and Manuscript Library, Duke Univ., quoted in Laura Joy Foxworth, "The Spiritual is Political: The Modern Women's Movement and the Transformation of the Southern Baptist Convention" (PhD diss., Univ. of South Carolina-Columbia, 2014), 194.

42. Kate Collins, "The Spiritual is Power," *The Devil's Tale: Dispatches from the David M. Rubenstein Rare Book & Manuscript Library,* November 1, 2012, accessed November 10, 2020, https://blogs.library.duke.edu/rubenstein/2012/11/01/the-spiritual-is-political/.

43. Gardner, *Reimagining Zion*, 42.

44. "Meeting of the Binkley Diaconate," March 5, 1984, reel 2, BMBCA.

45. "Meeting of Binkley Diaconate," January 2, 1984, reel 2, BMBCA.

46. Carol Ripley-Moffitt to Binkley Church, July 25, 2008, in *Binkley Memories: The First 50 Years 1958–2008*.

194 *Notes to Pages 87–92*

47. Robert Seymour, interviewed by Bruce Kalk, May 21, 1985.

48. "Binkley's History The First 40 Years," BMBCA.

49. "Church Council Meeting," January 6, 1970, reel 2, BMBCA.

50. "Church Council Meeting," March 3, 1970, reel 2, BMBCA.

51. "The Church Council was called to order . . . ," July 7, 1970, reel 2, BMBCA; "Abraham David called the September 1st meeting of the Church council to order," September 1, 1970, reel 2, BMBCA.

52. "The Oct 6 meeting of the Church Council," October 6, 1970, reel 2, BMBCA.

53. "Church Council Minutes," March 2, 1971, reel 2, BMBCA.

54. "Tuesday," June 1, 1971, reel 2, BMBCA.

55. "The Church Council," August 22, 1971, reel 2, BMBCA.

56. "Tuesday," November 2, 1971, reel 2, BMBCA.

57. "Tuesday," March 7, 1972, reel 2, BMBCA; "Tuesday," November 2, 1971, reel 2, BMBCA; "Tuesday," March 6, 1973, reel 2, BMBCA; "Tuesday," April 3, 1973, reel 2, BMBCA; "Minutes of the Church Council Meeting," September 20, 1976, reel 2, BMBCA.

58. "Tuesday," January 4, 1972, reel 2, BMBCA; "The Church Council," May 2, 1972, reel 2, BMBCA.

59. "Tuesday," October 3, 1972, reel 2, BMBCA; "Sunday," October 22, 1972, reel 2, BMBCA.

60. "Tuesday," December 5, 1972, reel 2, BMBCA; "The Church Council Met," July 1, 1975, reel 2, BMBCA.

61. "Minutes of Church Council Meeting," December 13, 1976, reel 2, BMBCA; "Minutes of the Church Council Meeting," September 20, 1976, reel 2, BMBCA.

62. "The Church Council," January 8, 1974, reel 2, BMBCA; "Tuesday," February 6, 1973, reel 2, BMBCA; "Tuesday," November 7, 1972, reel 2, BMBCA.

63. "Claudia Cannady," in *Binkley Memories: The First 50 Years 1958–2008*.

64. "Tuesday," March 6, 1973, reel 2, BMBCA; "The Church Council," February 5, 1974, reel 2, BMBCA; "The Church Council," June 6, 1974, reel 2, BMBCA.

65. "The Church Council," February 5, 1974, reel 2, BMBCA.

66. "Church Council Minutes," August 11, 1980, reel 2, BMBCA.

67. "Church Council," October 27, 1970, reel 2, BMBCA.

68. "The December Meeting of the Binkley Church Council was called to order," December 1970, reel 2, BMBCA; "Church Council Meeting," March 14, 1971, reel 2, BMBCA; "The Church Council met . . . ," August 22, 1971, reel 2, BMBCA; "Tuesday," June 7, 1972, reel 2, BMBCA.

69. "Tuesday," July 6, 1971, reel 2, BMBCA; "Binkley's History The First 40 Years," BMBCA.

70. "Binkley's History The First 40 Years," BMBCA.

71. "Minutes of the Church Council Meeting," November 8, 1976, reel 2, BMBCA.

72. "Church Council Meeting," September 20, 1976, reel 2, BMBCA.

73. "Minutes of Church Council Meeting," March 14, 1977, reel 2, BMBCA.

74. "Minutes of the Church Council," September 11, 1978, reel 2, BMBCA.

75. Ibid.

76. "Minutes of the Church Conference on the Report of the Program Committee of the Long Range Planning Council," October 29, 1978, reel 2, BMBCA.

77. Ibid.

78. Robert Seymour to Jim Lambert, January 18, 1978, reel 3, BMBCA.

79. "Meeting of the Church Council and Diaconate," August 27, 1979 reel 2, BMBCA.

80. "Church Council Meeting," May 12, 1980, reel 2, BMBCA.

81. "Binkley Baptist Church Conference," May 18, 1979, reel 1, BMBCA.

82. "Church Conference Minutes," April 8, 1979, reel 1, BMBCA.

83. "Church Conference Minutes," April 29, 1979, reel 1, BMBCA.

84. "Meeting of the Church Council and Diaconate," August 27, 1979, reel 2, BMBCA.

85. "Diaconate Meeting," October 1, 1979, reel 2, BMBCA.

86. "Minutes of the Church Conference," December 2, 1979, reel 1, BMBCA.

87. "Church Council Minutes," August 11, 1980, reel 2, BMBCA.

88. "Meeting of the Diaconate," April 6, 1981, reel 2, BMBCA.

89. Ibid.

90. Seymour, *"Whites Only,"* 18.

91. "Minutes of the Diaconate Meeting," August 31, 1981, reel 2, BMBCA.

92. Napier Baker email message to author, August 4, 2021.

93. "Diaconate Meeting," June 7, 1982, reel 2, BMBCA.

94. Bill Eastman to diaconate and staff, June 7, 1982, reel 2, BMBCA.

95. Fred Schroeder to friends, July 21, 1982, reel 2, BMBCA.

96. "Diaconate Meeting," August 23, 1982, reel 2, BMBCA.

97. "Meeting of Binkley Diaconate," August 29, 1983, reel 2, BMBCA.

98. "Meeting of the Binkley Diaconate," August 1, 1983, reel 2, BMBCA.

99. Bill Eastman to deacons and staff, December 9, 1983, reel 2, BMBCA.

100. "Meeting of Binkley Diaconate," January 2, 1984, reel 2, BMBCA.

101. Ibid.

102. Ibid.

103. Bill Eastman to diaconate and staff, May 2, 1984, reel 2, BMBCA.

104. "Meeting of Binkley Baptist Church Diaconate," May 7, 1984, reel 2, BMBCA.

105. "Diaconate Retreat," May 19, 1984, reel 2, BMBCA.

106. "Diaconate Meeting," November 5, 1984, reel 2, BMBCA; "Minutes of the Diaconate Meeting," January 6, 1986, reel 2, BMBCA; "Report from the Worship Committee concerning overcrowding at services," n.d., reel 2, BMBCA.

107. "The Olin T. Binkley Memorial Church is located . . . ," 1985, reel 7, BMBCA.

108. Ibid.

109. Ibid.

110. "Chapel Hill-Carrboro Meals on Wheels, Carole Nobles," in *Binkley Memories: The First 50 Years 1958–2008.*

111. "Habitat News at Binkley, Dale Osborne, Associate Minister," in *Binkley Memories: The First Fifty Years 1958–2008*; Bill Hoyle to Binkley Baptist Church, August 13, 2008, in *Binkley Memories: The First Fifty Years, 1958–2008*; "Binkley Baptist Church Diaconate Meeting," August 2, 1982, reel 2, in BMBCA; Seymour, *"Whites Only,"* 146.

112. Jim Wilde in discussion with the author, March 26, 2021.

113. "The Olin T. Binkley Memorial Church is located . . . ," 1985, reel 7, BMBCA.

4. Binkley in Transition

1. John Blevins, "The Olin T. Binkley Memorial Baptist Church Sunday Service," September 29, 2019, audio recording, 26:27–47:07.

2. Heather R. White, *Reforming Sodom: Protestants and Gay Rights* (Chapel Hill: Univ. of North Carolina Press, 2015), 4.

3. White, *Reforming Sodom,* 5.

4. See Mark Jordan, *Recruiting Young Love: How Christians Talk about Homosexuality* (Chicago, IL: Univ. of Chicago Press, 2011).

5. Marie Griffith, *Moral Combat: How Sex Divided American Christians and Fractured American Politics* (New York: Basic Books, 2017); Anthony Petro, *After the Wrath of God: AIDS, Sexuality, and American Religion* (New York: Oxford Univ. Press, 2019); this chapter follows most closely the work of Keith Hartman, *Congregations in Conflict: The Battle over Homosexuality* (New Brunswick, NJ: Rutgers Univ. Press, 1996). Hartman includes two chapters on Binkley Memorial Baptist Church and Pullen Memorial Baptist Church that take a local congregational approach to this question. This chapter follows Hartman's approach, providing context around Binkley Memorial Baptist Church in particular.

6. Cody Sanders, *Queer Lessons for Churches on the Straight and Narrow* (Macon, GA: Faithlab, 2013); Cody Sanders, *A Brief Guide to Ministry with LGBTQIA Youth* (Louisville, KY: Westminster John Knox Press, 2017); Jim Dant, *This I Know: A Simple Biblical Defense of LGBTQ Christians* (Macon, GA: Nurturing Faith, 2017); David Gushee, *Changing Our Mind: Definitive 3rd Edition of the Landmark Call for Inclusion of LGBTQ Christians with Response to Critics* (Canton, MI: Read the Spirit Books, 2019); Cody Sanders, ed., *Rightly Dividing the Word of Truth: A Resource for Congregations on Sexual Orientation and Gender Identity,* 2nd ed. (Charlotte, NC: Baptist Peace Fellowship of North America, 2013).

7. Southern Baptist Convention Annual (1976), 58, Southern Baptist Historical Library and Archives, https://sbhla.org/digital-resources/sbc-annuals/.

8. See Gregory B. Lewis, "Lifting the Ban on Gays in the Civil Service: Federal Policy toward Gay and Lesbian Employees since the Cold War," in *Public Administration Review* 57, no. 5 (October 1997): 387–95.

9. Southern Baptist Convention Annual (1977), 50

10. Southern Baptist Convention Annual (1985), 85.

11. Southern Baptist Convention Annual (1980), 56.

12. Southern Baptist Convention Annual (1988), 71–72.

13. Rick Mixon, "A Calling and a Coming Out Story: My Story," in *Rightly Dividing the Word of Truth: A Resource for Congregations on Sexual Orientation and Gender Identity,* 2nd ed., ed. Cody Sanders (Charlotte, NC: Baptist Peace Fellowship of North America, 2013), 161–63.

14. "American Baptist Churches USA: Responses/Actions Pertaining to Homosexuality," American Baptist Churches USA, accessed October 5, 2019, https://www .abc-usa.org/policy-statements-and-resolutions/.

15. Robert Seymour, "The New Morality," sermon, May 8, 1966, Binkley Memorial Baptist Church, Chapel Hill, NC.

16. *Towards a Quaker View of Sex: An Essay by a Group of Friends,* 2nd ed. (London: Friends Home Service Committee, 1963), 7; "Publication and Response, 1963," Towards a Quaker View of Sex, accessed October 6, 2019, https://exhibits.lgbtran.org/exhibits /show/towards-a-quaker-view-of-sex/gallery/publication-response.

17. *Towards a Quaker View of Sex,* 47.

18. Seymour, "The New Morality."

19. Ibid.

20. Ibid.

21. Robert Seymour, "The Church and Homosexuality," sermon, February 20, 1983, Binkley Memorial Baptist Church, Chapel Hill, NC.

22. Seymour, "The Church and Homosexuality."

23. Ibid.

24. Ibid.

25. Melissa Wilcox, "Of Markets and Missions: The Early History of the Universal Fellowship of Metropolitan Community Churches," *Religion and American Culture* 11, no. 2 (2001): 83–108.

26. Seymour, "The Church and Homosexuality."

27. Ibid.; Letha Dawson Scanzoni and Virginia Ramey Mollenkott, *Is the Homosexual My Neighbor? Another Christian View* (New York: HarperCollins, 1978).

28. Seymour, "The Church and Homosexuality."

29. Ibid.

30. Robert Seymour, *"Whites Only": A Pastor's Retrospective on Signs of the New South* (Valley Forge, PA: Judson Press, 1991), 140.

31. "Binkley's History: The First Forty Years," BMBCA.

32. Elizabeth Flowers, *Into the Pulpit: Southern Baptist Women and Power Since WWII* (Chapel Hill: Univ. of North Carolina Press, 2012).

33. Linda Jordan email message to author, February 8, 2021.

34. Ibid.

35. Ibid.

36. Linda Jordan quoted in John L. Humber, *The Ordeal and Tragedy of Binkley Baptist Church* (Chapel Hill, NC: n.p., 1992), 7.

37. Humber, *The Ordeal and Tragedy of Binkley Baptist Church,* 9.

38. Jordan email message to author, February 8, 2021.

39. John Blevins, "The Olin T. Binkley Memorial Baptist Church Sunday Service," September 29, 2019, audio recording, 26:27–47:07.

40. See "Summary of Diaconate Process Relating to the Licensure Request of John Blevins," March 2, 1992, congregation's archives; Humber, *The Ordeal and Tragedy of Binkley Baptist Church,* 9–10. Many of the sources utilized in this chapter were found within the congregation's archives, hereafter abbreviated CA.

41. "Summary of Diaconate Process Relating to the Licensure Request of John Blevins," March 2, 1992, CA.

42. "Dr. Robert G. Bratcher," *Raleigh News and Observer,* July 14, 2010, accessed October 12, 2019, https://www.legacy.com/obituaries/newsobserver/obituary.aspx?n =robert-g-bratcher&pid=144069874.

43. Byron R. McCane, "Jews, Christians, and burial in Roman Palestine," (PhD diss., Duke Univ., 1992), ProQuest Dissertations and Theses, 9303525.

44. Robert Bratcher, "On the Ordination of Homosexuals," June 21, 1991.

45. Byron R. McCane, "On the Ordination of Homosexuals." For McCane's opinions on the matter years later, see Hartman, *Congregations in Conflict.* Hartman explained that McCane "was unwilling . . . even to tell me which side of the debate he was on, saying it was a private matter."

46. Jim Wells, "Letter From the Diaconate," July 23, 1991, quoted in "Summary of Diaconate Process Relating to the Licensure Request of John Blevins," March 2, 1992, CA.

47. Linda Jordan, "From Our Senior Minister," September 17, 1991, quoted in "Summary of Diaconate Process Relating to the Licensure Request of John Blevins," March 2, 1992, CA.

48. Linda Jordan, "Sexuality and Spirituality: Can the two become one?," sermon, September 22, 1991, Binkley Memorial Baptist Church, Chapel Hill, NC.

49. Linda Jordan, "Eros As It Should Be," sermon, September 29, 1991, Binkley Memorial Baptist Church, Chapel Hill, NC.

50. Linda Jordan, "The Language of Love," sermon, October 6, 1991, Binkley Memorial Baptist Church, Chapel Hill, NC.

51. Linda Jordan, "Who Is My Neighbor?," sermon, October 13, 1991, Binkley Memorial Baptist Church, Chapel Hill, NC.

52. Jordan, "Who Is My Neighbor?"

53. Ibid.

54. Jim Wells to fellow Binkley member, January 5, 1992, in "Summary of Diaconate Process Relating to the Licensure Request of John Blevins," March 2, 1992, CA; See also Humber, *The Ordeal and Tragedy of Binkley Baptist Church.*

55. Steven D. Hoogerwerf, "Ethical Reflections on Homosexuality: Toward a Biblically Informed, Non-biblicist Ethic," January 1992, The Olin T. Binkley Baptist Church.

56. "Summary of Diaconate Process Relating to the Licensure Request of John Blevins," March 2, 1992, CA.

57. "Chapel Hill church debates ordination of gay minister," *Raleigh News and Observer,* February 5, 1992.

58. Linda Jordan to Marian Gregory, February 13, 1992, box 106, folder 13, Olin T. Binkley Papers, Z. Smith Reynolds Library Special Collections & Archives.

59. "Fact Sheet," February 7, 1992, CA.

60. "Summary of Diaconate Process Relating to the Licensure Request of John Blevins," March 2, 1992, CA.

61. Richard A. "Tony" Jenkins to Linda Jordan et al., February 15, 1992, CA.

62. Ibid.

63. Jim Wells to Binkley diaconate members, February 23, 1992, CA.

64. Jim Wells to Richard "Tony" Jenkins, February 22, 1992, CA.

65. Ibid.

66. Ibid.

67. "Homosexuality Draws Opposition," *Los Angeles Times,* February 22, 1992; "Baptist church to bless gay marriage," *Chicago Tribune,* March 3, 1992.

68. Bruce W. Johnson, "False Doctrine," *Raleigh News and Observer,* February 16, 1992.

69. Jennifer Jones, "Homosexuality in the Bible," *Raleigh News and Observer,* February 22, 1992.

70. Henry Jarrett, "Cheers to Binkley," *Raleigh News and Observer,* February 22, 1992.

71. David Stricklin, *A Genealogy of Dissent: Southern Baptist Protest in the Twentieth Century* (Lexington: Univ. Press of Kentucky, 2000).

72. "Pullen Memorial Baptist Church," in *Rightly Dividing the Word of Truth,* 223–24.

73. "Baptist Convention panel votes not to expel church," *Biblical Recorder,* April 9, 1992.

74. C. Fred Werhan, "The Peoples Forum," *Biblical Recorder,* March 14, 1992; R. G. Puckett, "A reasoned, responsible response," *Biblical Recorder,* March 14, 1992.

75. Barry Crocker, "The People's Forum," *Biblical Recorder,* March 14, 1992.

76. J. Ronald Hester, "The People's Forum," March 21, 1992.

77. "Paid Resolution Concerning Olin T. Binkley Memorial church and Homosexuality," *Biblical Recorder,* May 2, 1992; "Associations, church adopt resolutions on human sexuality," *Biblical Recorder,* May 23, 1992.

78. "Goldsboro church addresses homosexual issue," *Biblical Recorder,* March 7, 1992.

79. Dick Helwig, "From the Moderator," March 1, 1992; "Summary of Diaconate Process Relating to the Licensure Request of John Blevins," March 2, 1992, CA.

80. John C. Lotz to Linda Jordan and the Board of Deacons, March 12, 1992, CA.

81. "John L. Humber," Legacy.com, March 5, 2017, accessed October 24, 2019, https://www.legacy.com/obituaries/newsobserver/obituary.aspx?n=john-l-humber&pid=184342827&fhid=6292.

82. John Humber to Jerry Van Sant, February 10, 1992, CA.

83. John Humber, "Choice and Privacy for the Individual and the Group" (1992), 4–6, CA.

84. Humber, "A Proposal for a Statement of Belief and Policy by the Olin T. Binkley Memorial Baptist Church on the Issue of Sexuality" (1992), CA.

85. "James Olin Cansler," C. Massey Knox Distinguished Service Award, accessed October 24, 2019, https://masseyawards.unc.edu/james-olin-cansler/.

86. James Cansler to Richard Helwig, February 22, 1992, CA.

87. Jim and Dot Cansler to fellow church members, March 5, 1992, CA.

88. Allen and Pat Kelley to fellow church members, March 11, 1992, CA.

89. Allen C. Kelley to Linda Jordan, February 25, 1992, CA; a copy of this private letter to Rev. Jordan was included in the couple's open letter to the congregation.

90. Allen and Pat Kelly to Linda Jordan and Jim Wells, March 15, 1992, CA.

91. Jordan email message to author, February 8, 2021.

92. Mrs. Olin T. Binkley to Jim Wells, March 18, 1992, box 106, folder 3, Olin T. Binkley Papers, Z. Smith Reynolds Library Special Collections & Archives.

93. Jim Wells to fellow Binkley members, March 22, 1992, CA.

94. Betty Bouldin to James Wells, "Memorandum," March 7, 1992, CA.

95. Susan Smialowicz, "I regret, but feel strongly . . . ," undated, CA.

96. Melinda Wilde, "Summary of Perspectives Presented to the Diaconate of Binkley Church," 1992, CA.

97. Claudia Templeton to Jim Wells, March 8, 1992, CA.

98. Judith Eastman, "Statement for the Diaconate," 1992, CA.

99. Fred Schroeder to Jim," March 6, 1992, CA.

100. Ann Hamrick to Jim, "The following is in response . . . ," n.d., CA.

101. Eva Clontz to Jim Wells, "Brief Summaries of Important Points for me made by speakers," 1992, CA.

102. Alice Miller, "My Personal Statement," 1992, CA.

103. Lanie Freeman, "The Social Issue of Homosexuality . . . ," n.d., CA.

104. Humber, *The Ordeal and Tragedy,* 50–53.

105. Ibid., 53–55.

106. Jim Wilde in discussion with the author, March 26, 2021.

107. "Baptist church votes to license gay minister," *Raleigh News and Observer,* April 6, 1992.

108. Humber, *The Ordeal and Tragedy,* 55.

109. Ibid., 56.

110. "Gay preacher turns to matters of spirit after getting license," *Raleigh News and Observer,* April 7, 1992.

111. John Humber to Forrest Page, May 8, 1992, CA.

112. Michael K. Berkut to selected membership, May 4, 1992, CA.

113. John Humber, "Proposed Constitution Amendments," n.d., CA.

114. Humber, *Tragedy and Ordeal,* 63; "Binkley Memorial, Chapel Hill, rethinks homosexual statement," *Biblical Recorder,* July 4, 1992.

115. "General Board ousts Pullen and Binkley churches," *Biblical Recorder,* May 30, 1992.

116. Southern Baptist Convention Annual (1992), 80, Southern Baptist Historical Library and Archives, https://sbhla.org/digital-resources/sbc-annuals/.

117. Ibid., 81.

118. "Gay restriction added to SBC Constitution," *Biblical Recorder,* June 20, 1992

119. "2 Churches Ousted by Baptists' Vote," *New York Times,* June 11, 1992, A16.

120. Jordan email message to author, February 8, 2021.

121. Courtland Smith, "An Interpretive History of the First Ten Years," in *Essays on the First Fifty Years of the Olin T. Binkley Memorial Baptist Church,* box 106, folder 4, Olin T. Binkley Papers, Z. Smith Reynolds Library Special Collections & Archives.

122. Jordan email message to author, February 8, 2021.

123. Ibid.

124. Ibid.

125. Ibid.

126. Smith, "An Interpretive History of the First Ten Years," in *Essays on the First Fifty Years of the Olin T. Binkley Memorial Baptist Church,* box 106, folder 4, Olin T. Binkley Papers, Z. Smith Reynolds Library Special Collections & Archives.

127. Andrew Gardner, *Reimagining Zion: A History of the Alliance of Baptists* (Macon, GA: Nurturing Faith, 2015), 49–50.

128. John Blevins, "The Olin T. Binkley Memorial Baptist Church Sunday Service," September 29, 2019, audio recording, 26:27–47:07.

5. Every Member a Minister

1. "Jean and Don Westbrook, Binkley members since December 2007," in *Binkley Memories: The First 50 Years 1958–2008*.

2. See H. Leon McBeth, *The Baptist Heritage: Four Centuries of Baptist Witness* (Nashville, TN: Broadman Press, 1987).

3. I use the terms intersectionality and intersectional broadly as a means of thinking about the interrelationship between various congregational ministries and areas of ministry focus. Seeking justice through various ministries and issues in isolation is the product of a white, heteronormative, male power structure that prioritizes addressing ministries and issues in isolation. Informing my thinking on issues of intersectionality are Kimberlé Crenshaw, "Demarginalizing the Intersection of Race and Sex: A Black Feminist Critique of Antidiscrimination Doctrine, Feminist Theory and Antiracist Politics," *The University of Chicago Legal Forum* 140 (1989): 139–67; Evelyn Brooks Higginbotham, *Righteous Discontent: The Women's Movement in the Black Baptist Church, 1880–1920* (Cambridge, MA: Harvard Univ. Press, 1993); Grace Ji-Sun Kim and Susan Shaw, *Intersectional Theology: An Introductory Guide* (Minneapolis, MN: Fortress Press, 2018).

4. See Allen J. Matusow, *The Unraveling of America: A History of Liberalism in the 1960s*, 2nd ed. (Athens: Univ. of Georgia Press, 2009); Angie Maxwell and Todd Shields, *The Long Southern Strategy: How Chasing White Voters in the South Changed American Politics* (New York: Oxford Univ. Press, 2019).

5. Jim Pike, "Stories, Images, Memories & Defining Moments," *Binkley 60th Anniversary Reflections*, 2. This document was obtained through personal communication with Pike.

6. Pike, "Stories, Images, Memories," 2.

7. Jim Pike, "50th Anniversary Recollection," 1–2. This document was obtained through personal communication with Pike.

8. "Faces of Faith: A sense of purpose in a city pulpit," *Times Union,* October 10, 2014.

9. Peter Carman email message to author, February 10, 2021.

10. Ibid.

11. "Burmese, other refugees renew Lake Ave. Baptist Church," *Democrat & Chronicle,* August 4, 2015.

12. Carman email message to author, March 3, 2021.

13. Jim Pike email message to author, February 25, 2021.

14. Ibid.

15. Peter Carman interview with author, March 3, 2021.

16. Pike email message to author, February 25, 2021.

17. Carman interview with author, March 3, 2021; Carman email message to author, February 10, 2021.

18. Pike email message to author, February 25, 2021.

19. Ibid.

20. Rev. W. Dale Osborn to Binkley Church, May 27, 2008, in *Binkley Memories: The First 50 Years 1958–2008*; "Binkley Baptist Church: A Story of Courage," September 23, 2018.

21. Robert Wuthnow, *The Restructuring of American Religion: Society and Faith since World War II* (Princeton, NJ: Princeton Univ. Press, 1988); William Swatos, "Beyond Denominationalism? Community and Culture in American Religion," *Journal of the Scientific Study of Religion* 20, no. 3 (1981): 217–27.

22. Timothy Gloege, *Guaranteed Pure: The Moody Bible Institute, Business, and the Making of Modern Evangelicalism* (Chapel Hill: Univ. of North Carolina Press, 2015).

23. Jim Wilde interview with author, March 26, 2021.

24. Robert Seymour, "Ecumenical Challenges on the Eve of the New Millennium," May 7, 1998, box 31, Robert E. Seymour Papers #4554, Southern Historical Collection, Wilson Library, Univ. of North Carolina at Chapel Hill. Hereafter abbreviated RSP.

25. Pike email message to author, February 26, 2021.

26. Carman email message to author, February 10, 2021.

27. Carman interview with author, March 3, 2021.

28. Pike email message to author, February 26, 2021.

29. Liam Gearon, "Taize: A global and post-colonial theology of community," in *Contemporary Spiritualities: Social and Religious Contexts,* ed. Clive Erricker and Jane Erricker (London: Continuum, 2001).

30. Pamela Klassen, *Spirits of Protestantism: Medicine, Healing, and Liberal Christianity* (Berkeley: Univ. of California Press, 2011), 8.

31. "Binkley discussion will address brain function," *Raleigh News and Observer,* October 12, 2011.

32. "Margaret's Supply Closet," in *Binkley Memories: The First 50 Years 1958–2008.*

33. "Working her own road map," *Raleigh News and Observer,* June 15, 2003.

34. Roal Carlson, "Binkley's Brazil Connection," June 21, 2019, accessed April 13, 2021, https://myemail.constantcontact.com/News-from-Binkley-Baptist-; Church .html?soid=1102771164856&aid=FG_ospQPiUs. For more on this type of missiological perspective, see Alan Neeley, *A New Call to Missions: Help for Perplexed Churches* (Macon, GA: Smyth and Helwys, 1999); Andrew Gardner, *Reimagining Zion: A History of the Alliance of Baptists* (Macon, GA: Nurturing Faith, 2015).

35. "Binkley Baptist Church: A Story of Courage," September 23, 2018, a publication of Binkley Memorial Baptist Church.

36. Eva Clontz email message to author, March 22, 2021; "Edith Wiggins leaves behind a storied legacy in the Chapel Hill community," *Daily Tar Heel,* April 11, 2021.

37. Seth Kotch, *Lethal State: A History of the Death Penalty in North Carolina* (Chapel Hill: Univ. of North Carolina Press, 2019), 7.

38. "Kermit Smith case is acid test for opponents of death penalty," *Raleigh News and Observer,* December 30, 1994.

39. "Binkley Baptist: A Tradition of Loyal Opposition," *North Carolina Independent,* September 1, 1983.

40. "Dean Smith takes stand against the Death Penalty," *Chapel Hill News,* November 6, 1998; "Ex-coach takes on a higher cause," *Chicago Tribune,* February 9, 2003.

41. Statement quoted in "John Thomas NOLAND Jr.," Murderpedia.org, accessed February 14, 2021, https://murderpedia.org/male.N/n1/noland-john-thomas.htm.

42. "Hunt commutes first death sentence," *The Charlotte Observer,* December 16, 1999.

43. Maxwell and Shields, *The Long Southern Strategy*; Daniel Williams, *God's Own Party: The Making of the Christian Right* (New York: Oxford Univ. Press, 2010).

44. Herman Greene, "Creation Season of the Church Year: A New Season Emphasizing God's Presence and Our Role in Creation," (DMin diss., United Theological Seminary, 2004).

45. "Thomas Berry obituary," *The Guardian,* September 27, 2009, accessed January 22, 2021, https://www.theguardian.com/world/2009/sep/27/thomas-berry-obituary.

46. Mary Evelyn Tucker, "Thomas Berry and the New Story: An Introduction to the Work of Thomas Berry," in *The Intellectual Journey of Thomas Berry: Imagining the Earth Community,* ed. Heather Eaton (Lanham, MD: Lexington Books, 2014), 1.

47. Greene, "Creation Season of the Church Year," 172–73.

48. Ibid., 77.

49. Ibid., 188.

50. Ibid., 178.

51. Ibid., 180.

52. Greene, "What Now?," October 12, 2003.

53. Ibid.

54. See Jean Bradley Anderson, *Durham County: A History of Durham County, North Carolina,* 2nd ed. (Durham, NC: Duke Univ. Press, 2011), 117; A. C. Howell, *A History of Chapel Hill Baptist Church, 1854–1924* (Chapel Hill: n.p., 1945), 6.

55. "Binkley's Baptist," *Chapel Hill Herald,* March 6, 1994.

56. "Binkley Baptist Church and Barbee's Chapel Harvest Word Missionary Baptist Church Racial Reconciliation Ministry, Nancie McDermott," in *Binkley Memories: The First 50 Years 1958–2008.*

57. Ibid.

58. Jim Pike email message to author, February 25, 2021.

59. Carman interview with author, March 3, 2021.

60. "Kimberly Eastman Zirkle, Binkley member since 1966," in *Binkley Memories: The First 50 Years 1958–2008.*

61. "The Binkley Baptist Church-Barbee's Chapel Harvest Word Missionary Baptist Church Yard Sale: August 16, 2008, 8am to 1pm," in *Binkley Memories: The First 50 Years 1958–2008.*

62. "Really Big Sale," *Raleigh News and Observer,* August 1, 2012.

63. Pike email message to author, February 25, 2021.

64. "Burnette," *Raleigh News and Observer,* May 17, 1994.

65. Gene Hatley, "Discrimination is alive and well in Chapel Hill," *Chapel Hill News,* June 29, 1994.

66. Robert Seymour to Gene Hatley, n.d., box 30, RSP.

67. Hatley, "Discrimination is alive and well in Chapel Hill."

68. Robert Seymour to Gene Hatley, n.d., box 30, RSP.

69. "Letter from LaVonda Burnett," *Raleigh News and Observer,* May 17, 1994.

70. Carman email message to author, February 10, 2021.

71. "Congregation fills church as anti-gay protesters picket quietly outside," *Raleigh News and Observer,* May 17, 1995.

72. Pike, "Stories, Images, Memories."

73. See Rebecca Barrett-Fox, *God Hates: Westboro Baptist Church, American Nationalism, and the Religious Right* (Lawrence: Univ. Press of Kansas, 2016).

74. Pike, "Stories, Images, Memories."

75. Ibid.

76. "Bill Eastman, Binkley member since 1966," in *Binkley Memories: The First 50 Years 1958–2008.*

77. "Congregation fills church as anti-gay protesters picket quietly outside," *Raleigh News and Observer,* May 17, 1999.

78. "Harry M. Jensen, Jr. Binkley member since 1959," in *Binkley Memories: The First 50 Years 1958–2008.*

79. Boy Scouts of America et al. v. Dale, 530 U.S. 640 (2000).

80. Jim Pike interview with author, February 25, 2020.

81. "Harry M. Jensen, Jr. Binkley member since 1959," in *Binkley Memories: The First 50 Years 1958–2008.*

82. "Sponsors sever ties to Scouts," *Raleigh News and Observer,* April 16, 2001.

83. Ibid.

84. Howard Lee interview with the author, March 29, 2020.

85. Napier Baker interview with the author, March 18, 2020.

86. "The Beacon," Binkley newsletter, September 22, 2010.

87. Raymonda "Ray" Speller interview with the author, April 15, 2021.

88. Carman interview with the author, March 3, 2020.

89. "The Beacon," Binkley newsletter, February 23, 2011.

90. Speller interview with the author, April 15, 2021.

91. Ibid.

92. Ibid.

93. Carman interview with the author, March 3, 2020.

94. "Weighing Amendment One: Binkley's Stance," *Raleigh News and Observer,* March 31, 2012.

95. Carman interview with the author, March 3, 2020.

96. Speller interview with the author, April 15, 2021.

Conclusion

1. "Charles Carver, Binkley member since 1974," in *Binkley Memories: The First 50 Years 1958–2008;* James L. Pike to Binkley Church, July 1, 2008, in *Binkley Memories: The First 50 Years 1958–2008.*

2. John Thelin, *A History of American Higher Education,* 2nd ed. (Baltimore, MD: Johns Hopkins Univ. Press, 2011).

3. Within the context of American religious history, Sydney Ahlstrom's magisterial work *A Religious History of the American People* (New Haven, CT: Yale Univ. Press, 1972) typifies this liberal consensus that tells a white, Protestant history of American religion while incorporating non-white and non-Protestant groups into the narrative.

4. Numerous studies have sought to understand the events of the 1980s and their significance in the broader scope of Baptist life specifically and American religious life more broadly. See Nancy Ammerman, *Baptist Battles: Social Change and Religious Conflict in the Southern Baptist Convention* (New Brunswick, NJ: Rutgers Univ. Press, 1990); Bill Leonard, *God's Last and Only Hope: The Fragmentation of the Southern Baptist Convention* (Grand Rapids, MI: William B. Eerdmans Publishing Company, 1990); James C. Hefley, *The Truth in Crisis: The Controversy in the Southern Baptist Convention,* vol. 5 (Richmond, VA: Hannibal Books, 1990); Walter Shurden, ed., *The Struggle for the South of the SBC: Moderate Responses to the Fundamentalist Movement* (Macon, GA: Mercer Univ. Press, 1993); David T. Morgan, *The New Crusades, the New Holy Land: Conflict in the Southern Baptist Convention, 1969–1990* (Tuscaloosa: Univ. of Alabama Press, 1996); Jerry Sutton, *The Baptist Reformation: The Conservative Resurgence in the Southern Baptist Convention* (Nashville, TN: Broadman and Holman, 2000); Carl L. Kell, *Exiled: Voices of the Southern Baptist Convention Holy War* (Knoxville: Univ. of Tennessee Press, 2006); Eileen Campbell-Reed, *Anatomy of a Schism: How Clergywomen's Narratives Reinterpret the Fracturing of the Southern Baptist Convention* (Knoxville: Univ. of Tennessee Press, 2016).

5. Like many congregations that would help form the Southern Baptist Alliance, later the Alliance of Baptists, Binkley never found a home in the Southern Baptist Convention.

This organization formed in 1987 was comprised of individuals and congregations who were either tired of denominational fights or questioned whether the SBC was worth fighting for in the first place. See Andrew Gardner, *Reimagining Zion: A History of the Alliance of Baptists* (Macon, GA: Nurturing Faith, 2015); Gardner and Gerardo Marti, "From Ordaining Women to Combating White Supremacy: Oppositional Shifts in Social Attitudes between the Southern Baptist Convention and the Alliance of Baptists," *Religion and American Culture* 32, no. 2 (2022): 202–35

6. Bill Leonard, *Baptist Ways: A History* (Valley Forge, PA: Judson Press, 1993), 166.

7. See Robert Wuthnow, *The Restructuring of American Religion: Society and Faith Since World War II* (Princeton, NJ: Princeton Univ. Press, 1988); William Swatos, "Beyond Denomiantionalism? Community and Culture in American Religion," in *Journal of the Scientific Study of Religion* 20, no. 3 (1981): 217–27.

8. Robert Seymour, *"Whites Only": A Pastor's Retrospective on Signs of the New South* (Valley Forge, PA: Judson Press, 1991).

Index